TAKING CARE OF YOUTH
AND THE GENERATIONS

MERIDIAN

Crossing Aesthetics

Werner Hamacher

Editor

Translated by Stephen Barker

*Stanford
University
Press*

*Stanford
California*
2010

TAKING CARE OF YOUTH
AND THE GENERATIONS

Bernard Stiegler

Stanford University Press
Stanford, California

English translation © 2010 by the Board of Trustees of the
Leland Stanford Junior University. All rights reserved.

Taking Care of Youth and the Generations was originally
published in French in 2008 under the title *Prendre soin de la
jeunesse et des générations* © 2008, Flammarion.

This book has been published with the assistance of the French
Ministry of Culture—National Center for the Book.

Printed in the United States of America
on acid-free, archival-quality paper

Library of Congress Cataloging-in-Publication Data

Stiegler, Bernard.
[Prendre soin. English]
Taking care of youth and the generations / Bernard Stiegler ;
translated by Stephen Barker.
p.   cm. — (Meridian : crossing aesthetics)
"Originally published in French in 2008 under the title
Prendre soin de la jeunesse et des générations."
Includes bibliographical references.
ISBN 978-0-8047-6272-4 (cloth : alk. paper)
ISBN 978-0-8047-6273-1 (pbk : alk. paper)
1. Attention.   2. Adolescent psychology.   3. Attention-
deficit hyperactivity disorder.   4. Technology—Philosophy.
I. Title.   II. Series: Meridian (Stanford, Calif.)
BF321.S6813   2010
194—dc22
2009025390

Contents

To my parents
with my most affectionate gratitude
To the memory of Gabriel Mehrenberger

Sapere aude! [Dare to know!] Have courage to use your own understanding. That is the motto of enlightenment.

> —Immanuel Kant, "An Answer to the Question: What Is Enlightenment?"

Master of a knowledge whose ingenious resources
Transcend all hopes,
He can thus take the path of evil or of good.

> —Sophocles, *Antigone*

I take . . . the risk of trying to ground the fundamental significance of the "normal" in a philosophical analysis of life, understood as the activity of opposing inertia and indifference. Life tries to win over death, in all senses of the word "win" and, first of all, in the sense in which the victory is through play. Life plays against a growing entropy.

> —Georges Canguilhem, *The Normal and the Pathological*

The fact that I am still alive and that I have returned unscathed attests above all, I'd say, to chance. Pre-existent factors, such as my impulse for the life of the mountains and my trade as a chemist, which gave me certain privileges in the last months in the camp, played only a minor rôle. Perhaps I also found support in my never-diminished interest in the human soul, and in the will not only to survive (the objective among many of us), but to survive with the specific goal of recounting what we had participated in and what we had undergone. Finally, what had perhaps also played itself out was the will I had tenaciously maintained, even in the darkest hours, always to see, in my comrades and myself, human beings and not things, thus avoiding that humiliation, that total demoralization that for many led to spiritual shipwreck.

> —Primo Levi, *If This Is a Man*

Abbreviations

AF	Pontalis, *Après Freud*
AG	Giddens, *The Consequences of Modernity*
AK	Foucault, *The Archaeology of Knowledge*
Al	Plato, *Alcibiades*
AO	Stiegler, *Acting Out*
Aris	Aristotle, *Metaphysics*
ASN	Stiegler, *Aimer, s'aimer, nous aimer*
BC	Foucault, *The Birth of the Clinic*
BT	Heidegger, *Being and Time*
Cassin	Cassin, *Google-moi, la deuxième mission de l'Amérique*
CE1	Stiegler, *Constituer l'Europe 1*
CE2	Stiegler, *Constituer l'Europe 2*
CEL	Lecourt, *Pour une critique de l'épistémologie, Bachelard, Canguilhem, Foucault*
CF	Foucault, "The Confession of the Flesh"
Char	Plato, *Charmides*
CM	Morana, "Éclairer les Lumières"
Con	Kintzler, *Condorcet*
CP	Lecourt, *Contre la peur*
CPR	Kant, *The Critique of Pure Reason*
DAO	Deleuze, *Anti-Oedipus*
DDP	Stiegler, *De la démocratie participative*

DE1   Foucault, *Dits et écrits 1*

DE2   Foucault, *Dits et écrits 2*

DE3   Foucault, *Dits et écrits 3*

DE4   Foucault, *Dits et écrits 4*

DEII   Foucault, *Qu'est-ce que les Lumières?*

Dissemination   Derrida, *Dissemination*

DP   Foucault, *Discipline and Punish*

Dufour   Dufour, *On achève bien les hommes*

EBH   Baton-Hervé, *Télévision et fonction parentale*

EC   Marcuse, *Eros and Civilization*

Ecog   Stiegler and Derrida, *Ecographies of Television*

Ego   Freud, *The Ego and the Id*

EH   Petit and Bontemps, *L'Économie de l'hypermatière*

FD   Dolto, in Hintzy, Interview

FF   Fillon, Policy Statement, 3 July

Fillon   Fillon, François. 2007. Interview. *Le Figaro*, 2 June

FK   Derrida, "Faith and Knowledge"

Fleury   Fleury, *Le TNP et le Centre Pompidou*

GD   Hayles, "Hyper and Deep Attention"

GG   Gasmi and Grolleau, *Économie de l'information versus l'Économie de l'attention?*

GHP   Derrida, *The Problem of Genesis in Husserl's Philosophy*

GI   Dobbs, *The Greeks and the Irrational*

GIP   Freud, *A General Introduction to Psychoanalysis*

Gould   Gould, *Écrits 1*

GSP   Simondon, Preface, *Individuation psychique et collective*

HG   Guiland, *S'intéresser à l'attention*

Hintzy   Hintzy, Interview

HM   Leroi-Gourhan, *L'Homme et la matière.*

HOG   Derrida, *Edmund Husserl's "Origin of Geometry": An Introduction*

HP   Packard, *The Hidden Persuaders*

HS1   Foucault, *The History of Sexuality 1*

HT   Gille, *Histoire des techniques*

Huss   Husserl, *The Crisis of European Sciences and Transcendental Phenomenology*

IG	Simondon, *L'individu et sa genèse psycho-biologique*
IM	Heidegger, *Introduction to Metaphysics*
IPC	Simondon, *Individuation psychique et collective*
Iser	Iser, *The Act of Reading*
Jonas	Jonas, *The Imperative of Responsibility*
Kaiser	Kaiser Family Foundation, *Generation M: Media in the Lives of 8–18 Year-olds*
Levi	Levi, *If This Is a Man*
L-G	Leroi-Gourhan, *Le geste et la parole*
Lecourt	Lecourt, *Contre la peur*
LH	Plato, *Lesser Hippias*
LP	During, "Logics of Performance: Cage/Gould"
Mann	Mann, *The Tables of the Law*
MC	Crepon, *La Culture de la peur*
MD1	Stiegler, *Mécreance et discrédit 1*
MD2	Stiegler, *Mécreance et discrédit 2*
MD3	Stiegler, *Mécreance et discrédit 3*
MEOT	Simondon, *Du mode d'existence des objets techniques*
Meshes	Foucault, "The Meshes of Power"
MM	Freud, *Moses and Monotheism*
MS1	Stiegler, *De la misère symbolique 1*
MS2	Stiegler, *De la misère symbolique 2*
Myst	Stiegler, *Mystagogies*
Neg	Deleuze, *Negotiations*
NM	Changeux, *Neuronal Man*
NP	Canguilhem, *The Normal and the Pathological*
OG	Derrida, *The Origin of Geometry*
OM	Freud, *On Metapsychology*
OT	Foucault, *The Order of Things*
PE	Weber, *The Protestant Ethic and the Spirit of Capitalism*
PLT	Heidegger, *Poetry, Language, Thought*
PM	Plato, *Meno*
PostCard	Derrida, *The Post Card*
PPA	Stiegler, *Philosopher par accident*

PR	Winnicott, *Playing and Reality*
Pre	Heraclitus, *Les Présocratiques*
Prof	Agamben, *Profanations*
Prop	Bernays, *Propaganda*
PS	Sloterdijk, *Règles pour le parc humain*
Q1/2	Heidegger, *Questions I et II*
Q3/4	Heidegger, *Questions III et IV*
QL	Mendelssohn and Kant, *Qu'est-ce que les Lumières?*
Quarto	Foucault, "L'Écriture de soi"
RE	Kant, *Réflexions sur l'éducation*
Rifkin	Rifkin, *The Age of Access*
RM	Stiegler, *Réenchanter le monde*
Robin	Robin, *Platon*
Ross	Ross, *May '68 and Its Afterlives*
RQ	Queneau, *Bâtons, chiffres et lettres*
RTG	Auroux, *La Révolution technologique de la grammatisation*
Scil	Lacan, *Scilicet* 1/1
SE	Loyola, *The Spiritual Exercises*
SP	Noyer, Proceedings of a conference at the Théâtre de la Colline, 5 November 2005
TCD	Stiegler, *La Télécratie contre la démocratie*
Tehran	Foucault, "Tehran: Faith Against the Shah"
TT1	Stiegler, *Technics and Time 1*
TT2	Stiegler, *Technics and Time 2*
TT3	Stiegler, *Technics and Time 3*
WA	Agamben, *What Is an Apparatus?*
WE	Foucault, "What Is Enlightenment?"
WEK	Kant, "An Answer to the Question: What Is Enlightenment?"
Zim1	Zimmerman and Christakis, "Early Television Exposure and Subsequent Attentional Problems in Children"
Zim2	Zimmerman and Christakis. "Television and DVD/Video Viewing in Children Younger Than 2 Years"

TAKING CARE OF YOUTH
AND THE GENERATIONS

§ 1   Destruction of the Juvenile
Psychic Apparatus

1. Regarding what children deserve

Henceforth in France, juveniles who commit certain crimes, and juvenile recidivists, will no longer be tried as minors: the same laws will
apply to them as to their parents. This important change has been made
because the legal definition of *the age of criminal responsibility*, which determines the law's treatment of minors (those "below voting age"), was
seen as inducing a sense of impunity encouraging delinquent youths to
repeat their criminal behavior.

The problematic result of this change in the law is that there is now no
clearly defined age of *responsibility*. In fact, this change in the law is a *dilu-
tion* of responsibility, since "responsibility" is:

1. socially established by and founded on reaching the age of maturity,[1]
2. before all else, the adult responsibility of taking care of the young,
very much including adolescents going through various "vulnerabilities,"
as François Dolto calls them:[2] it is *before all others* the adult responsibility
to take care of them precisely because they are minors.

Questioning the minority status of delinquent children simultaneously
means questioning the status of adults as well, finally relieving adults of
the very responsibility that gives them their status *as* adults. It also re-
lieves adult society of its responsibility, displacing that responsibility onto
minors themselves. In attenuating the difference between minority and
majority, this change in the law, simultaneously redefining *both* minority and majority, also obscures both that responsibility is a *learned* social
competency and that society is responsible for transmitting it to children

Keeps adults from having to have responsibility

1

and adolescents. They are called "minors" specifically because adult society is *required* to take care of their successful transition to adulthood—but first of all, and most especially, to their *education* education is our name for transmitting the social competency that produces responsibility; that is, that leads to "maturity."

The recent change in French law obfuscates this transmission of responsibility's vital and obligatory nature, through which minors become adults, occludes its meaning in the minds of both adults and minors (both younger children and adolescents), and is a powerful indication of the weakness of a society that has become *structurally* incapable of educating its children, in being incapable of distinguishing minority from majority.

This distinction is not merely erased by the new French law: undermining the difference between minors and adults is at the very heart of contemporary consumer culture, which systematically defines consumers—minors and adults alike—as being fundamentally, structurally irresponsible.

It could be objected here that such concerns, or at least the philosophy behind them, are too "formal," too theoretical: that in terms of results (from the perspective of the security that our society, suffering from ever-increasing juvenile delinquency, justifiably wants), one must be a realist. But compounding the repression of delinquency's legal definition is not at all "realistic"; Jacques Hintzy has shown that "countries that, like the United States, over the greatest length of time most heavily penalized minority offenders are finding very negative outcomes from these measures." In fact, denial of minority status to minors, and thus of responsibility to adults, only expands the divisions between what remains of adult (i.e., responsible) society, children, and minor adolescents, a denial that increasingly locks the young—and their parents—into a self-perpetuating irresponsibility that all evidence shows only translates into further delinquency, even criminality.

Authoritarianism, a particularly telling symptom of the change in the law defining minority status, is as symbolic as it is juridical, and in fact is always an indicator of the law's weakening, precisely insofar as law emanates from the symbolic order—the order to which Antigone calls out in a language that is both ancient (Greek) and tragic ("divine law"): as in *Antigone*, all decisions made through impotent authoritarianism, in all genres, always result, sooner or later, in the *worsening* of the situation they are intended to "treat."

Mildew, or a cockroach or lice infestation, can be "treated," but law can never be protected by a "treatment": it requires careful nurturance. This is the case because what guarantees respect for law is not its repressive apparatus, which is always improvisatory, but the *feeling* it can create when it has been culturally internalized. And this nurturance, this *care*, which alone can create this sense both of intimacy *and* of familiarity (as *philia*[3]), is grounded in a *shared* responsibility—at least in a society of laws.

The real issue is knowing what minors—children and adolescents—*deserve*. In June 2007, while the new law was being debated, a French advertising campaign provided a partial but perfectly clear (and exceptionally symptomatic) answer to this: children deserve "*better than that.*"[4] "That" in the ad campaign refers to their parents and grandparents: children "deserve" Channel Y,[5] the television channel specifically aimed at this vital segment of the television audience (i.e., those with "available brains": minors[6]).

This special "segment" is defined by dividing the various age groups into "slices," which are then targeted as such (as in "target audiences"), and these "slices" or "segments," because their ages are not specified, become instrumental within the channel's audience-identification system: they become *prescriptive*, through a generational inversion that is only the most obvious sign of the destruction of education, to which consumer society's televisual marketing techniques must inevitably lead. Through this generational inversion, the segment designated "minors" becomes prescriptive of the consumption habits of the segment that is ostensibly adult—but is in fact infantilized: adults become decreasingly responsible for their children's behavior, and for their own. Structurally speaking, adults thus become minors, the result being that adulthood as such, judicial as well as democratic, appears to have vanished.

2. What "that" means

An "adult" human being is one recognized as *socially* adult and thus responsible. *Responsibility* is the adult's defining trait; an adult who is irresponsible, *stricto senso*, loses both adult rights and duties. Such an adult might need supervision, such as elderly persons entering "second childhood" or adults who have become significantly mentally unbalanced (and "interned"), or at least do not have all of their mental faculties: responsibility is a mental characteristic and thus also a characteristic of *human intelligence* as both psychic and social. I will return to this *double* dimension of intelligence in terms of a wider political discourse in which François Fillon, prime minister in the Nicolas Sarkozy government, defined—as his first priority—what he called the "battle of intelligence."

Responsibility is a psychic, as much as a social, quality of adulthood, and since Freud it has been clear that formation of this responsibility, this *becoming* adult, develops from infancy through a relationship of identification with parents who educate the child. This is what Freud calls primary identification, about which he claims that

1. it is practically indelible and that it is in operation throughout the first five years of life,

2. it is the condition of access to the superego through which the adult transmits to the child being educated the capacity to internalize, the familiar name of which is "the law": in identifying with the adult, the child identifies with what the adult identified with while being educated, and this is repeated from generation to generation; this repeated identification is thus what both distinguishes and links the generations.

This process of identification is precisely what the contemporary culture industry subverts,[7] in diverting and capturing the attention of young minds in their time of "brain availability," passive in the face of demands to consume but increasingly subject to attention problems generally accompanied by hyperactivity, to which I will return in Chapters 4 and 5.

Channel Y's reprehensible advertising campaign brazenly exploits this situation: two different posters depict a father and grandfather, that is, adults, and representatives of adulthood, one with his child, the other with his grandchild—with the minors they are responsible for guiding to maturity; in their advertisements, this channel specifically designed for minors ("Channel Y" declares its "brain-available" target audience: Youth) ridicules the father and grandfather, denying them all responsibility.

In the background, mother and grandmother see nothing dangerous here; stereotypes (among them, repression) are used to short-circuit any parental authority. A blog responding to the campaign accurately portrays these paternal stereotypes as inverted and derided: the father and grandfather, trying to make the child laugh, are infantilized in an "inversion of values [that] is a typical strategy in advertising that confuses all normal references, dynamites traditional hierarchies, destroys culture and education."[8] The *moral* of these two advertisements, printed in large letters on each poster, is that "our children deserve better than that"—"that" clearly indicating the father and grandfather.

The "that" is much more, however, since Freud's *The Ego and the Id* of 1923 (Freud's "second topic"), in which Freud defines a psychic system that the *id* [*ça*, "that"] forms *with* the ego [*moi*], linking consciousness, the preconscious,[9] and the unconscious.[10] The *ça*, "that," the id, is not entirely coincident with the unconscious, since if the unconscious consists of repressed representations—repressed by the ego—then the ego (ostensibly in opposition to the unconscious and thus oriented toward consciousness) is itself not fully conscious. The repressive forces residing in the ego are not conscious forces: the ego itself cannot be consciously aware of the forces working to repress what is coming from the unconscious, though these repressive forces are part of the ego. In other words, the ego no longer entirely coincides with the consciousness, and the id no longer coincides entirely with the unconscious. The id, of which the unconscious is a part, extends into the ego *as* the system of unconscious repression, and in this sense, it is the id that connects the unconscious and the superego.

An organic and functional link between ego and id exists not only because the id "contains" the ego's forces of repression but also, Freud tells us, because the id *learns something of the world* through the ego's intermediation. The ego, as the seat of consciousness and thus also of attention, is the repository of what Husserl calls "primary retentions"—what occurs in the conscious flow of time.[11] But these primary retentions, which are essentially perceptions, then become secondary retentions—"memories" in the traditional sense—that can themselves become either preconscious (latent) or actually repressed (unconscious).[12]

As repressed perceptions, these psychic phenomena, as representations, provide the material for the drives emanating from the unconscious (in conjunction with the id), in so doing setting the stage for the pleasure principle, which searches through the unconscious for immediate gratification of all drives; "immediate" here meaning without passing through the reality principle, the social mediation encompassing all media as, to some extent, the *medium* (and the feeling) of pleasure.

The pleasure principle, as it is satisfied (i.e., not deferred or deflected by the reality principle) is what produces *jouissance*.[13] But *jouissance* is what vanishes, "dies" [*s'éteint*] through the very fact of being achieved [*atteint*]—which is why it is also called the "little death": *jouissance* is defined by its transitoriness, which differentiates it from *desire* as well as from kinds of pleasure only achievable insofar as they differ from *jouissance*, such that when they are attained, they reappear as différance,[14] maintaining their objects as objects of desire. But that presupposes a supplementarity, as Derrida indicates. And as we will see, this supplementarity, which is also a *pharmakon*,[15] poison and remedy simultaneously, is the condition of *all* systems of care.

3. Sedimentation of the symbolic intergenerational environment as the condition of attention formation

The unconscious, with the id as its base, nonetheless contains inherited psychic representations not initially *lived* as conscious, primary retentions that were then repressed but that were transmitted through a *symbolic medium*, such as language, and through symbolic means in general: objects, icons, and the myriad memory supports of which the human world consists from its very inception, since symbolic materials are inherently part of that world and belong there; these are *tertiary* memories ("supplements"), social or cultural memories subsequently materialized—both socially materialized and materially socialized (even through ephemeral states of matter such as words, as vibrations in air).

Tertiary retentions are the sedimentations that accumulate across generations and that are central to the process of creating collective individuation, internalized through both consciousness and the unconscious during the development of the psychic apparatus. Freud theorizes the intergenerational transmission of *inherited* psychic traits in *Moses and Monotheism* (1939),[16] where he attempts to conceptualize what he calls "the dream language of myths" through which, according to Freud, humans inherit the Oedipus Complex. But I suggest that Freud fails.[17]

How can or should the significance of dream symbols be properly understood? Freud asks this question in *A General Introduction to Psychoanalysis* in 1916: "this understanding comes to us from many sources: fairy tales and myths, jokes and simple folktales; that is, from the study of mores, usages, proverbs, and songs of diverse peoples, as well as from the poetic language of their common tongue" (GIP, 151). Thus, Jean-Bertrand Pontalis can say that "when one analyzes what Freud did indeed discover . . . , one is led inexorably to connect the unconscious to a *trans-individual* reality. . . . To Freud, the unconscious is in no case reducible to an invisible storehouse unique to each person."[18] Freud asks how this "dream language of myths" (GIP, 151) might be transmitted and where it is preserved. This is a matter of a curious phylogenesis about which Freud later writes, in *Moses and Monotheism*, that even if biology

> rejects the idea of acquired qualities being transmitted to descendants, . . . we cannot *au fond* imagine one without the other. . . . If we accept the continued existence of such memory traces in our archaic inheritance, then we have bridged the gap between individual and mass psychology and can treat peoples as we do the individual neurotic; . . . It is bold, but inevitable. (MM, 128)

If Freud here condemns himself to neo-Lamarckism, it is because he does not take tertiary retentions, the basis of epiphylogenesis, into account[19]— nor, in fact, technics in general. Yet they are of supreme importance since memory's epiphylogenetic structure uniquely inculcates a process of psychic *and* collective individuation governed by what I have suggested should be formalized as a general organology,[20] in which the psychic apparatus is continuously reconfigured by technical and technological apparatuses and social structures.[21]

Only by thinking the evolution of the psychic apparatus organologically (i.e., as a cerebral organ interacting with other vital organs, forming a body), in relation to both evolving social structures (qua social organ-izations) and the technical and technological configurations constructing tertiary retention (qua artificial organs), can the psyche's process of inherited internalization—which is called *education*—be properly assessed.

However, as the internalization of the heritage of previous generations, only possible because of memory's organological (tertiary) nature, this transmission itself presupposes a close intergenerational relationship that can be achieved only *as education* through a relationship linking the child, as a minor with no access to the reality principle, with living ancestors. These *living* ancestors then serve as transmitters of experience accumulated across many generations, connecting the child with *dead* ancestors; this transmission process is the very formulation and formalizing of the reality principle in its many forms of knowledge (knowing how to live, knowing what to do, knowing how to think [*savoir-vivre, savoir-faire, savoir-théorique*]. Such transmissions are precisely the pleasure principle's objects and media—the objects and media of sublimation.

In this sense, adults' primary responsibility is the transmission of the reality principle as a formalized and encoded accumulation of intergenerational experience. And as the internalization of these inherited symbolic representations, bequeathed by ancestors and transmitted by parents and other adults, this intergenerational relationship constitutes the formation of *attention*, constructed of *retentions*, which then create *protentions*, that is, the expectations without which *attention* is impossible; we will explore this further in the following chapter.

4. What the "that" makes laugh. Construction and destruction of the psychic apparatus

Conceived as such a combination of differing types of retentions—conscious, preconscious, unconscious—experienced consciously or inherited without having been directly lived, the ego and the id form the system constituting the psychic apparatus and in which

> the ego is that part of the id which has been modified by the direct influence of the external world through the medium of the *Pcpt.-Cs.* [Preconscious-Conscious]. . . . [T]he ego seeks to bring the influence of the external world to bear upon the id and its tendencies, and endeavors to substitute the reality principle for the pleasure principle which reigns unrestrictedly in the id. (Ego, 15)

When a father, grandfather, or some other adult plays or "clowns around" with children to make them laugh, since children have often not learned the reality principle and are (were) thus minors before the law (juridically not yet responsible), these adults are actually playing with their own unconscious through "jokes and stunts"; that is, through the id's connecting the unconscious and the ego. And at the same time they are "playing" with their own desire, which is not simply the pleasure principle but how it is inscribed in the Real as much as in the Symbolic, through ancestral intermediation. In their efforts to make children laugh, they act through the unconscious Freud shows us as being expressed in that laughter, thus following a trajectory that is not simply repressive authority nor reality principle but the comprehensive and collusive authority of *fantasy* (the fruit of the imagination, *phantasia*)—of which "the dream language of myth" is part.

Yet laughter is an essential element in the construction of the psychic apparatus, produced socially through rituals and festivals or privately as in parent-child play; we call that [*ça*] "gentle persuasion [*l'autorité de tendresse*]." Channel Y's advertising campaign attempts to liquidate that complex tenderness, that complicity originating in the unconscious, and since it implicates many generations in *its* desire, finally it is the id itself that must be controlled—short-circuited—and somehow censored. This requires replacing the transgenerational superego, by which one reaches the id (in 1955 Marcuse saw television becoming an "automatic superego"), with an *attentional control*—that in fact, unfortunately, creates only channel surfing and loss of all authority, of any generalized individuation on the psychic or social level, simultaneously provoking inappropriate and sometimes extremely violent reactions from the overcensored id—for example, through delinquent, even criminal acts in minors, acts society had thought it could contain through *mechanical* repression, stripped of all symbolic authority.

In other words, Channel Y (along with the exploiters of the "available" brains of other juveniles, adults, and many elderly or impaired—those who are thus *made irresponsible* and thus relegated to structural immaturity), in simultaneously diverting primary identification and capturing the attention of young minds, purely and simply destroys the psychic apparatus's resistance to the pleasure principle, since if the psyche is properly formed, it is not reducible to consciousness or the ego but is, rather, inscribed in a *process* of psychic and collective individuation in which attention, both psychic and social, can be produced only as an intergenerational relationship.

"To capture the attention of young minds" in this sense means to capture the attention of the *systems* formed by those minds, as ego with id, such that consciousness is, according to Freud, responsible for teaching the *that*, the id, to compromise with the reality principle, but equally in which young minds "resonate" in their relation to the id, *respond* to it, thus responding to their ancestors, fathers, grandfathers, and *their* ancestors, if it is true that "responsibility" means responding to what one is given.

5. How Jesus became the son of God even before being born

The law is first of all the relationship between the generations, as Antigone says,[22] but it is also the sense of the genealogies resonating throughout the Bible, evident in the Gospel of St. Matthew but beginning in Genesis through the descendants of Abel's murderer, Cain, who strays far from the face of Yhwh:

> Then Cain went away from the presence of the LORD
> And dwelt in the land of Nod, East of Eden.
> Cain knew his wife, and she conceived and bore Enoch;
> and he built a city, and called the name of the city after the name of his son, Enoch.
> To Enoch was born Irad; and Irad was the father of Me-hu'ja-el,
> and Me-hu'ja-el the father of Me-thu'sha-el, and Me-thu'sha-el the father of Lamech. (Gen. 4:16–18)

Then Adam returns and Eve gives birth to Adam's third son:

> And Adam knew his wife again, and she bore a son and called his name Seth, for she said, "God has appointed for me another child instead of Abel, for Cain slew him."
> To Seth also a son was born, and he called his name Enoch.
> At that time men began to call upon the name of the LORD.
> This is the book of the generations of Adam.
> When God created man, he made him in the likeness of God.
> Male and female he created them, and he blessed them and named them Man when they were created.
> When Adam had lived a hundred and thirty years, he became the father of a son in his own likeness, after his image, and named him Seth.
> The days of Adam after he became the father of Seth were eight hundred years; and he had other sons and daughters. (Gen. 4:25, 5:1–4)

Then, in Genesis 6:1,

> When men began to multiply on the face of the earth, and daughters were born to them,
> The sons of God saw that the daughters of men were fair; and they took to wife such of them as they chose.

The multitudes issuing from Adam and Eve *desired*. Later in Genesis many other genealogies appear, of Shem, Abraham, Jacob, and so on, followed by others in Numbers. And then Matthew's Gospel, the "Book of the generations of Jesus Christ, the son of David, the son of Abraham," begins:

The son of Abraham was Isaac,
and the son of Isaac was Jacob,
and the sons of Jacob were Judah and his brothers,
and the sons of Judah were Perez and Zerah by Tamar,
and the son of Perez was Hezron,
and the son of Hezron was Ram,
[Etc.] (Matt. 1:2–3)

In Matthew 1:17,

So all the generations from Abraham to David are fourteen generations,
and from David to the taking away to Babylon
fourteen generations,
and from the taking away to Babylon to the coming of Christ
fourteen generations.
Now the birth of Jesus Christ was in this way.
When his mother Mary was going to be married to Joseph,
before they came together the discovery was made that she was with child by
the Holy Spirit;
and Joseph her husband, being an upright man and unwilling to put her to
shame, had a mind to put her away privately.[23]

This is the scene—Joseph's renunciation of Mary—with which Pasolini begins *The Gospel According to St. Matthew.* Joseph repudiates his wife, the descendant of Adam and Eve, who is carrying a child—which is not his—in her pregnant belly. Then an angel appears to him—and Joseph *adopts* this child who is not his: Joseph becomes *responsible* for the child, recognizing him as his own and *caring* for him. The child becomes the son of God.

According to Thomas Mann as well as to Freud, it was Moses, as an adopted child—an Egyptian adopted by the Jews—through whom Yahveh is revealed as "the God of the Fathers":

Thus Amran and Jochebed became Moses' parents before men, and Aaron was his brother. Amran had fields and herds, and Jochebed was the daughter of a stone-mason. They did not know what to call the unlikely little lad; in the end they gave him a half-Egyptian name, or rather half of an Egyptian name. For the sons of the land were often named Ptah-mose, Amen-mose, or Ra-mose: in other words, sons of those gods. Amran and Jochebed preferred to leave out the god-name and simply call the boy Mose, or just "son." The question was, whose?[24]

Then, in the "Book of the generations of Jesus Christ, son of David, son of Abraham," the Gospel of St. Matthew, in which God's messenger says to Joseph:

> Joseph, son of David, have no fear of taking Mary as your wife; because that which is in her body is of the Holy Spirit. And she will give birth to a son; and you will give him the name Jesus; for he will give his people salvation from their sins. . . .
>   And Joseph did as the angel of the Lord had said to him, and took her as his wife. And he had no connection with her until she had given birth to a son; and he gave him the name of Jesus. (Matt. 1:20–25)

Thus even before he was born, Jesus had become the son of God, the symbol of the fathers of the Church and the institution of the Church, which Kant, defining the Enlightenment as *maturity*—adulthood—calls the Symbol.[25]

6. The fruits of desire, psychopower, and the minoritization of the masses

The writer of the blog *Antipub—Décryptage du désenchantement* [Anti-Ads—Deciphering Disenchantment] correctly understands what is at stake in Channel Y's advertising campaign: reversal of generational hierarchy, destruction of generational differences, and the restructuring of that confusion. I would assert, on the other hand, that this strategy is not obliging adults to submit to their children's *desires*;[26] the apparatus of attention control is aimed at soliciting and exciting not only desires but *drives*. The goal is the stimulation of immature drives, making them prescriptive for adults as well by inverting intergenerational relations, the result of which is organized mass regression, cultural minoritization, and (even through legislation, now) the imposing of premature maturation.

Desire is in fact not at all Channel Y's target. On the contrary: desire unfolds and is defined *socially* as circuits of transindividuation across the generations, circuits on which the transindividual's identity and significa- tion are formed; that is, through the production of the psychic, as well as the social, object of attention. Such a production process connects the generations spiritually, culturally, and communally. But desire can also generate ancestry through filiation, the creating of families, and taking on

[handwritten marginalia: "give into desires when not able to handle desires", "Harmful if causing premature maturation"]

Hyper-attention – living in the moment

the obligation to educate children by transmitting to them the fruits of desire: a sense of culture and community.

Short-circuiting generational inheritance effaces both what differentiates children, parents, grandparents, and, at the same time, cultural memory, consciousness, and attention to what is passed down through the myriad human experiences accumulated as secondary and tertiary retentions underlying cultural knowledge.[27] Systems of sliced and segmented audience capture such as Channel Y replace the psychic apparatus that should be constructing both ego and id (as well as the transindividuation circuits in which the transindividual is worked out as the objects and fruits of desire[28]) with a psycho*technical* apparatus that controls attention yet no longer deals with desire but rather with drives, short-circuiting past (and present) experience by foregrounding future experience (i.e., any future *as* experience) in advance.

Give into Desires + drives destroys connection to our past

These psychotechnological systems of psychopower constitute the biopower Michel Foucault has analyzed so thoroughly. But that operation entails the possible creation of control-oriented and "modular" societies in which marketing becomes the central function of social development,[29] replacing traditional social regulation. Channel Y's ad campaign clearly shows attention control made possible by psychotechnological systems (the key technologies of societies of control), short-circuiting the psychic system for the production of *desire*, which is inherently intergenerational.

This short-circuiting is consistent with "job skills" and "life skills" [*des savoir-faire et des savoir-vivre*], chief characteristics of hyperindustrial, service societies that lead to consumers not being in charge of their very existence. But this deprivation, which is also a deprivation of the responsibility that defines human existence, also short-circuits the psychic links *between* the generations—and of the psyche itself, which metamorphoses from the status of "consciousness" to that of "brain"; when controlled by the audiovisual cultural industries, psychopower destroys the transmission and education of *philia*, the intimate connection among the generations.

not really true it is a set up.

The fundamental problem, and the crippling limit of this attention-control apparatus, is that it destroys attention itself, along with the ability to concentrate on an *object* of attention, which is a social faculty; the construction of such objects is in fact the construction of society itself, as civil space founded on [cultural] knowledge including social graces, expertise, and critical thinking (i.e., contemplation). This destruction leads directly to an increase in juvenile misconduct, but by putting children

Manners

and adolescents on trial and imposing a premature, potentially penal maturity on them, we do no more than divert public attention from what creates attention in the first place: adult attention toward minors and of minors' developing attention.

In other words, at the same time that we make children into the infantilizing definers of adults, we cast them in the role of scapegoat—in Greek, *pharmakon* (which means both "poison" and "remedy"). The juvenile delinquent, who may have been a victimizer, also serves here as the expiatory victim discharged from his own crimes. But for the Greeks, the fact that the scapegoat was a *pharmakon* meant that such attention diversion could only be an *expediter*, in the long term only increasing the evil it should immediately and forcefully have ameliorated.

What do these children deserve; what do "our" children deserve; what do children deserve, who(so)ever they are? Do they not deserve, at least, to have fathers, grandfathers, and a family (which is fundamentally always adoptive) within which they can *play*,[30] and through doing so learn to respect, that is, to love, and not merely to fear? What does it mean to play with one's daughter or grandson? It means to laugh and to "forget about time" with them—to give them one's time, and to give it not merely to their brains but to the formation of their nascent attention by concentrating one's adult attention on their juvenility—as imagination.

To play with a child is to take care of the child, opening the paths by which transitional spaces are created, paths that stimulate the origins of art, culture, and ultimately of everything that forms the symbolic order and the "dream language of myths," such as the aura Winnicott so subtly theorizes through observing and analyzing a mother nurturing her baby:

> Transitional objects and transitional phenomena belong to the realm of illusion which is at the basis of initiation of experience. This early stage in development is made possible by the mother's special capacity for adapting to the needs of her infant, thus allowing the infant the illusion that what he or she creates really exists.
>
> This intermediate area of experience, unchallenged in respect of its belonging to inner or external (shared) reality, constitutes the greater part of the infant's experience, and throughout life is retained in the intense experiencing that belongs to the arts and to religion and to imaginative living, and to creative scientific work.[31]

Giving children this time for amusement and laughter from earliest childhood means giving access to the Muses, to the imagination, which alone can lead to the child's enchantment and which grounds the imaginative life, the source of art, science, and all forms of cultural connection.

On the other hand, allowing psychotechnologies to take control of the child's developing attention means letting the culture industry destroy those transitional spaces—and the transitional *objects*, the first forms of tertiary retentions,[32] that can appear only through them; such spaces form the basis of all systems of care and nurturance: a *transitional* space is first and foremost a system of caring.

Fantasy, created through *phantasia* (i.e., through the imagination's formation of symbolic mediations), is humanity's most precious gift: it engenders the very spirit of human culture, including science, since as Bachelard shows, science results from imaginative play in the specific form of attention we call *contemplation* (*theoria*), which then results in a mode of *observation* in which pleasure and reality seem to coincide: the reality principle does not oppose the pleasure principle here, but rather is its product.

Enchantment through fantasy, without which the symbolic order cannot be formed (not even in the language of science), *uncontrolled* cultural industrialization activates the psychopower of attentional control, which then constrains fantasy (having become "entertainment") to the role of capturing its audience through the most archaic drives, then compelling it to construct a consciousness reduced to simple, reflex cerebral functions, which is always disenchanted and always "available." Care is completely destroyed, since the diversion of attention occurs before the formation of any other definition of attention can be passed, through symbolic regimes and their bequeathed transindividual significations, transferred as education, from adult ancestors to their minor descendants. This lost care is also the reciprocal recognition of ancestors by their descendants, which is also vital to the formation of proper attention.

Channel Y's publicity campaign, focusing as it does on the youth "segment" or "slice" of the television audience, is the perfect manifestation of this destruction of proper care as attention and recognition, by both adults and minors. It is quite ironic that Channel Y, through an advertising agency similar to that of TF1 (and only a few years after TF1, through its former CEO, Patrick Le Lay)[33] had felt the need to *confess to its crime*[34]—and it is indeed a crime if it is criminal to attack the public order at its very foundation by appealing to the drives, and if it is true that the first of these foundations is knowledge as an intergenerational legacy; I will return to this, with Kant, in the next chapter. In this sense, it is a scandal that neither the French Audiovisual Council nor the agencies responsible for the approval and verification of television advertising felt the need to control these central, extreme forms of incivility that could result only in the *systematic* spread of incivility throughout the culture.

The fact that these television channels no longer hesitate to claim that they systematically use attention-seizing audiovisual mechanisms to bring about—and specifically—adulthood's regression to childhood indicates that this psychotechnological destruction is also aimed at the very social structure that led, with time, to the Enlightenment—to what Frederick II's German subjects called *Aufklärung*. Kant shows us that *Aufklärung* is historically what defines "adulthood" as collective individuation and, within the *social* sphere, a developmental stage of the psyche instructed and instrumentalized *by the book* as psychotechnics, and thus the critical ground of knowledge.[35]

Yet we are now in the midst of a revolution in cultural and cognitive technologies, and in the very foundations of knowledge in which, as François Fillon stated in 2007, we are engaged in the "battle of intelligence."[36] In the context of such an ambitious and appropriate project, what lessons might we learn from the Enlightenment, which Kant also calls "the century of Frederick," and which he presents to us as the victory of adulthood?

§ 2 The Battle of Intelligence for Maturity

7. General principles for attention formation—assuming that there is a technique for its acquisition

The *psychotechnological* age is an inversion of the *psychotechnical*, which is also *nootechnological*, consisting of mental techniques of which writing, as the foundation of "the republic of letters" characteristic of the public space during the Enlightenment, is the most essential: as *hypomnēmaton*, writing was the basis of government for both the self and other, as Michel Foucault shows more and more systematically in his later works, and as the practicing of *melētē* and *epimēleia* by the Stoics and the Epicureans— but also by the early Christians and the monastics. "The book" is the psychotechnique for attention formation lying as much behind Jewish monotheism as Greek philosophy, science, and literature; the synthesis of these religions and philosophies of the book lead directly to Christianity.

In other words, strategies for concentrating attention are not unique to our time: to concentrate or capture attention is to *form* it. Reciprocally, to form attention is to capture it, as every teacher knows. Attention formation—which Moses Mendelssohn, explaining the nature of *Aufklärung*, called *Bildung* (encompassing both *Kultur* and *Aufklärung*[1])—is a fundamental aspect of all human society and of the process of individuation that is both psychic and collective; and since it is indissociably both psychic and social, attention formation is also what Gilbert Simondon calls the "transindividual," a term Pontalis also uses, as we have seen, but to designate the unconscious.

The formation of at-tention always consists of the psychotechnical accumulation of re-tentions and pro-tentions. Attention is the flow of consciousness, which is temporal and, as such, is created initially by what Husserl analyzes as "primary" retentions—"primary" because they consist of apparent (present) objects whose shapes I retain as though they were themselves present. This retention, called "primary" precisely because it occurs in perception, is then "conditioned" by "secondary" retentions, as the past of the attentive consciousness—as its "experience." Linking certain primary retentions with secondary retentions, consciousness projects protentions, as anticipation. The constitution of attention results from accumulation of both primary and secondary retentions, and the projection of protentions as anticipation.

Yet the *formation* of attention is always already simultaneously a psychic and a social faculty, to the extent that its concentration channels primary retentions according to the individual's secondary psychic retentions, while inscribing them in *collective* secondary retentions that symbolize and support "tertiary" retentions.[2] Collective *individuation* consists of collective *retentions*, linked with those psychically co-individualized only through sharing a common retentional base; this retentional base, forming what Simondon calls "the pre-individual milieu" in which transindividuation occurs, consists of objects that are also the objective recollections of epiphylogenetic memory—technics.[3] As Plato shows, it is only within this epiphylogenetic setting that properly mnemotechnical objects, *hypomnēmata* (Greek for attention-capture psychotechnologies), can appear, which, as tertiary retentions, form the material basis of psychotechnics.

Thus, materially and spatially projected onto psychotechnical supports—rendered tertiary—collective secondary retentions can be internalized by those who have not actually experienced them directly but who project onto them their own lived secondary retentions. This is what Freud himself refers to as projection.[4] As the basis of the adoptive process, this projective mechanism also allows for the creation of the transindividual: attention formation through its social accumulation (i.e., *education*) is the path by which individual psyches become not only *co*-individual but *trans*-individual, even at the unconscious level, about which in this respect one might say, as Lacan does, that it is "structured like a language."[5]

In the course of human history many attention-forming techniques have been conceived and practiced; in their great variety they all alter the psychic machinery's organization, not merely the organization of society: this is a particularly important example of the objects and processes a *general organology* helps us understand. And we will see how current brain imaging allows us to observe ways in which synaptogenesis is profoundly modified by contemporary media,[6] which create an environment that Katherine Hayles has described as one in which the brains of the youngest children, living in a numeric world of "rich media," are structured differently from those of the preceding generation.[7] And more specifically, these young brains are having increasing difficulty reaching what Hayles calls "deep attention."

The generation preceding these preadult brains currently in formation at the synaptic level (one of the neurophysiological bases for the stabilization of their general attentional capacity), that generation whose brains are structured differently from mediatized children's—*we* are that generation: the readers as well as the author of this very text—we can and must hope that some of those youthful consciousnesses whose synaptogenesis is in process as I write this in 2007 will themselves one day read it. To be capable, to be compelled, to want, above all to know this belief and this hope, these are the infinitives of adulthood, and of our current responsibility to the next generations.[8]

Whatever a given society's form may be, one of its most distinctive features is the way in which it forms attention, thereby configuring the psyche as well as social structures and conceiving the various attention-forming techniques created in tertiary retention. Among these psychotechniques, the sacred writing of the Book produces the formulation of a dogmatic attention characterized by creation of a Law, as moral as it is juridical, and the foundation of the kingdom of Judea; then, later, as an evangelical gloss on the Dogma, as a symbolic institutional *body*, the Roman Church, which Kant simply calls the Symbol.[9]

There is, then, dogmatic attention, which is not a pejorative qualification since "religion" does not exist without "dogma," and no adoptive process exists that does not involve the adoption of a dogma (religious or laic) for what is adopted, whether it be the Roman family, official history, or so on. Indeed, monotheistic religion is a major stage in the history of attention formation as a process unifying collective individuation according to a certain concept of genealogy, that is, of intergenerational relationships, affirming the grounding principles of unification whose juridico-moral basis is the Ten Commandments.

8. The adult minor's malignancy and the mind's pharmacology

Kant teaches us that during the *Aufklärung*, the secular book [*le livre profane*] allows for the critique of dogma—not only *allows* for it but *requires* it as the successful psychic and social achievement of maturity, defined as the power to think and the will to know; with the secular book, Kant says, majority is a critical faculty presupposing the ability to read and write: these are the proper usages of a reasoning public "as a scholar before the literate world" (WEK).[10] For Kant, adulthood is reserved for the savant, for those who would today be called "experts."[11] Yet in fact the opposite is true, with the exception that "maturity" is indeed reserved for "savants" in the sense that *everyone* is destined to become a savant and that savants are destined to become adults: to dare and to want to know [*oser et vouloir savoir*], in this sense meaning that they make use of their understanding and thus the need, the will, and the knowledge to critique and, as a result, to move beyond minority status, whatever they may then be: generally they achieve adulthood [*majoritairement accéder à la majorité*], leaving minority status behind.

This is the "battle of intelligence," and it is precisely that: a battle of a mind that claims in principle that the democratic (i.e., collective) majority is founded on an adulthood understood as "courage and will" resulting from individual knowledge: "*Sapere aude!* Dare to know! Have courage to use your own understanding—that is the motto of enlightenment" (WEK). *Aufklärung*, adulthood, which is "humanity's departure from minority as the inability to use its understanding—its power to think—without external direction" (WEK), requires the courage and the will to know. But *against what* does this courage and this will to know for oneself, not to depend on old ideas, the dogmas spread and maintained by those who pretend to think for us, the learned ones and experts we seem unable to do without—against what must we place our adult character traits, the struggle of our courage and our will? Against our tendency toward the laziness and cowardice characterizing adult minority, a tendency haunting the mind as the malignant spirit of voluntary constraint:

Laziness and cowardice are the reasons why so great a proportion of men, long after nature has released them from alien guidance (*natura-liter maiorennes*), nonetheless gladly remain in lifelong immaturity, and why it is so easy for others to establish themselves as their guardians. It is so easy to be immature. If I have a book to serve as my understanding, a pastor to serve as my conscience, a physician to determine my diet for me, and so on, I need not exert myself at all. (WEK)

In other words, if *Aufklärung* (adulthood; the affirmation of courage and will against laziness and cowardice) presupposes this psychotechnique of attention formation—that is, writing (and simultaneously reading, if the nootechnics of the book's *hypomnēmaton* is the constitutive condition of a critical public space, a "republic of letters")—then this *pharmakon*, the book, must not take the place of understanding.

The *remedy* for the mind's weakness, the book, as a psychotechnique of attention formation and the basis of monotheism and philosophy, is thus also the mind's fatal *poison*, as Plato said when he reproached the Sophists for what he calls their *logography*, and for substituting for dialectic as thought itself (as dialogue or *dianoia*) a rhetorical technique for fabricating a *prêt-à-penser* by the psychotechnical powers of the *logographic hypomnēsis*, the power of the book.

Kant's issue here is the *mind's pharmacology*, and maturity as the *pharmaka's* proper end; this is also the philosophical question's instigation as such. The fact that the Sophists had already raised the issue through philosophical critique means that it was also the question of *money* and of its role in the life of the mind. The adult minor, lazy and cowardly, says, "I need not think if only I can pay; others will readily undertake the irksome work for me" (WEK).

According to Plato, the Sophists had already offered young Athenians—for a fee—the reduction (the short-circuiting) of the time required for a dialectical education by accelerating the process of attention formation—but as the power to capture the attention of *others*, through acquisition of the techniques of the *pithanon*, persuasion as the method of controlling others' attention, making them accept any suggested viewpoint. The rhetorical persuader is like a sleight-of-hand artist, *thaumaturge* to the Greeks; that is, a person with no regard for the truth nor even for the viewpoint he is espousing: by extension, no regard for the quality of work required to constitute the transindividual—nor for the significance of the dialogue (with another or with oneself *as* another) at the heart of the dialectic, a significance Plato calls "the idea."

But the work of constituting the transindividual involves the formulation of a transindividuation *process* that cares not just for language but for *things*, allowing us not just to designate them but to think them, to make them appear, and finally to give them their place—by giving them meaning. This is the careful, meticulous work Plato calls "dialectic," a term Kant maintains in the *Critique of Pure Reason*. But short-circuiting this dialectical process through sophistical attention formation results in mental *deformation* and, in the end, the destruction of attention (as cynicism).

Kant tells us that as an adult minor defined by laziness and cowardice, I can always avoid the dialectical responsibility of thinking *at all*, and thus of knowing what I should "serve." From the Sophists to twenty-first-century *service industries*, steering clear of what Kant calls the "tutors" of the Enlightenment, I can satisfy my laziness and cowardice at the expense of my courage and my will to know and think (my individual responsibility), avoiding what amounts to a constant battle of and for intelligence. This situation is characteristic of sophistics, but if we remember that Kant defines Enlightenment thinkers as a social order *organizing* the battle of and for intelligence (in Prussia, under Frederick II's direction, for Kant), it is equally characteristic of our current hyperindustrial service economies, in which, however, it has now exceeded all limits. This unprecedented destruction of attention imposes entirely new responsibilities on *our* economic and political leaders, and more generally on the "tutors" of contemporary society.

Today, attention control via cultural and cognitive technologies ("technologies of the *spirit* [*esprit*]," those malignant spirits haunting the adult minor as apparatuses for capturing, forming, and deforming attention), has become the very heart of hyperindustrial society;[12] however, it no longer relies on psychotechnics but on psychotechnological apparatuses whose devastation we see on TF1, Channel Y, and so on. Here and now, at the very moment when the worldwide "battle of intelligence" on which François Fillon wants to focus his political energies must be engaged,[13] it is all the more urgent to read what Kant writes "as a scholar before the literate world"—a public we still are and thus, as adults, have the responsibility of acting in a manner that will permit following generations to assume adult responsibilities as well; it is more than urgent to read Kant on maturity *as* responsibility—individual and collective—in this battle of intelligence against the inherent laziness and cowardice that also characterize essentially fallible beings.

9. Public attention as critical attention and as the historical formation of maturity during the Enlightenment

The condition of adult immaturity, Kant writes, is a kind of crime in the face of which enlightenment, as the moment of departure from immaturity, confronts adult men and women with their responsibility, defined as the free and *public* use of reason. However, adult infantilization, systematically pursued by today's cultural industries and resulting in the premature maturation of children and adolescents, whose psychic apparatus has purely and simply been destroyed by the psychotechnical systems of those same cultural industries—this infantilization is being manifested in an unprecedented regression. Reading Kant closely, we see that to think through and understand this contemporary state of affairs *require* us to fight against it, as scholars before the literate world. And of course we must also interpret Kant's text relative to the current situation. In 1983, Michel Foucault taught a course on Kant's text in France,[14] then published a second reading of the text in the United States in 1984; in these two texts, Foucault emphasizes the uniqueness of the event itself and of the connections between topicality and historical thinking that Kant, as a "modern" thinker, inaugurates. And Foucault emphasizes the fact that Kant sees maturity, as both departure and outcome, as the very meaning of the Enlightenment.

However, Foucault never mentions the place Kant reserves for reading and writing in the formation of this process—even though "The Writing of the Self" (included in DE4) is from the same period. My effort here will be to show that at the conclusion of "The Writing of the Self," Foucault's analysis of the enhanced role of the historical in Western society is also an occultation of writing, as psychotechnique and nootechnique, at once juridical, administrative, and epistemological, and that this occultation leads Foucault into major contradictions that obstruct both his rereading of Kant's text and the possibility of combating our current regression.

"Public," during the Enlightenment—and in *Was ist Aufklärung?*—means "the literate world"; that is, a public capable of reaching that specific form of attention shared by the book and its author, assuming that the book has captured the writer's attention during the process of writing:

writing is already an "auto-capturing" of attention and as such forms the basis of what Foucault calls "the technique of the self."

Kant's scholar and reading public have achieved maturity, given that reading, being read, and being capable of writing what they have read—either to develop their writing skills in the work in progress, in the case of the writer, or in order to write another book, article, report, review, or commentary on a text, in the case of the reader (who could be, for example, a high school or college student, a teacher, a civil servant, a priest, etc.)—in this scenario they have both successfully reached the critical form of attention. It is nonetheless extremely important to remember that the book can just as likely suspend the reader in immaturity—starting with the writer as first reader—to "replace understanding," in which case the auto-capture of attention can become auto-alienation of the writer by the book itself, which writes him. Kant does not expressly emphasize this alternative reading, but it is clearly supported by his reasoning; thus, maturity and immaturity are two possibilities of *the same pharmakon*: of that *hypomnēsia* Plato confronted, faced with the sophistic minoritization of Greek citizenry.

The *use of reason*, which creates public access to critique as the mode of transition from minority to maturity, is also the *use of the book* through which psychotechnics leads not to the re- or dis-placement of understanding but rather to a nootechnics opening onto a kind of understanding that is always and intrinsically public. It is the *critical* exercise of being exposed to critique, as Kant himself was in 1784 before all the Prussians, including Frederick II, his enlightened monarch, in the *Berlinische Monatsschrift*. Kant's short discourse on *Aufklärung* is thus also a discourse on that journal's noetic sense and on its role as a "spiritual" or intellectual instrument in what Kant already defines as a battle of and for intelligence. For Kant, reason's *private* usage, very different from its *public* usage, is nonetheless always coordinated with the social mechanisms without which society could not function; this coordination reveals responsibility's flip side: responsibility as the need for obedience:

> Now in many affairs conducted in the interests of a community, a certain mechanism is required by means of which some of its members must conduct themselves in an entirely passive manner so that through an artificial unanimity the government may guide them toward public ends, or at least prevent them from destroying such ends. Here one certainly must not argue, instead one must obey. (WEK)

Public use of reason is not that of collective, social, and disciplined action but of individual thought manifested in the process of collective individuation within the critical space of *publication*; this is why Kant invokes the *public use* of reason, since reason's private use, though certainly not blind (if it were, it would not be a use of *reason*), remains passive. This means that it is obedient, obedience being a form and dimension of care that puts reason to work in service to society as a kind of machine regulated by its various usages, the "private" being only a single element: "one must obey."

However, this private usage is still reason in the strict sense that it must be capable of being critiqued *by this very reason*, but uniquely through its public usage. And in this sense, in becoming public, private reason must be capable of being individualized both psychically and collectively, as the *re-forming* of community affairs. Reason's public usage "takes care of" the other form or dimension of care, its private or adult dimension, which shows care both through producing attention to what within the larger system of care (the social apparatus), and through reason's private usage, caring for the social *within* the system of care that it forms. It *can*, however, lead to wrong outcomes in community affairs since it is a kind of *pharmacological machine*, a collection of all sorts of artifacts that constitute *Kultur* and whose union with *Aufklärung* forms *Bildung*, as Moses Mendelssohn indicates.

To make public use of reason, as a scholar before the literate world, Kant insists, is *to write*—"as a scholar who speaks through his writings" (WEK), to practice the psychotechnics of writing's becoming nootechnics, grounding reason's public usage before a reading public that thus also can write. Making public use of reason means addressing oneself to precisely that literate public as a power, a will, and a critical knowledge through the nootechnics that, as the formation of a specific kind of attention (now called "public opinion"), opens up an associated psychotechnical space.[15] A *psycho*technical milieu can become *noo*technical insofar as it also becomes associatively symbolic; a symbolic milieu is "associated" when those receiving its symbols are able and apt to individualize them through what Husserl calls the communitization of knowledge, without which it is neither knowledge nor intelligence (acquisition of both of which is always a battle—what both Plato and Kant call a dialectic). And we will see, with Foucault, how and why Seneca proposes just such a reciprocity as the necessary condition for the writing of the self through the epistolary dialectic (DE4, 420, and Section 44 in Chapter 9).

The transformation of psychotechnics into nootechnics requires the organization of social structures into what the Greeks called the *polis*, in which the *grammatistēs* (i.e., the teacher, quickly enough becoming the sophist) taught alphabetics and grammatical form to citizens, thus shaping their psychic *and* social attention, which, for the Greeks, constituted their *political* attention, resulting in *doxa*—opinion, in turn transforming the psyche into what the Greeks called the logical *organon*, a special form of attention capture and organization constructed on *logos*—the associated symbolic medium, which they saw as a specific method of making *literal* public use [*à la lettre*] not simply of reason (the *psychē* as *logos*) but of language (*glossa* as *logos*). This is precisely what Plato calls dialectic.

Readers, as the receivers of reason's public exercise (as literate usage before the literate world, and who are also—at least ostensibly—writers), through the circulation of various writings such as exchanges of letters, gazettes, reviews, books, and so on, were exposed to the formation of a particular attention that, in Kant's Enlightenment, was addressed to *all*, to "the people," "the literate world." Even if they were serfs, no more than slaves, all of the monarch's subjects, being equal before their Father as God's creatures, were potentially eligible. This attention formation, fostered by an increasingly literate social environment that extended further and further beyond the print shop, forcefully encouraged their maturation process in the battle to emerge from immaturity, like butterflies emerging from the cocoon: adulthood was assumed to be tantamount to the becoming-adult of society itself through the process of education—the battle of and for intelligence that Kant and others addressed, fearing Frederick II the Great's death, but which utilized mental (spiritual) weapons produced through the elevation of psychotechnics to nootechnics.

By the same token, making only private, passive use of reason, as being a "part of the machine" (WEK) that is the social structure, however, can and must also be seen as making public use of it, since the social apparatus is always capable of being improved upon and can thus always acknowledge its flaws and stop them—even if they become detrimental, like the *pharmakon* that as remedy can always and suddenly become poisonous; the person who makes only private use of reason, as an element of the social machine that can be arrested, can and even absolutely must as a member of the community as a whole, or even of the world community, as a consequence, address the public in the role of a scholar, in the proper sense of that term; he can most certainly argue, without thereby harming the affairs for which as a passive member he is partly responsible. Thus it would be disastrous if an officer on duty who was given a command by his superior were to question the appropriateness or utility of the order. He must obey. But as a scholar he cannot be justly constrained from making comments about errors in military service, or from placing them before the public for its judgment. (WEK)

Not only can he defend doing so; it is his most absolute duty. And what is true of the soldier is also true of the priest, as educator, nurturer of consciousness, who officiates in the very specific symbolic environment of the "Symbol of the Church":

> Likewise a pastor is bound to instruct his catechumens and congregation in accordance with the symbol of the church he serves, for he was appointed on that condition. But as a scholar he has complete freedom, indeed even the calling, to impart to the public all of his *carefully* considered and well-intentioned thoughts concerning mistaken aspects of that symbol. (WEK; emphasis added)

What is true of sacred dogma is obviously at its most powerful in the profane dogmas on which the machinic social apparatus rests. Even if we can distinguish two usages of reason, they must interrelate [*composer*] ceaselessly, or else they are not reason: reason is a unity with two faces:

1. It implies obedience to the social and the symbolic order, as law, but also as heritage and transmission of myths, dogmas, "illusions," and ways of life involving the more or less congenial fantasies of a people who constitute the unity of a social body as support for *philia*,[16] and what Kant calls "the private use of reason."

2. It also implies, by the same movement, but one that has become a movement of historical conquest, the *public* usage of reason, presupposing the capacity to critique the social order, to identify its weaknesses, and, finally, to expand the frontiers of knowledge.

But this public use of reason requires that the psychotechnique of critical attention underlying textual *hypomnēsis* has been socially instrumentalized as nootechnique, that is, through the formation of a public attention through which *Kultur* becomes *Bildung*. This means that the historical movement called *Aufklärung* is a stage within a genealogy of the mind that is itself only thinkable as a general organology (as a genealogy of mental instruments, as "phenomenotechniques" of the spirit [*phénoménotechnique de l'esprit*].[17]

In Chapters 7 and 8 we will explore how Foucault correlates the fundamental elements of this organology of the mind/spirit, itself predicated on a particular theory of attention and a history of its formation through attention-capture techniques forming it into a "psychosocial apparatus"— at the very historical moment when these psychotechnical systems (technologies of control), as constituted through the intermediary of psychopower, are destroying the psychic, as well as the social, apparatus.

10. The organology of maturity and the battle of intelligence for and against it

The *public* attention defining *Aufklärung* is the basic condition required for constituting what since the Enlightenment we have called "public opinion," print media's transformation of *doxa* as the Greeks had formulated it. The publicness (and thus the publishing) of opinion in the latter part of the eighteenth century is the full fruition of the "republic of letters," of printed books beginning in the early sixteenth century, and of the establishment of postal networks, whose arrival meant the ability to write and to circulate the effects of one's reading in the private, and then public, libraries then appearing throughout society, then to gazettes, then reviews; reading relationships could be established not merely with enlightened monarchs and philosophers but with anyone who, as the embodied image of the "honest man" that had emerged in the seventeenth century, formed the "literate world"—and who in France would soon become revolutionaries and bourgeois "enthusiasts." The daily broadsheets [*journaux*] of that period become the daily press of the nineteenth century.

Foucault emphasizes that Kant defines *Aufklärung* as a "historical process" centrally implicating humanity, thus making Kant a modern philosopher. But this historicity is organological (political as well as noetic and aesthetic), which, as Kant himself indicates (without directly referring to it), is essential to the process: this organology of adulthood must pass through the socialization of reading and printed writing. Foucault will himself become interested in this "organology of the *esprit*" when, long after *The Order of Things*, which had already given the classical *epistēmē* a constitutive role in creating images of the world [*tableaux du monde*],[18] he lights upon what he calls the "techniques of the self"—which for Foucault are related to manuscript writing.

According to Kant, adult or mature society is the "society of the century of Frederick," the literate public. This society, resting on the increasingly general ability to read and write brought about by the circulation of books, manuscripts, gazettes, reviews, and a new kind of psychic and collective individuation (echoes of Martin Luther and Ignatius Loyola [OT, 321]): this historical form of individuation is an illumination [*éclairement*], by Enlightenment thinkers, and an explanation [*éclaircissement*]— *Aufklärung* in its fullest sense. This is the context for Diderot's 1751 publication of the *Encyclopaedia*, a new kind of technical individuation. And in 1798 Kant wrote to Friedrich Nicolaï that "the writing of books is not an insignificant profession in a society that is already very advanced in matters of civilization, and in which the ability to read has become a nearly irrepressible and universal need" (WEK).[19] An "organology of intelligence" such as this requires a new kind of social organization in which scholarly institutions become the impetus for the educational formation of society itself, leading directly to the position taken by Condorcet,[20] which nearly a century after Kant's article in the *Berlinische Monatsschrift* will result in the *institution* of mandatory public education as the systematic internalization of this form of attention, by means of attention-capture techniques defined during the Enlightenment with the clear intention of establishing maturity, which Jules Ferry as well calls the transformation from minority to individual adulthood, and thus to the collective expression of "mature" public opinion through the democratic process.

The "battle of intelligence," which is concomitant with the history of humanity, is also the history of psychotechnics that as it develops into nootechnics transforms both the psychic and social: it is a process of psychic individuation, collective and technical. Consequently, if there is a contemporary history of this battle of intelligence that for the first time is defined economically,[21] it can only be written about politically *and* economically if it is inscribed in this older history, which thus bestows upon it the means of specifying the original nature of the techniques and technologies through which this battle finally arrives at the debut of the twenty-first century—which is also the one in which, for centuries France, along with other rare nations, politically and economically "dominated" the world, . . . nonetheless, the world has awakened and taken its revenge on history. Entire continents are on a quest for progress. Their population is young, gifted, terribly motivated. As we struggle to preserve our heritage, they fight to constitute theirs.[22]

The divergent forms of attention that constitute the history of the battle for, and the conquest that is, intelligence always consist of *pharmaka* that can just as easily arm this attention as alienate it (that is, according to Enlightenment prescriptions, destroy or sterilize it by demolishing its determination to reach majority), and this is precisely why intelligence must wage a battle *for* intelligence: intelligence must fight for itself, and perhaps even against what, within itself, is bestial.

11. The psychopower of stupidity and the industrial politics of intelligence

To engage in the battle of and for intelligence means posing three preliminary questions.

1. The first requires asking oneself about the intelligence that is required to ask about intelligence. This is called reflectivity: intelligence reflecting on itself in its auto-intelligence. Reflection is necessary in order to gain true intelligence regarding what intelligence is and what is at work in the very moment of reflection, insofar as it is itself an individual intelligence caught up in a process of which it is only a part, a process of collective intelligence. Intelligence regarding what is intelligence is a requisite for *any* engagement in the battle of and for intelligence—along with the fact that a history of intelligence exists, as Kant shows, and that intelligence evolves [*devient*]. My thesis is that this history is organological; indeed that intelligence regarding intelligence *is* organological intelligence.

2. The second consists of knowing *why* it is necessary to engage in the battle for intelligence. Why can't one just "be" intelligent? This question can be understood in many ways. The first way, appropriate to our epoch, is the one behind François Fillon's statement that intelligence could become a major factor in our economic struggles. Bacon had already suggested this relative to power in general, and to the struggle for political power in particular, for example, the current power of President Sarkozy and his prime minister and the fights in which they engage: Knowledge is

power.[23] But from the outset, within the context of the twenty-first century in France and as François Fillon's general political discourse, this is a matter of *economic* power.

Yet it is necessary to know what one is fighting *for* in this economic battle that though also a battle for intelligence is nonetheless certainly not identical to the struggle for intelligence, and may sometimes be entirely its opposite. The economic battle could in principle be only a "means" of attaining the goal of intelligence. But in the course of this battle a certain reversal seems to appear, such that what might be only "means" becomes "end," and the end the means. And it further appears that what seemed an economic battle of intelligence, *by* intelligence, produces its opposite, stupidity, the destruction of attention, then irresponsibility, incivility, "the degree zero of thinking" (TCD, 44).

But perhaps this is a matter of transcending the idea of the "means," or rather, in order not to simplistically oppose ends and means and to replace thinking in terms of means by thinking in terms of media—by a thinking in terms of *an ecology of ends*. In fact, a medium—which is not an end—is also not a means to an end: it engenders ends that it is not: it engenders ends in those who finalize—those who *desire*—through it, in it, and by it. And the *technical* medium is no more a means than the *symbolic* medium: this is the place of the life of the spirit, which engenders both the symbolic milieu and the psychic and collective individuation, produced as transindividual, as spirit, but that can also asphyxiate the spirit in forms evolving over time, since this medium, like all technical media, can become toxic.[24]

Consequently, if an organological history of intelligence exists, the reason is that there are also historical and organological forms of stupidity.[25] And clearly, to work toward intelligence is to struggle against stupidity. But in order to accomplish that, in our age, it is necessary to think the organological forms of stupidity *of our age*, and that requires transcending the gross metaphysical stupidity consisting in believing that technics is a milieu in service to an end that could not itself be technical, that could not itself be organologically constituted and determined. It is this stupidity that *makes* us think, that *forces* us to think, as Deleuze says, and this stupidity, which makes us think according to a specific modality of *paying attention*, is in a fundamental relationship with shame, the shame of being human. But this shame and the thought it causes are constituted by psychotechnical media and are thus symbolic wherever they occur.[26]

In the face of stupidity I am ashamed, and this shame makes me think: it *forces* me to think—makes me *pay attention* in a very specific way (called thought), releasing a particular force. (Which? This force, resembling what Kant calls the moral law, is not, however, reduced to it.) But this stupidity cannot make me *feel* ashamed, and thus *makes* me *pay* attention to what is stupid, leading me to wrest intelligence from stupidity, which I know *is initially my own*: it can only affect me, this stupidity, because it *reminds me* that *I also*, I am (organologically) stupid, and that, as children say, in the language of the minor that is nonetheless not stupid (a language that is also that of literature, beginning with the literature called "minor"), "he who *says* it *is* it."

In other words, before struggling *against other intelligences*, including against (and through) economic intelligence, which before all else is a form of espionage, and before the question of knowing how to fight with the other forms of intelligence that develop within the framework of economic warfare, in another country, for example, in Asia, the United States, Saudi Arabia,[27] to Abu Dhabi or elsewhere, it is necessary first to begin by *battling against one's own lack of intelligence* (insofar as it is, organologically, stupidity).[28]

The battle of intelligence is the battle for intelligent being. How is one to be intelligent and, in particular, how is one to be *more* intelligent, or at least as intelligent as those who are already *very* intelligent, and who are "young, gifted, and very motivated"?[29] One should begin by *becoming* more intelligent than one already is: this begins by advancing *one's intelligence*, which is also called *upbringing*, but also to raise the general level of intelligence, most notably in *bringing children up*, and in ensuring that children raise the level of collective intelligence, including that of their own parents: in ensuring that their parents are adults, as Kant tells us, but also in ensuring that they can distinguish between the majority and minority before the minority of their children who are historically and thus organologically on the way to majority.

To distinguish maturity from minority status for a literate public within the psychotechnology called literature is also to distinguish between production of the mature and the immature mind through the book, and further, what can *reinforce* maturity or *perpetuate* minority. And to distinguish maturity from minority requires an understanding of what this elevation means and of enhancing an understanding of this knowledge as the individual and collective battle against stupidity *in this sense, as minority*, perhaps brought about by *pharmaka*, themselves the very conditions of maturity formation: of a maturity both historically and organologically advancing.

3. All of this leads us back to the third and last requirement for any contemporary battle of and for intelligence in the struggle of and with *technologies* of intelligence, in which psychotechnologies that might produce stupidity by destroying attention transform into the technologies of an individual and collective intelligence whose aim is to constitute *a* social (political) apparatus unifying *all* social apparatuses, the economic, juridical, educational, scientific, artistic, and cultural (as well as the medical), and those focusing on society's protection, such as internal and external security, and so on. All of these elements must then be reconfigured according to instrumental conditions surrounding current psychotechnologies for attention capture.

12. Psychotechnologies of stupidity and the new formation of maturity

Any such battle must begin in recognition of the fact that there are instruments of intelligence that are also weapons in a war for minds. These perpetually evolving weapons are concretized today as cultural and cognitive technologies; they have emerged through mutations taking place in numerization. Today's battle for intelligence is in fact one for control of the industrial politics of these technologies,[30] a politics of attention formation, and thus of *mature* intelligence as "the public use of one's own reason . . . as a scholar . . . before the entire literate world." But such a politics must be carried out with an understanding of the consequences of the fact that reading and writing are not what they once were: they have become numeric, hypermediated, and collaborative. These new technologies reject the industrial model based on the producer/consumer opposition (and its link to the professional/amateur opposition[31]): producers and consumers are historically created and opposed by machine-tool industrialization—and the age of grammatization.[32] "New media" technologies call these oppositions into question and constitute the core of hyperindustrial societies, and thus the contemporary industrial economy (which has become cultural capitalism), and they fundamentally restructure the *intergenerational connection* constituting intelligence as the structuring and restructuring of the retentions and protentions from which attention is constructed.

As a result, the battle over technological development requires intelligence about technology, and intelligence about intelligence in its connection to technology, both of which are currently entirely reconfiguring the intergenerational relationship. The *organological* conditions required for the formation of individual and collective intelligence are radically changing, particularly given that "individual intelligence" is never individual: individual intelligence *does not exist.*

If maturity consists of the ability to think for oneself, such thinking is only thinking insofar as it takes place *before* the entire literate world (the sole basis for democratic majority—in both senses) as the *circulation* of thought that is always surpassing itself, thought *for* the other and *through* the other (*through* the other as thinker). Thought and intelligence are always already collective: both are part of a process of individuation that is actually a metastabilizing co-individuation of the transindividual, where a circulating intelligence, as *interlegere*, forms an organological milieu linking minors and adults, parents and children, ancestors and descendants, and the generations containing mind and *spirit: pneuma, ruah, spiritus.*

Intelligence leads to knowledge, and the battle for intelligence today is what might be called the battle between consciousness industries and societies of knowledge [*des industries de la connaissance et des sociétés de savoir*]. But any such society requires a social intelligence within which it is possible to *live intelligently.* This kind of intelligence speaks of accord, of good understanding, and in this regard, the political and economic challenge becomes that of the possible appropriation and control of the technologies of intelligence and their emergence as hegemonic devices for the control of collective behavior and its being kept in a state of structural minority, as what must then be called *technologies of stupidity:* poisoning by *pharmaka* as *hypomnēmata*, which are just as much in service to *anamnesis* as to *hypomnēsis* and capable of creating both short-circuits and the long circuits of transindividuation.[33]

Hypomnesic forms have today become the very heart of an industrial system consisting of psychotechnologies that are in the process of refining somatotechnologies into microtechnologies that have actually begun to modify the very structure of the body, including body shape, and of reproductive—procreative—technologies, as well as the invention of *new kinds of bodies* and of living beings, genetic modifications, cloning, and so on. The issue of intelligence is more than ever that of *pharmaka*, and of methods of taking care, of oneself and others, within the new, intrinsically pharmacological context in which we must see ourselves.[34]

Intelligence is first and foremost a *taking care,* of *pharmaka* through the careful use of *pharmaka* against the perverse effects of *pharmaka.* Living intelligently in society means taking care of the social in such a way that the social cares for the individual *as* individual. Intelligence means articulation of the individual and society in order to overcome their apparent contradiction through a politics of the *pharmaka* and, more than ever today, through a psychotechnological industrial politics creating a de facto economic psychopower that imposes a *psychopolitics of law* nurturing this economy and transforming it into a true ecology—an ecology of the spirit.

There is nothing inevitable requiring that time (attention) be captured and monopolized in young brains by marketing, nor that this process should result in the systematic deprivation of consciousness, to the point that it might become literally impossible to (re)educate those organologically conditioned brains that have become prone to incivility and delinquency. Nor is it inevitable that older brains, subject to the same conditions, should find themselves deprived of all responsibility; that is, of their capacity to oppose such conditions. The fact that the United States suffers so massively from *attention deficit disorder,* that there are a million *otaku* children in Japan, that China has had to take action against the effects of video games—but alternatively that the battle of and for intelligence has also resulted in the creation of universities with global outreach, in such places as Saudi Arabia, result from the same psychotechnological system of global psychopower formation.

While we wait (though we must not wait contentedly) for such a global outreach system to arrive for all the generations, above all for the children and adolescents worldwide, communicating on SMS networks that are neither postal nor national but electronic and global,[35] potentially extraordinarily dangerous for the future as symbolic and *actual* deprivation created by the instigation of general irresponsibility in a time requiring the *fostering* of responsibility more than any previous one. But this new phenomenon could also be the pharmacological and organological condition for a new individual and collective intelligence, a new maturity, and a new critique. If we are to carry out a battle for intelligence, that is where we must begin: we must organologically reform the *Bildung,* reconstituting and re-forming psychosocial attention in the face of these psychotechnologies of globalized psychopower.

§ 3   Mysteries and Drives from
Aufklärung to Psychopower

13. Psychotechniques and the mystagogy of pharmacological minds (intelligence as a whole)

Well before the advent of psychotechnologies, there were nonetheless both psychotechniques and attention-capture techniques for maintaining capture in a minoritized adult, but capturing children's attention began long before such efforts with adults.[1] Since ancient times, these techniques have been applied in early childhood as lullabies, counting rhymes, fairy tales, oral storytelling, then written, including forms such as comic strips and graphic novels—and now, as "children's programming," DVDs, video games, MP3s, and targeted youth Web sites such as MySpace and Facebook.

All of these techniques are aimed at attracting and *retaining* attention, in order to produce *retentions*. Additionally, technologies of the body—somatotechnologies—such as dances, rites, and practices involving physical possession, as well as gymnastics, exercise regimens, and techniques for walking and running—are all echoes of what the Greeks called *epimēleia,* self-care, all either individual or collective techniques for channeling, and frequently for capturing, attention.[2]

Such techniques resulted not only in the Enlightenment thinkers; they are also, and perhaps most frequently, the basis of mystagogic (if not of all obscurantist) practices and behaviors. And it is important to remember that the use of attention-capture techniques to construct *critical* maturity is both very rare (initially limited to tiny ancient Greece and only among "free men") and quite recent, such as the Enlightenment program for critical maturity in which *we* [*nous*] is constituted as *everyone* [*tous*], though this does not occur until well after the French Revolution when the spread of public education created "modern society" as such. It is no accident that both "modern art" and Constantin Guys,[3] as Baudelaire notes, arrive along with public education.

In most cases, however, such techniques aim at controlling attention not in order to motivate the courage and will "to know," to gain knowledge, but on the contrary, to maintain a minoritized-adult condition.

> The guardians who have so benevolently taken over the supervision of men . . . having first made their domestic livestock dumb, and having carefully made sure that these docile creatures will not take a single step without the go-cart to which they are harnessed, these guardians then show them the danger that threatens them, should they attempt to walk alone. (WEK)[4]

In the *Republic* Plato himself uses—and says that *aiēdes* and rhapsodes should use—poetic storytelling techniques to "educate our heroes," creating citizens' minds as children's and thus no longer a threat to the formation of the philosophical mind; this is the reason that Plato, through the dialectic, focuses on having done with the always more or less mystagogic stories and myths of the pre-Socratics in addition to being rid of the kinds of rhetorical "magic" constructed by Sophists.[5]

But on the other hand, Plato also says that such techniques are *indispensable* for governing the *polis* by those same philosophers who understand how to take care of it, and who, as what Heidegger will call the "guardians of being," consequently know how to accede to the Ideas by which the city's affairs may be appropriately conducted; such techniques will thus be necessary to them, Plato says, in permitting the *synchronization* (and the unification) of the diachronic (and manifold) bodily and mental activities constituting the *polis*, such as music and choreography—what Peter Sloterdijk (referring to Plato's *Politics*) calls a set of "rules" for managing a "human park."[6]

I will come back to this last quick point later, since it seems to me that Sloterdijk neglects the fact that there is today no longer any need for directions by "guardians" and that any direction now given is no longer political: the process of capturing public attention is handled by service industries, cultural industries, and programs synchronizing individuals' activities into mass behaviors motivated by *business plans*. In other words, I will claim that Sloterdijk neglects the specificity and the originality of psychopower.

Service industries that utilize psychopower no longer sell anything to a population that thus no longer needs to pay anything: people, having abdicated their majority without being conscious of it, "give themselves" to these industries, or rather, the industries capture them as "available brain time" psychopower enterprises to sell young audiences on the market: minors beneath the legal age of responsibility thus prematurely become adults before the law—that is, before the *ça*, the id. This is all evidence of our inherent laziness and cowardice, fallible, pharmacological beings that we are.

This is the complex issue of techniques as *pharmaka*, and of systems of care perpetually readdressing, just as philosophy reiterates itself from Plato to Kant and beyond, the "battle for intelligence" the French government made its priority in 2007. But to manage this battle successfully, we must remember that *pharmacological human minds* are never satisfied in the state of domestication leading to what Peter Sloterdijk calls "anthropotechnics." On the contrary, they always need to create fantasies of *escape* from that control, lying in the shadowy place of mysteries at the heart of those *crypts* to which, as Heraclitus says, *physis* ("being" for the mystagogue Heidegger) loves (*philein*) to withdraw (*kruptestai*), where there is light, or fire, or at least *warmth*—the very crypt before which Heraclitus wants to place his Laws.[7]

To say it differently, beyond or behind Enlightenment maturity are the intellectual Motives (even more obscure but no less necessary, encrypting the unconsciousness); and the id, unifying the ego, as the machine of repression and thus of obedience, with the unconscious, which despite everything provides its motives for action, and unifying *Kultur* (culture as cults, which are always mystagogic in some way—even the most republican ones) with the Enlightenment as the critique of that mystagogy. This is the unity Moses Mendelssohn and Kant call *Bildung*, which I am calling *attention formation*, which is an *attente*, a waiting, and a *critical* waiting. And I submit that formation of such a waiting could not occur without a pharmacological artifice.

The social practices associated with any attention-capture technique, even those that, like philosophy (which operates through dialectic as an attention-capture technique extracted from the transindividual by means of a maieutic operation that "numbs the mind" confined within a collective retention, anamnesis[8]), are the results of analytic thinking, and of critique (thus of Heidegger's *Existential Analytic,* which opens the questions of ontological difference and the History of Being), these social practices, prephilosophical as well as philosophical, are *always* more or less mystagogic, because all critique is grounded in an economy of desire whose object is intrinsically mysterious—and to that extent desirable (always a disproportion, impossible to measure) desirable. This is Plato's subject in the *Symposium.*

This structure of desire and its economy, though through a pathway other than that of critique, generally facilitates both social controls, specifically subjecting minoritized adults to guardianship, and our pharmacological minds' psychic and collective individuation: the other pathway is that of the idea of *Kultur* a nation acquires, Mendelssohn asserts, "through social commerce, i.e. through poetry and rhetoric" (QL, 32), which is also the origin of what Freud calls the oneiric language of myths, folklore, and so on, all those fantasies of the imaginary that are simultaneously at the origin of science itself, forming intelligence as a social process of "being-together," "living in good intelligence," *interlegere.* For this reason, pharmacological beings cannot be domesticated for long: deprived of access to fantasy that also instructs, such beings become ineluctably enraged, potentially even savage.

At the same time, certain *instructional tendencies* are always already present in the working out of these mystagogic psychotechniques of attention capture, which, though they are as powerful as the tendencies toward "laziness and cowardice," are still not critique. This is what Romanticism discovered in opposition to Kant. Such mystagogic and pharmacological forces do not produce only domestication; on the contrary, the very heritage of this *Kultur* produced through cults and other mysteries also feeds a desire for "high-mindedness" such that "if only they refrain from inventing artifices to keep themselves in [domestication], men will gradually raise themselves from barbarism" (WEK), and to keep them there over time by instrumentalizing this heritage—for example, as pseudo-identity.[9]

Like Kant, I believe not only that all human beings *want* to become adults, to the extent that they do not persist in maintaining themselves in their laziness and cowardice, but that at the very moment when the planet has been poisoned by humanity itself, that is, by all of the remedies and poisons that humans have become, its *pharmaka*, humanity's future depends on this adulthood *for everyone*: on a critical maturity's becoming politically and economically mature, and on the development of responsibility as the concrete form of intelligence that, through the invention of a new industrial model,[10] is the only credible possibility for, as Fillon says, "rethinking the French model from top to bottom."

It is also my belief, once again with Kant, that even in an age of psychopower, in which the guardians are no longer what they were,

> even among the entrenched guardians of the great masses a few will always think for themselves, a few who, after having themselves thrown off the yoke of immaturity, will spread the spirit of a rational appreciation for both their own worth and for each person's calling to think for himself. (WEK)

In Kant's world, this exceptional human being was called an enlightened despot. The powerful themselves, the best among them, the *truly* powerful among them, grew tired of a power that merely disempowered their subjects (or their clients), a power that allowed them to feel it only through the impotence they imposed on others by locking them into the servitude of minoritization; they themselves (and their descendants) were diminished *through* the diminishing of those over whom they had power, becoming in a sense the minoritized powerful, reigning merely over impotence, over the unpowerful.

We are, however, no longer in an age of despots, benevolent or otherwise, but of industrial democracies, as Henry Guaino has recently reminded us. The issue is now not the despot's power, nor even that of a laic head of state, republican or democratic, but of a psychopower manifested through psychotechnologies not concerned any longer even with adopting some mystagogy: they have replaced the power of *mystery* with that of *drives*. This means that we must return to the primary concern in the battle for intelligence, which emerges well before that of universality.[11]

14. The organ-ization of juvenile nihilism; irresponsibility as nihilism's achievement

In the age of the television spotlight, the slogan of the channel specifi-cally targeting juvenile consciousness is "Channel Y: television completely turned on [*la télé complètement allumée*]." To be "turned on" is to be a bit crazy—to be a fantasist to the point of "going too far": to transgress. What Channel Y channels, and provokes into going too far—for those who define the symbolic order, knowledge of which is transmitted by teachers, through mystagogy, dogma, *or* criticism—is the drive toward the unconscious. But those forces of the unconscious must then be pressed into the service of destroying the id, short-circuiting the intergenera-tional play through which such transgression has *constructed* the id, that is, the construction of *care*. This is undoubtedly the first time that a psy-chotechnics of attention, having transformed into a psychotechnology, has *not* served care,[12] but has rather implemented an attitude of "*I don't give a damn*" that is not just uttered but strongly asserted—and perfectly cynically.

Channel Y's milieu is thus *performative nihilism* as the state of the ju-venile mind.[13] And now, the premature maturing of minor delinquents occurs within the (resultant) context of the law's loss of authority, whose only possible outcome is a correlative, systematic adult infantilization and their becoming-irresponsible; the becoming-prematurely-adult of chil-dren is the mirror image of the protracted retardation of their older sib-lings' and parents' minoritization, the *loss of their exemplarity*. All of this leads to an asymptotic tendency to crystallize a strict psychic and social incapacity to achieve responsibility, as maturity; the new French law re-garding juvenile delinquency translates this sad fact into the stone tablets of the law,[14] inscribing it as legal recognition and thus *legitimized* destruc-tion of the difference between minority and maturity.[15]

This organ-ization of juvenile nihilism results, inevitably, in an aggra-vated juvenile delinquency[16]—but equally inevitable as a direct conse-quence of the correlative adult regression is aggravation of larger envi-ronmental problems, since delinquency destroys the social environment, often further leading to a degradation of the family environment. Con-sumer irresponsibility, of juveniles as well as adults—the former prescrib-ing the behaviors of the latter more and more frequently—degrades the familial (and social) environment by both destroying intergenerational links and weakening laws. But such irresponsibility also, and as a consequence, degrades the natural environment by normalizing waste and "disposability": nonattachment to things as such. The generational confusion inherent in consumerism destroys any shared concern for taking care of the world and of oneself, self-care as opposed to a consumption resulting in obesity and other "sedentary" problems (such as cardiovascular pathologies): addiction, cognitive overflow syndrome, attention deficit disorder, depression, impotence, and, finally, the collapse of desire.

The current, growing crisis of environmental imbalance, of which global warming is a major part, became the first priority of the French government in 2007,[17] according to Nicolas Sarkozy's somewhat surprising commitment addressed to the United States on the evening of his election,[18] then including in his first government a Ministry of State for Ecology, Development, and Long-Term Planning. This announcement, a major political act, placed renewed weight on the issue of responsibility, and indeed of *shared* responsibility among politicians, economic advisers, and technological, developmental, and marketing researchers, and the reformation of the social structure in general, in particular national education and the audiovisual media—and, finally, the people themselves, especially as parents and educators.

Sarkozy's declaration affirmed the current need to place the issue of *care* at the very heart of political and economic life as a matter of nothing less than human survival. Suspension of authorizations for genetically modified organisms (GMOs) in France corroborates the seriousness of this politics. But the central question is still that of care: carbon dioxide–producing engines, the GMO question, nuclear energy, nanostructures—all require the construction of a new form of attention at the level of psychic, social, and technical (i.e., industrial) apparatuses that by all indications amount to an entirely new social necessity—based on a new form of intelligence: being-together, *interlegere*.

Still, implementation of psychotechnologies through marketing psychopower amounts to a colossal historic regression creating massive irresponsibility and adult infantilization, through the liquidation of circuits of primary identification with ancestors and generational confusion exacerbated by a constant increase in consumption calamitous on all environmental levels and destructive of the metastability of the entire "human ecosystem" from the infantilized psychic apparatus to the climate system[19]—which are intimately connected by the many kinds of *pharmaka* that make up the human world. This regression is mistakenly called "growth"; mistaken because "growth" in this context means merely what becomes larger—whereas irresponsibility is the *reduction* of what *should* be larger: *esprit*—individual and collective mind/spirit, whose modern form is *critical consciousness*.[20]

Those acceding to irresponsibility cannot take its consequence seriously, having become unconscious of it. They are stripped not merely of critical consciousness but of consciousness itself: they become nothing more than a brain. As consumers generally, we are becoming systematically unconscious, mocking the consequences of our behaviors while living in a structural *I-don't-give-a-damn-ism* that completely privileges the short term and systematically penalizes the long term, whether it be the long term of ancestors (as the authority of the law, whether or not the direct reference is to the Law, and whether or not it is divine in Antigone's or the biblical sense as Moses—the Egyptian adopted by the Jews—understood it) or of descendants, in the form of the "growth" that gives rise to the multitude, and as responsibility passed on indefinitely (and potentially infinitely) from parent to child.

In the first chapter I introduced the vital idea, also addressed by Hans Jonas in *The Imperative of Responsibility*, the question of our responsibility, for the first time, of the very existence of succeeding generations, within the specific context of the industrial world. In the second volume of *Taking Care*, I will show how such a discourse, resting on what Hans Jonas calls a "heuristic of fear," will simply not permit *any* response to the challenge of forming a radical new social organization of attention and of care, which would be the only way for world citizens at the beginning of the twenty-first century to take the French government's message seriously.[21]

The dangers here are obvious; but it is equally obvious that knowing this is not enough: one must first *know what is at stake*, what any such danger actually threatens. It must not be constituted by fear;[22] rather, it must first be capable of *desiring*—desiring an object. Yet the fundamental ontology of *Sorgefrage*, Heidegger's "care" that then catalyzes all of Hans Jonas's analysis, entirely ignores the question of desire, without which it is impossible to formulate attention *as care* if it is true that the object of attention is first and foremost the object of desire.[23]

An increasingly juvenile (potentially criminal) acting out is now the pathological aspect of desire through which nihilism appears, catalyzed by degraded social organization mesmerized by a version of "the law of consumption" urging parents to abandon their families to attention-capture apparatuses that destroy in their children the very attention they themselves have abandoned; sadly, all of this takes place far afield of "the sensory." This (re)organization is a direct and immediate contradiction of the attention any generation is capable of when it is encouraged to take responsibility for transmitting attention—for responsibility itself—and it operates all the more perversely on the young in that it seems to have been prescribed by the older generation itself, as a kind of countercurrent.

Thus, a law prematurely "majoritizing" delinquent minors serves only to ratify, in terms of the legal system itself, a long-term penalization that is of deep concern to Hans Jonas, though Jonas himself does not think of it as such—as a function of the *time* of preoccupation and care, of what Heidegger calls *Besorgen*, at the core of which (and *only* at the core of which) the possibility of *Sorge* arises, as concern and care of what, in time and *as* time, transcends all time and becomes a mystagogy.

Heidegger refers to this process as "the hermeneutic circle"; however, what this mystagogy excludes, and what Jonas is incapable of thinking in his dogmatic adherence to ontological difference, is precisely that the time of consciousness, and beyond that the time of existence itself, within which consciousness is formed, is organologically configured by psychotechnologies. We will see through reading Foucault in Chapter 5 that this Heideggerian exclusion follows a motif introduced in Plato's privileging of consciousness (as *gnôthi seauton*) over care (as *epimēlesthai sautou*)—that is, over *Sorge*.

The organological project of psychotechnics is one in which it is equally possible to care for oneself and others as to delude oneself and to minoritize others, but this is precisely what Hans Jonas does not consider in any way, and this omission prevents his accounting for the genesis of irresponsibility that is his central issue, what he calls the "imperative of responsibility." At the same time Jonas simply ignores the current regression toward minority and the generational confusion so clearly characteristic of contemporary industrial society, just as he ignores the problematics of attention formation in the absence of which there quite simply can be no responsibility. In so doing, Jonas replicates Heidegger, defining human technicity as the very principle of decline. But Jonas goes further, ignoring Heidegger's famous citation of Hölderlin in which danger itself becomes the principle of a *salut*, a welcome (this is a matter, however, that I believe Heidegger's philosophy never allows itself to face).[24]

My effort in this chapter has been to demonstrate that in the modern world of interest to Hans Jonas, responsibility is indeed the "age of attention" Kant calls "maturity." As such, and as achievement of a victory, responsibility is not simply a psychic process, even if it presupposes the individual's psychic transformation: responsibility is a *historic* process of *Aufklärung*. Access to maturity in the Kantian sense requires formation of *critical* attention that analyzes the law—and can recognize it as a crisis, an evolutionary process that, out of the Enlightenment and throughout the nineteenth century, we have called "progress." This would mean that maturity, as the historic time of attention, constitutes a specific, systematic kind of care in which the law is a necessary element but could never be sufficient in itself. In the modern age, the law's authority, which must be respected and which can only be obeyed insofar as it is respected, simultaneously contains two forms of care:

1. Men and women are capable of caring for one another *independent of all written laws* but within an intergenerational framework of ancestors and descendants; more specifically, we are capable of taking care of children, both our own and *all* children, precisely *as* children, as actual minors: absent such care, a function of time and thus incarnated in the generations as a succession of births and deaths—care that is *not* Kant's idea of maturity—the law can in no case be imposed as the authority to be obeyed when at the same time the maturity Kant *does* speak of is not present. Freud found this aspect of care, as the litany of monotheism, to be grounded in the unconscious.

2. Mature adults have the capacity to critique the law precisely because they respect it, and in their critique, they take care of the law in a mature way, affirming the possibility of altering it and conferring new authority on it: that of *modernity*. But in the spirit of Kant as well as Freud's theory of desire, since the law is irreducibly intergenerational, it must be inscribed in a transindividual process—configuring what I have called elsewhere a *plane of consistency* (distinguishing rights that ex-ist from justice that con-sists but does not ex-ist,[25] a structure with certain links to what Heidegger calls ontological difference). This second dimension, as a *critique* of care, is the time of the superego that, as the unconscious force of repression situated in the ego, Freud says links consciousness and the unconscious in what after 1923 he calls the id.

The simultaneous liquidation of these two dimensions of the only authority that could be acknowledged by a maturity constituted *within* authority, responsible for identifying and taking care of immaturity and attempting to move it toward maturity, amounts to nothing less than the triumph of nihilism and the destruction of desire (of which Heidegger says nothing, but which was already Nietzsche's central concern). This liquidation takes place as what Max Weber calls disenchantment with modernity (which had already worried Moses Mendelssohn[26]) reaches its culmination, no longer producing enchantment even for very young children prematurely matured by psychotechnological drives so effectively and systematically targeted as to make them prescribers of their own parents.

15. Disenchantment as loss of the meaning of critique, and the three limits of contemporary industrial development

Enlightenment thinkers' "modernity," as *Aufklärung*—as the expansion of "clarification"—is a rationalization process that, as Max Weber shows, is necessarily also a process of disenchantment, against which Sturm und Drang is an early reaction, according to Cyril Morana (CM, 44); Weber closely analyzes the "sermons" of Benjamin Franklin, the American representative to Enlightenment Europe (who also published in the *Berlinische Monatsschrift*), to show how the capitalism formed by Calvinistic socialization transforms all beliefs into intrinsically calculable—and thus rationalizable—credit, where "reason" exclusively means *ratio* and no longer *motive*.[27] "confidence" has replaced "belief." In such a rationalization process, tradition and all of its dogmas, all of the authority figures it should produce, all of its values are *reversed*; inevitably, the "enlightened monarch" (and with him, God) must be declared dead.

"Modernity" is thus no longer critique as *critical caretaking*, the ceaseless submitting of its (dogmatically inherited) basic values to the judgments of a maturity understood evolving from minority, a critically formed attention maturely responsible for the social legacy of the "scholar before the entire literate world" through "the public use of one's reason," but rather critique as the discerning of discrete unities, discrete in the arithmetic or algorithmic sense: as *calculable* unities. Critique becomes "mastery through calculation," which will culminate in the late twentieth century in various cognitivist models.

The rapid spread of the *Polizeiwissenschaft*, in which Michel Foucault locates the origin of the implementing of political technologies of bio-power characteristic of the nineteenth-century bourgeois state, "biopolitics," is the inevitable result. But these power technologies require a grammatization process that Foucault leaves entirely in the shadows, but that is also pharmacological in that it develops directly from the conditions of care that are now based on calculability, its shortcomings and its poisonous effects, which prevent it from ever becoming a psychopower.[28] This new, fundamental calculability must be applied to *all objects*, very much including objects of desire, which then become increasingly undesirable; eventually they disappear as objects of desire, and along with them a sense of the world's future—if not the world itself.

I have tried throughout a series of works to show that this generalized critique-as-calculability, rationalization, and disenchantment has pushed capitalism to face its *two primary limits*:

1. That the arrival of Enlightenment thought and its translation not only into the French Revolution but into the Industrial Revolution and its establishing of systematized capitalist production are *simultaneously* the pursuit of a grammatization process of what I call psychotechnics,[29] through apparatuses of behavior control that, as machine tools, allow for the liquidation of workers' skills and thus individual workers' realization of huge gains in productivity and development of a new kind of prosperity. This process, beyond the misery it creates in the working class, inevitably comes up against the limit Marx analyzes as the tendency toward profit reduction.

2. That in the struggle against this limitation on capitalist development, "The American Way of Life" has invented the figure of the consumer whose libido is systematically enticed toward *over*production, socially concretizing the tendency to reductions in profit. This channeling of the libido, operated through attention capture, leads directly to the liquidation of consumers' skills and the massive development of service industries alienating consumers from their existences: their responsibilities as mature adults. In the end, this leads to the liquidation of their desire and that of their children in that they can no longer identify with them, both because parents no longer "know anything" and are no longer responsible for anything (having become big children) and because the primary process of identification is short-circuited by psychopower, through psychotechnologies. This destruction of desire (and of attention

and care) is a new limit encountered by capitalism, not only as a mode of production but as a mode of consumption (as a *mode de vie*, a way of life).

3. But here, as in future works moving on from this one,[30] I am working to define a *third limit*, by which the development of the industrial way of life inherited from the nineteenth and twentieth centuries has become toxic not only for the *esprit* and the libido but also geophysically and biologically, and that this limit can be overcome only through the invention of a new way of life that takes care of and pays attention to the world by inventing techniques, technologies, and social structures of attention formation corresponding to the organological specificities of our times, and by developing an industrial system that functions *endogenously* as a system of care: *making care its "value chain"—its economy.*

The pursuit of industrial development will not occur simply through the planetary extension of the way of life found in the West and in modern Japan and South Korea; contrary to the pretenses of dogmatic neoliberalism, through the exportation of the technologies required for their modes of production, Western societies have created industrial competitors and launched a global economic war, the context within which François Fillon made his sweeping political declaration. And this new competition has resulted in destruction of the complex equilibrium that has permitted capitalism's development to be the simultaneous *social* development of industrial democracies, through a Keynesian organization of distribution under the authority of the welfare state; it is in the context of this war that marketing has become "the instrument of social control" within societies of control,[31] and that the reduction of libidinal energy has suddenly been accentuated.

Capitalism has, then, lost its mission, what Weber calls its "spirit."[32] This demotivation is a major phenomenon;[33] Weber shows that this "spirit" produced the motivation that made the long-term functioning of capitalism possible. In terms of consumption, the capitalist way of life has become an addictive process characterized by diminishing long-term satisfaction, which has engendered a significant malaise pervading consumption, a malaise that has "replaced culture"—that is, care—if indeed "culture" originates in cults, in attachments to objects constituting a system of care; on the production side there is an ever-increasing sense of "suffering from work," today translating into worker, as well as executive, suicides.

The neodogmatists—ideologues of neoliberal dogma—respond that these symptoms are merely the epiphenomenological malaise of a civilization under too much stress, somehow saturated with comforts driving the Old West, in particular Old Europe (and within Europe, Old France, which along with England and Germany is the home of the Enlightenment), to a mortal listlessness in the face of the extraordinary dynamism of the newer industrial countries providing renewed opportunities for the contemporary world: globalization could bring them to a renewed energy of entrepreneurship and labor, allowing capitalism to triumph once again and overcome its limits of profit reduction and declining libidinal energy.

This reasoning, however, neglects a significant fact: any such new world capitalism is utterly incapable of being developed by reproducing the production and consumption modes of the Western industrial democracies, including Japan and South Korea, since the broader exportation of this way of life also means increasing the production of all kinds of toxins for the vast majority of the planet's population, and in the end can only lead, literally, to the end of humanity—far beyond the "mere" destruction of the psychic apparatus, which is itself occurring at such a pace that this fatal "growth" only continues to spread further. The new global capitalism can in fact renew energies only by inventing a new logics and objects of investment—and this word, *investment*, must be understood in its widest sense: in terms of both the industrial and the libidinal economy.

16. Democracy as the political organization of care, and the new responsibility of public power faced with declining growth

Not only entrepreneurs and financiers but also producers invest and are invested in industrial systems of production in which they are shaped (and that shape their attention to work itself) through an accumulation of experience marking out a long circuit through which transindividuation is inscribed in the world—in that these producers are not *completely* proletarianized and/or rendered unstable. For consumers, things are different: they are structurally inscribed on the short-circuit of obsolescence [*jetabilité*] and of *deinvestment* in objects of consumption that also amounts to a loss of their knowing *how to live*—a new form of proletarianization.[34]

Investment, always attached to its object and therefore long term, is the precise *opposite* of consumption. When consumption functions for and by itself, as is the case today, it is propelled by drives that, unlike desires, demand immediate satisfaction. Functioning for and by itself, consumption destroys the desire connecting it to its objects and, as a result, is always investment.

Given the wide variety of systemic environmental disorders that feed each other and are nothing more than the consequences of the destruction of caretaking systems, we face a situation that must be changed, and the consumer is the *central factor* in this system of autodestruction. The figure of the consumer, the pharmacological being who has been rendered structurally irresponsible and infantile (dependent), must be transcended; that is, taught once again to cultivate care and attention, through the structure of an industrial organization that must be reinvented.

This recuperation must be the task for a new design,[35] conceiving a new industrial intelligence—the true stakes of the battle for intelligence: to reconstitute maturity (responsibility), in the Kantian sense. But this reinvention of maturity must be the *responsibility of the industrial age* and must take into account

1. the fact that maturity is a historic victory, in the sense that it originates in a developmental stage of an *organological* medium (and within this organological medium, one of grammatization) whose core is human life, which never stops evolving and which, with regard to the psychic apparatus viewed through psychotechnics and its ambiguous pharmacological structure, is always susceptible to a reversal of its effects;

2. the fact that the mind is not simply consciousness nor indeed presupposes an unconscious; the mind is a *process of production* of libidinal energy in which consciousness is a sublimated form (a superego-différance-apparatus), translating into the second major Freudian motif: the psychic apparatus is the id articulating the ego and the unconscious.[36]

Any reinvention of maturity must take these facts into account, for two reasons:

1. On the one hand, the historic conquest of maturity is organological because libidinal economy itself, like the psychic apparatus it forms, is pharmacological—tertiary retentions being at once what underpin the transindividual *and* what allow for its destruction, that is, through new forms of *hypomnēmata* as psychotechnologies: it is in this limited sense that maturity, the *critical attention of consciousness* (the *critical age of the superego*[37]), is itself pharmacologically constructed.

Work hard
Reward - more hard work
see what is free

2. On the other hand, the repression of adults and the generalized spread of irresponsibility rely on the destruction of the id by intergenerational confusion, the short-circuiting of primary identification, and liquidation of systems of care as traditional spaces for culture formation. Such are the effects of the destruction of the psychic apparatus by psychotechnological devices of psychopower as *pharmaka*.

To reinvent maturity is to struggle against the psychopower of new "guardians" who misuse these *pharmaka* and for whom new "subjects" (in the Kantian sense) are *consumers*. Any such struggle must be a transformation of the psychotechnologies of attention control into nootechnologies, forming a new kind of critical attention (as responsibility): a transformation of psychotechnologies into nootechnologies forming a *social* apparatus of collective individuality,[38] just as much as a *psychic* one, and as widely distributed and shared as possible.[39]

According to Kant, laziness and cowardice are the causes of minoritization that must be conquered if maturity and responsibility are to be achieved. Kant's challenge is currently taking place within a context of environmental crises compounding psychic and physical pressures unimaginable in Kant's time, in large part created through the hegemonic abuse of psychotechnologies that, as functions of *misbelief,* systematically encourage irresponsibility, as well as laziness and cowardice, by methods that are no longer those of political or religious guardians but of marketing (responding to a "return to religion" that is itself deeply regressive). It is in this new context that the battle for intelligence must be reengaged in order to counteract this new form of irresponsible minoritization, as organized regression.

But further, this battle must reengage a politics of the mind and spirit—a noopolitics—that, in this age of psychotechnologies, must also be an industrial politics focusing on *technologies* of the spirit; these are the conditions without which any necessary reform of our educational institutions will be made entirely in vain, if it really is a battle to take intelligence *to a higher level*—and individual and collective responsibility along with it—not just to overdevelop, in the framework of economic war,[40] an industrial model that merely creates a frustrating "growth" that has become malignant [*mécroissance*] and is increasingly perceived to be a cancerous excrescence [*excroissance*].

In their time, Jules Ferry's politics were a politics of the spirit and a transformation of the psychic apparatus, through interiorization of a psychotechnique for critical attention formation, and thus of maturity not only in Kant's sense but in Condorcet's (as "suffrage"[41]) as well. Ferry was not confronted by industrial psychopower: current psychotechnologies and the marketing strategies that have become their instruments did not yet exist. What Ferry argued against was not the diverting of attention by the industrial economy and the libido through a process of desublimation, but rather the power of the Church over "souls"—a religious psychopower presenting itself as a noopower of sublimation, the spiritual power of *the spirit* over *temporal spirits* (*esprits*, i.e., minds as well),[42] the power of the *Saint-Esprit*, the Holy Spirit.

In other words, for Jules Ferry it was a matter of substituting laic sublimation for religious sublimation. Such a politics would have to be that of attention formation as *historic* consciousness as well as *critical* consciousness; along with public education, which inscribed the principles and the consequences of evolutionism into education in general, the idea of *a* genesis, and of genealogies created out of a divine origin for the world, gave way to a historical consciousness of humanity's situation, a consciousness of humanity's transformation process *by itself* through its various forms of knowledge such as life skills, technical skills, and theoretical knowledge constituting various disciplinary attention formations as well as basic conditions of human freedom, establishing a universal sense of the first two types of knowledge within both geoanthropological space and prehistoric, protohistoric, and historic time.

"Authority" thus became knowledge grounded in rules for the establishment of a sense of truth no longer proceeding from revelation, that is, not from a kind of family romance broadened to encompass the entire human species but from an interiorization of that Greek invention: *logos* as a specific type of symbolic medium, a critical medium as *critical space* and *critical time* whose literate-ization made the classical age possible; with the spread of the alphabetics, eventually supported by publishing engendered by the arrival of the printing press and, by the nineteenth century, making printed matter accessible to all, constructing the base for modern democracies and industries.

But the public education systems and training programs instituted in the 1880s have been slowly but irresistibly ruined by mass media and the programming industries, in particular by television in the second half of the twentieth century. Today, this state of affairs has taken its calamitous effects to such extremes as Patrick Le Lay and Channel Y, to the point at which one has to wonder if these industries have not been self-lobotomized, driven to the destruction of public opinion and its replacement by "the audience."

The result has been the transformation of democracy into telecracy, psychopower's economico-political concretization and the ruining of all sense of responsibility, given its increasingly disastrous effects, chiefly on children and intergenerational connections—in the very name of *authority*. It has become extremely difficult to imagine how any public authority could arbitrate the conflict between psychopower and the attention *diversion*, on the one hand, and attention *formation* as the psychic and social faculty of responsibility, on the other.

Just as any idea of a "democracy" of collective maturity embodying Condorcet's concept of suffrage would require the creation of mature individuals, in the sense in which Kant, Condorcet, and other Enlightenment thinkers conceived of *constructing* a political system of care called democracy, in the very same way a general *destruction* of systems of care, specifically destruction through psychotechnological attention diversion of the modern political organization of care called democracy, leads directly to the liquidation of "democratic maturity" and "democratic responsibility," that is, to *populism*.

That is to say: in the face of the care-less-ness of generalized irresponsibility, a new responsibility of public power arises, first and foremost instilling and protecting attention in children and adolescents, but inscribed within the broader challenge of reconstituting systems of care in civil and civilized societies in which political systems can potentially save democracy by reinventing it through organological evolutions and psychotechnologies themselves. Such a struggle could be based only on our having no further doubts about the program's first priority: the battle for intelligence.

§ 4 The Synaptogenesis of Attention's Destruction

17. Attention deficit disorder and the industrial destruction of consciousness

If the battle for intelligence could find renewed energy in the university, which would obviously mean that primary and secondary schools would themselves have to appreciably raise the level of their students, the precondition for any renewal of the educational system would be that the symbolic industrial milieu in which children, adolescents, young adults, their teachers, and their parents live today must no longer be a systematic obstacle to the construction of skills and knowledge through rational and critical attention.

A (re)formation such as this itself would require the *regulated interiorization* of psychotechnics and psychotechnologies, according to rational criteria by which they can become nootechniques and nootechnologies. These criteria must in turn be framed by mental disciplines encompassing objects of attention through which nootechniques and nootechnologies can produce *long circuits* of transindividuation and can fight against the *short*-circuiting of transindividuation—minoritization in the Kantian sense: as laziness and cowardice.

The current destruction of attention as a psychosocial faculty, for example, as destruction of intergenerational relations and their replacements, is at the same time the destruction of that form of institutionally constructed attention called consciousness, *con-scientia* being the capacity to form long circuits of reason, the basis of reflective consciousness.[1] In other words, consciousness is destroyed by industrial psychotechnologies in two senses:

1. as the authority that in conjunction with the unconscious and the preconscious forms the Freudian psychic apparatus, focused in the ego;

2. in the sense that for both Enlightenment thinkers and public education, consciousness is formed as a *historical* configuring of the id, in which the critical consciousness typical of the mature individual and producing both long transindividuational circuits as such (i.e., producing them theoretically, in terms of causality) and historical, individual, and collective consciousness formation. This works as an articulating of both the universal history of humanity as a *we*—as a very long circuit—and as the individual history of an *I*; this double structure then becomes a new basis for attention formation as the *political* structure producing modern industrial democracy in the nineteenth century.

But industrial psychopower's destruction of consciousness during the current historical era, in which no form of teaching worthy of the name is possible—not elementary, secondary, nor higher—is also the contemporary destruction of the democratic system of care by a force that by definition does not and cannot *take care.* This force is financial speculation, which has made care-less-ness the central mechanism of its dynamic—a dynamic of malignant growth, a *negative* dynamic: the "dynamism of the worst"[2]—in that it systematically privileges the very short term and the inevitable psychic, social, financial, and other such short-circuits that result. Replacing capital investment in apparatuses of industrial production with speculation destroys businesses by depriving them of the opportunity to project and plan their own futures, and subjects them to deadly (speculative) competition, a war without mercy and without *rules* that locks them into short circuits.

The ultraspeculative organization of this kind of financial capitalism, as public powers completely deterritorialized and thus completely careless of all local conditions—including social structures—has now significantly taken control of its consumer audience (including journalists and all others addressing the public, literate or not, as scholars or not—scientists, philosophers, professors, writers, artists, etc.), which must adapt to this production apparatus. Ultraspeculation has universalized the telecracy's reign over democratic organizations of care; it is thus the greatest obstacle to the development of an intelligence fitting the requirements of our age,

for both the encouragement and facilitation of production and innovation—chiefly for the innovative development of durable goods—and the
development of a responsible collective consciousness.

In privileging short-term, immediate satisfaction over investment, this
drive-oriented organization of speculative capitalism also destroys all the
forms of individual investment in a responsible consciousness, thus insti-
gating an "industrial populism" that is all the more antagonistic to educational, familial, and national missions in that its current highest-priority
goal is the massive capture of children's attention from the earliest age,[3]
provoking widespread organological disorders and the literal destruction
of children's affective and intellectual capacities—and further, provoking
dramatic increases in attention deficit disorder through the premature
structuring and irreversible modeling of their synaptogenetic circuits, the
neural bases of transindividuation and the site of attention's organology.
This system has developed to the point that in Europe currently, "between 1/3 and 2/3 of children now have a television in their bedrooms,
according to country and social class (nearly 75% in the lower classes in
England). These figures apply to children between 0 and 3 years of age."[4]
In the United States, at the age of three months 40% of babies regularly
watch television, DVDs, or videos. The percentage passes 90% for two-
year-olds, according to a 2007 study done by Frederic Zimmerman and
Dimitri Christakis.[5] This confirms the results of their 2004 study, which
had found that one- to three-year-old children's exposure to television
measurably heightened the risk of developing attention deficit disorder
before the age of seven. Reminding us that very young children's synapses
develop as a function of their environment, Zimmerman and Christakis
had suggested in 2004 that television could cause significant attentional
problems in the course of the development of the psychic apparatus:

> It is widely known that the newborn brain continues to develop rapidly
> through the first few years of life and that considerable plasticity exists during
> this period. Considerable evidence also exists that environmental exposures,
> including types and degrees of stimulation, affect the number and the density
> of neuronal synapses. The types and intensity of visual and auditory experi-
> ences that children have early in life therefore may have profound influences
> on brain development. . . . We hypothesized that very early exposure to televi-
> sion during the critical periods of synaptic development would be associated
> with subsequent attentional problems.[6]

Their hypothesis is confirmed by the 2007 results, as in a recent article in *Le Monde* also citing the Aid to Dependent Children office [*Caisse nationale d'allocations familiales*], emphasizing that "an adolescent who watches more than three hours of television per day cuts the chances of succeeding in higher levels of education to half of what someone watching less than one hour per day will achieve." Without doubt, these are major stakes in the battle for intelligence.

In September 2005, Inserm prepared the results of a study on attention problems and their resultant effects on conduct,[7] for example, on what the study called "oppositional behavior with provocation." But before it could be published they discovered that in the course of the entire study almost no attention had been given to the detrimental effects of the televisual and audiovisual industries on the study's young subjects.[8] Inserm had hypothesized that these social and cultural factors were genetically based, so the institute recommended tracking children from the age of three who were supposedly genetically predisposed to antisocial behavior. The amended study, published in the *Archives of Pediatrics and Adolescent Medicine* in 2007, confirms that antisocial behavior directly linked to attentional deficits developed in association with televisual media is, on the contrary, a significant catalyst of the care-less-ness within social structures that have become detrimental to the life of the mind, in that it undermines consciousness, in particular that of the very young and thus most impressionable: those who need the *most* care and the greatest attention devoted to their education.[9] This study conclusively showed that the televisual industry destroys education and engenders "the zero degree of thought" (TCD, 44ff.).

Yet television is of course now present in every corner of the globe, and the psychosocial state of the world is equally ubiquitously—in the United States, Europe, China, India, and so on—being overtaken by a colossal deficit of attention, an immense neglect in the form of a *global attention deficit disorder*, stemming directly from the proliferation of psychotechnologies that no political power can now control. Perhaps worse, this situation has been transferred to the professional adult world as the *cognitive overflow syndrome*, the cause of a *regression* of intelligence, and proliferation of modes of consumption that are increasingly destructive to the planet's future.

18. Education, psychotechnologies, and referential individuation

My effort in *La Télécratie contre la démocratie* [*Telecracy Versus Democracy*] is to demonstrate that the current educational system is a nineteenth-century institution of behavior-control programs (TCD, 162) and that it is now time to complete its project, adding to it the instituting of scholastic programs aimed at forming mature attention, through a historical configuration of the *adoption* process that is fundamental in the process of human psychic and collective individuation (see TT3, 138), in which an individuating collectivity's horizons perpetually expand and, ideally, become universal; this historical configuration of adoption is closely connected to historical Enlightenment thought. The adoption process, as individuation, in general captures, formulates, and interiorizes a socially configured system of care as the kind of attention developed in nineteenth-century industrial democracies. In schools this system's psychosocial configuration of care, like the interiorization of the capacity for rational attention (i.e., critique), develops through various disciplines that are all configured by the same psychotechnique: writing.

In the twentieth century, chiefly following World War II and with the development of electronic technologies, the educational system and audiovisual—that is, programming—industries have worked together to capture children's attention through psychotechnologies. By the end of the twentieth century, under immense pressure from marketing—and in the context of the emerging energy crisis, the then-powerful "conservative revolution," and globalization as world economic warfare—this partnership had precipitated a set of conflicting forces, *attentional deficiencies* brought about by psychotechnical attention capture, whose current result is an immense psychological, affective, cultural, economic, and social disaster, and has led to the weakening and increasing fragility of social linkages that at this point are capable only of engendering generalized insecurity and immense doubts about the future condition of all intergenerational relations.

The goal of the programming industries, as the armed wing of the telecracy, is complete control of the behavior-formation programs regulating social groups, indeed their removal from the public education system and their adaptation to immediate market needs. The goal entails their engaging in a struggle with both families and the programming

financial speculators

institutions that since the origins of Western culture have been responsible for transforming psycho*ethnic* programming into the psycho*political*; as Jules Ferry emphasizes,[10] these programming institutions are responsible for laic maturity, beyond inheritance of a tradition or transmission of a revelatory dogma. The founding of mandatory public education, as an institution, is in effect an alteration of the *referential individuation process* that had previously been the basis of Western society. This systematized care regulating human society became the new configurer of a referential individuation system (TCD, 112): a social group's formation requires that, within the diverse processes of secondary identification by which a psychic individual can connect with various processes of collective individuation, a dominant referential individuation laying the basis for all others must be present, arbitrating among them and thus forming the basis of the law. This referential individuation is interiorized—adopted—as the superego, transmitted from one generation to another through the course of a primary identification process. But this primary psychic identification is doubled and reinforced by a collective and social primary identification. Systems of care form this primary social identification—for example, as such programming institutions as mandatory public education. Any social group's unity requires this identification—which on the other hand never produces *identity*, a central point to which I will return.[11]

Taking control of such adoption processes means also taking control of the formation of all the criteria necessary for referential individuation. According to Enlightenment thought, in industrial democracies these criteria must be grounded in Kant's and Condorcet's sense of maturity; through programming industries and psychotechnologies, however, they have permutated into the intensification of consumption via attention capture, at the price of widespread irresponsibility: they have become *the opposite* of the criteria inherited from the Enlightenment.

In *La Télécratie et la démocratie* I analyze the general spreading of new kinds of "artificial crowds" and regressive identification processes (50) engendered by the psychotechnologies on which I am focusing here, as well as the institutional dissemination of sociopolitical programs countering the regressive identification processes that for Jules Ferry had already become major motivations for action in a time when "progress" was already engendering resistances that were often archaistic, and when the struggle between the Church and the Republic was at its height.

Writing, as *hypomnēsis*, the first institutional psychotechnique and the inventor of public space and time, allowed the writer to take control of transindividuation and to make it functional (and conversely, through rhetorical psychotechniques and "logographs," to create the regressive processes of identification that result in transindividuational short-circuits). The sophistical hypomnesis critiqued by philosophy places hypomnesic *practice* in the service of *anamnesis*, as it was in fact practiced in Plato's Academy as the foundation of Western rationality. Instructional disciplines in contemporary schools, as critical attention formation, can form long transindividuational circuits on which students can be "inscribed" in the struggle against short-circuiting (i.e., irrationality), constructing a process of referential psychic and collective individuation—in Jules Ferry's time called "the nation."

As a general rule and as a process of adoption, individuation brings about a permanent change in the world. This particular individuation, suddenly accelerated by the Industrial Revolution, required an elevated level of both individual and collective responsibility, a "revolution of intelligence" concretized institutionally as public education. But the power exercised by the programming industries' psychotechnologies today ruins all the benefits of this revolution of (inherited) intelligence, which lasted in France from the Enlightenment through the Third Republic.[12]

Any system of care is a social pedagogy whose goal is to reground primary psychic identification as primary collective and social referential identification, as a function of its organological changes. Attention, always at the base of any care system, is formed in schools, but as a rational discipline of adoption inculcated into the psyche of the student-as-scholar (i.e., rationally adopting a knowledge or skill) before the entire literate world (initially, classmates). This form of adoption, called "reason," is an education *and* the simultaneous transmission of long circuits of "human experience" and formation of *new* long circuits: autonomous individuals dedicated to becoming mature and therefore *critical*—and before all else *self-critical*, capable of fighting off the "inherent" laziness and cowardice that persistently arise, but also capable of ever-renewed dedication to the knowledge required in this struggle.

Transmission of these long circuits constituting human experience molds the process of primary collective identification, which is also the base for the process of referential individuation in modern society. But this role is today *fundamentally threatened* by the telecracy of industrial populism, which constantly attempts to insinuate itself as a *new* process of referential individuation intrinsically archaistic and gregarious, and which systematically appeals to the very mechanisms Freud describes as regressive processes of identification. Meanwhile, it is national/social group unity that is disturbed: *unity* is not and never was *identity*.[13]

19. The phantasm of national identity

Primary psychic and collective identification is not what leads to identity but on the contrary *alterity*, singularity that can never be self-identical, is always beyond itself, in excess of itself—*more than one*, as Simondon says (IPC, 15); this is precisely why *new* transindividuational long circuits must be formed: individuation is always a "battle of and for intelligence."

The issue of a *national* identity (and more generally that of all human groups) is a phantasm occluding the true issue: unity (national, collective, social) itself. A social group—ethnic, national, a union of states—is a unification process constantly transformed by the integration of external elements: food, materials, merchandise, techniques, human beings, symbols, ideas, and so on. Leroi-Gourhan thoroughly analyzes this in *L'Homme et la matière*,[14] demonstrating that the "ethnic cell" is pervaded by technical tendencies that alter but do not disintegrate it—in fact, they further integrate it, and the integrations by which this process continuously redefines and metastabilizes its integral unity, as the concretizing of the intelligence it fights for, are ceaselessly raised to ever-higher levels of transcendence through production and projection of a telos, and by *reason*.

This telos, or outcome, is "the future" as projected by desire. In a democratic society (i.e., a *political* society), governed by a res publica (in the form of the collective written law), only the future projected by desire can allow for what comes from outside it to be integrated in the best possible manner, as a perpetually renewed *manufacturing of unity*; this is intelligence (*interlegere*). The identification process, psychic or collective, primary or secondary, constructs both the psychic and the social reality of what Simondon describes as a never-completed, *never-identified*, process of individuation (or, rather, completed only when it is terminated: in death) that never produces identity but, rather, unity.

The problematics of thinking through these processes result from what might necessarily be the consequence of such an identity, were *identity* to occur. But the actual situation is precisely the opposite: identification is

nnerted to ancestors + their futures

endless because the individual (psychic as well as collective) never stops changing (this is called "existence"). Thus, primary identification's function, as opposed to secondary identification, is to provide a system and a set of criteria for the *arbitration* of inevitable conflicts among secondary identifications occurring in a psychic system as it matures. This arbiter, transmitted first by the parental *imago*, allows the individual to adopt successive personalities as functions of the telos being projected from primary identification—but which never provides even the least shred of "identity"; once again, on the contrary, this power to alter identity is the very "poetry" of the human being who can always say "*je est un autre*," Rimbaud's declaration echoing Pindar, which Nietzsche turns into a maxim: "become what you are!"[15]

Secondary identifications, then, form the "fabric of alterations" through which patterns are drawn on the historic loom of the always both psychic and collective individual, who can "become what he is" only through integrating the new—and who, if he should reject this need, is condemned to disappear. That identification can never be fully integrated, transforming what it integrates by submitting it to the primary identification's arbitration (by "unindividuating" it); it is a fact that must be specifically analyzed, particularly since it is *collective* primary identification calling up a *referential* process of individuation, fully understanding that the issue to be explored relates to referential individuation's transformation. But this transformation is precisely the battle for intelligence, and thus a matter of skill and knowledge to the extent that they are capable of forming a system of care. My undertaking here is to offer an introduction to this problem: that referential individuation is always organologically conditioned.

In our disrupted age, amid the confusion and negligence catalyzed by the psychotechnological destruction of attention, it is difficult to remain dispassionate: regressive identification processes lead to "crowd psychology," archaistic processes resulting in identity drives that are poison to unification, yet these regressive phenomena have now worked through the telecracy to become dominant. In such circumstances, children are encouraged to construct themselves as referential individuations (but having neither authority *nor* intelligence), resulting in identification not with parents, nation, or any idealized object but with merchandise and brand names.

Telecratic devices destroy the referential individuation process toward which Jules Ferry was already struggling in his confrontation with a new adoption process produced by industrialization (which is itself both a vast organological revolution and the appearance of new stages of grammatization; TCD, 160); the Industrial Revolution imposed new responsibilities on human beings (whatever they were) aimed at the necessity of their finding themselves relentlessly challenged to adopt, and to *have* adopted, such new objects and techniques. In this constantly changing context, adoption came to be experienced as endless *becoming* (in which ontotheology, what today might be called disenchantment, fell into neglect).

But when capitalism encountered its first limit[16]—the tendency toward lower profit levels and simultaneously the invention of the image of "the consumer"—the programming industries, whose mission was to reprogram public behavior, substituted this consumer image for programming institutions in an effort to impose *another process of adoption*, but at the price of what led to the destruction of the entire system of care. By the end of the twentieth century, the consumer had become an increasingly addictive and irresponsible pharmacological being, which in turn has led to a confrontation with capitalism's second limit, the tendency toward lower libidinal energy, while experiencing what Marcuse analyzes, through the emergence of television, as a process of desublimation.[17]

20. Organology of the education system

Jules Ferry's educational system developed alongside the industrial transformation of editorial practice: the first great editors appeared in the later nineteenth century, and newspaper presses brought about the possibility of daily papers with enormous readerships. The technical infrastructure necessary for the formation of a *mature* reading public, in both Kant's and Condorcet's sense, was in place. And this convergence made Ferry's undertaking possible; the printing of scholarly financial manuals by public institutions became economically conceivable, and the programs being regularly redefined by an official known as the inspector general could be updated and republished while the very transformations created by the acceleration of the adoption process became industrialized.

Also, the nineteenth century was already producing devices (photographic, phonographic, cinematographic) that would become the basis of psychotechnologies by which the programming industries could in the twentieth century take control of the process. These conditions united to create the programming industries' psychopower, to overturn the educational system's role as the principal social apparatus for the systematic formation of care as shared responsibilities and the construction of maturity. Now, at the dawn of the twenty-first century, in an organological context in which numerization functionally and instrumentally articulates both cognitive (of information) and cultural (of communication) technologies, a new coordination of programming *industries* and programming *institutions* must be carefully thought through, instituted, and regulated according to organological criteria.

Such an approach to (educational) programming institutions must presuppose that

1. in a democratic political society, the education system is also what instrumentalizes citizens as a literate public (that has knowledge: i.e., can read and write);

2. citizenship is psychic and collective, conforming to a process of referential individuation grounded in shared knowledge;

3. individuation connects and articulates the *synchronicity* forming the *we* with the *diachronicity* creating the *I*; this articulated connection then forms idiomatic reality:[18] all idiom, in fact, is just such a structure,[19] and the individuation, informed and knowledgeable, that education creates is the language of instructional disciplines, *formal* idioms, constructed through the idiomatic individuation.

Formal idioms are those whose rules are in principle articulatable and that are capable of being made diachronic (forming "schools of thought") only through strictly controlled procedures: conforming to standards of testability, scientific discovery, establishment of proofs, noncontradictory presentation, and so on—all on an axiomatic basis that is still always mystagogic without being dogmatic:[20] a provisional, hermeneutic mystagogy, infinitely soluble, consisting of knowledge that is endlessly open to new interpretations. The same is true of the kind of reason inscribed in the laws of psychosocial individuation, knowing that individuation, properly understood, *is* its modification[21]—and is therefore both temporally and factually *impossible* or, in other words, *only possible as the infinite.*

Training in disciplinary idiomatics in the course of an education, then, constructs a *we* in the Husserlian sense;[22] for example, the *we* of the geometricians, but equally a *political we*, in which the educational system articulates a logic of formal idioms (of which what we call "formal logic" is but one case), *disciplinary* idioms emerging from the logic of attention formation—once again, the condition for maturity. Systematic education is by definition the location of the formation and the interiorization of both a political organology and an organology of rational knowledge; this double dimension, political and epistemological, constitutes the *we* that,[23] as the basis of communal life constructed through referential individuation, is the system of care we call "industrial democracy," which we must remember was created through and on a "battle for intelligence."

However, any organology thus interiorized is first and foremost the product of a hypomnesic exteriorization that has conferred *all* its pharmacological powers on hypomnesia—the good and the bad ones, those forming short-circuits within transindividuation as well as those weaving themselves into long circuits. As the transformation of psychotechnics into nootechnics, the education system gives rise to anamnesis derived from hypomnesia,[24] through collective individuation understood as transindividuation forming long circuits.[25] And that means that rational knowledge, and along with it the entire educational system, crafts new symbolic milieux linked to what initially produced, as the grammatization process, *dissociated* symbolic milieux.[26] These are social vehicles in the process of desymbolizing and dissociating, the care-less-ness endemic to the West as, for instance, the philosophy/sophistics conflict, a *conflict* at the heart of rational knowledge.

A scholarly education, as the interiorization of organology, consists entirely of psychotechniques for capturing and fashioning attention, transforming it into nootechniques through the interiorization of disciplinary criteria. Embedded in these criteria are the rules governing the practice of any organology—such as the rules for rewriting in mathematics, as the anamnesis of the long circuits grounding those rules in reason (that is, by going back to axioms) transferred through the course work assigned by teachers and training programs. Certain organs—the eye, the hand, the brain—must be coordinated for reading and writing to take place, but the entire body must first be trained to sit for long periods of time. "Children are sent to school first of all not with the intention of learning something there but finally to be trained to remain quietly seated and to respond quickly to what they are ordered to do" (RE, 96). This observational apprenticeship, neutralizing children's motor functions (by capturing their attention) is the base on which an object (attention) can become the object of knowledge—a constructed object—through the anamnesis of transindividuational circuits (instruction) reconstituted by memorization and the mobilizing of the tertiary retentions consigned to schoolbooks and manuals. Then the student begins to produce these circuits himself or herself by interiorizing and remaking them through classroom assignments. Through this process the nervous system learns a wide variety of attentional attitudes, raising the level of concentration (attention span) born of synaptogenesis. Brain-imaging technology allows us today actually to watch this process in action.

Transindividuation circuitry is inscribed, and in some sense *written*, into the brain as synaptic connections. Insofar as social organization is a collective individuation metastabilizing the reified individual forms of symbolic media associated with individuation, supported by tertiary retentions (technical organs, mnemotechniques, and psychotechniques increasingly analytic and discrete as they are grammatized), it is engrammed into the individual brain's cortical and subcortical zones and through them controls all physiological organs.

The education system, like all systems of care, is charged with clearing the way, transmitting, individuating, and transforming social organology's technical and physiological circuitry, as the id's intergenerational construction. And these are the very circuits psychotechnologies *short*-circuit and destroy, along with the education system (and democracy itself as a political system of care).

Somatotechniques and psychotechniques acquired through *hypo-mnēmata* linked to organs of the individual psyche aimed at forming a collective individual (i.e., a "course of study") organize access of the group of young people—the generation—gathered together in the course (a word designating a process) to their *otium*, which is usually translated as "leisure":[27] scholarly study is effectively the legal and even mandatory suspension of the requirement to do subsistence work; we pharmacological early twenty-first-century beings have long forgotten this fact, but in Jules Ferry's time it was a great novelty. A scholarly education (then and now) *ennobles* children and youth *thus* (but *only* thus) able to enter the next generation, of mature adults whose maturity is precisely a nobility, a *sovereignty*, achieved in the struggle to pass beyond minority in the battle for intelligence that each person manages more or less alone.

In ancient Greece we would have spoken not of *otium* but *skholē*, "contemplation," the privilege of citizenship (i.e., of nobility), reserved for those not needing to undertake menial tasks, as both Plato and Aristotle often emphasize. "Anamnesis," as the product of dialectic, permitted those free of utilitarian constraints and of all personal interest—and thus *sovereign*—to rise to the level of idealities, the *objects* proper to the *skholē* just as much as to the *otium*. Idealities are thus the objects proper to scholarship and to those who, even in English, we call *scholars*.

Anamnesis involves the interiorization not only of dialogue (which, as dialectic, is an attentional psychotechnique Socrates calls maieutic) but of its hypomnesic traces of transindividuation's long circuitry. Rational knowledge of this circuitry is what we call *heritage* (as a body of disciplines); anamnesis is the force generating the dialectic of thought with itself: *dianoia*. In this sense, *dianoia* is thought's freedom, its nobility organologically engaging the mental exercise of active reason: Kant's "maturity." But this freedom, spanning rational disciplines—the transindividuation creating all signification (ideas, axioms, theorems, theses, basic principles, the formalized content of all the genres of which academic courses and classroom lessons are abbreviations)—projects learners who are becoming scholars toward the plane of consistencies: of *nonexistent objects*. Nobility of mind provides the freedom to propel oneself beyond what exists and, *a fortiori*, beyond *subsistence* as the condition of what exists. Nobility of mind is reason seen as the faculty of projecting the objects of the desire for knowledge as infinite.[28]

Reason as freedom, to critique, discern, analyze, and resynthesize after having analyzed—freedom to *reinvent*,[29] the basic power of rational imagination—this reason is synthesized in its potential capacity to project ideal objects that do not ex-ist but con-sist, as *protentions*, and as the double desire for knowledge as such and the infinite expansion of ideal knowledge. Such protentions are created only by interiorized retentions in the form of long circuits of disciplinary transindividuation.

These are the objects at which the *skholē* and the *otium* aim; Plato calls them *eidē*, and they are the objects of eidetic analysis by which Husserl addresses what he calls "the nucleus of intentionality," unifying the retentions, protentions, and attentions formed as their manifestations. Within the disciplines and schools of philosophical thought now called "phenomenology," these "intentional nuclei" are the ideal objects projecting all rational knowledges. And these objects organize these knowledges into what Husserl calls "regional ontologies" (regions of the knowledge of what is).

21. Peer unity, reconstruction of collective intelligence, and the new organological connections

Protentions formed and projected by the mature being's reason as ideal objects, which do not exist and which will never exist,[30] but which guide the rational existence of pharmacological beings such as we humans, are just as much the objects of desire as of rational sublimation, the fruits of fantasy (i.e., of the id) become science. Knowledge organizes intergenerational relations according to specific procedures that are organologically limited: there is nothing simple about the image of Plato seeing Parmenides as a father figure.

The education system retraces modes of access to these nonexistent objects, these idealities-as-consistencies, and this process is methodological: it is the reconstruction of the advances (*methodos*[31]) traced by a society's ancestors and that is retraced by descendants who return to them again and are strengthened by the best among them. This track might be called science and knowledge, the path along which the generations become mutually reacquainted on a nonethnic, nonreligious basis, the only solid way to unite those in an industrial society, and what absolutely ruins the programming industries' attempts at organizing generational confusion, while in passing destroying consciousness and id, psychic and social apparatuses. Rather than critical mature consciousness they prefer archaic reactions fusing all parts into one.

Public mandatory, laic, national education can control the process of organizing adoption of hypomnesic psychotechniques, knowledges, foreign languages, immigrants, progress itself, incessant industrial novelty, the indeterminacy rising out of an always-accelerating future, and so on—and it can do so by authority of idealities through referential individuation, the common horizon of all desires. It need only allow for conflict arbitration among the diverse forms of individuation that citizens and groups of citizens adopt; the education system underpins the primary, collective process of republican identification. But that means that the education system must also prioritize the organization of access to these idealities (with regard to the organological context that in the next chapter we will see creates an attentional mutation that places new requirements on the education system).

Schools' fundamental mission is obviously not to produce anything like "national identity": on the contrary, it expands national difference and alterity in that it intensifies the process of individuation psychically as well as collectively, always pushing it to new singularities. Individuation is never finished; it never exists *as identity* (as a stable state), but consists as process: individuation is always *to come*, and thus is always open only to a future. On the other hand, in projecting a future—and therefore a desire—individuation produces unity in the *social* body,[32] at the national (and perhaps—tomorrow, one might hope—European) level.

As a tool in the process of referential individuation, the late twentieth-century education system entered into conflict with those cultural industries engaged in decomposing both the diachronic and the synchronic, replacing the *I* and the *we* with the *one* and thus confusing them,[33] just as they confuse the generations by transforming associated symbolic milieux into dissociated and desymbolized (desublimated) ones.[34] Moreover, these cultural industries then construct a symbolic medium in which *we* live; this development is inherent in any industrial society, let alone a hyper-industrial one.

But this is not a question of rejecting psychotechnologies or cultural industries but of transforming them into technologies of mind, into nootechnologies. It is a question of revolutionizing those industries that have become the organological infrastructure of the battle for intelligence—which is, of course, an economic battle, and such industries are the *arsenal*—submitting them to regulatory control that has been adapted to this situation, but also providing them with research and development sectors that have today been completely eradicated (particularly in Europe) and by supporting them through national and European research programs.

The final goal of such programs would need to be the creation of a new system of care, engaging families, elementary and secondary schools, and colleges and universities, on the one hand, and on the other, reengaging an editorial system that has transmuted into the principal impetus for cultural industries and programs; all of these must serve an industrial model rethought to produce an organological transformation in individual and collective intelligence. And all this must be accomplished in and through an industrial model that has moved beyond the consumer age. The great problem of the school today is initially that of knowing how in the future it will be possible organologically to design

1. educative structures (programming *institutions*), charged with constructing this intelligence as *noēse* through the critical interioriza-

tion of *hypomnēmata*, technologies of the mind that have now become psychotechnologies;

2. cultural industries (programming *industries*), just when a new associated technical medium has appeared, and along with it both numeric transindividuation technologies revealing a new form of *hypomnēmaton* and a new figure, the "amateur" who is no longer anything like a consumer and who *wants to know*[35]—to be individuated.

The hypothetical school whose primary task would be organizing hypomnesic interiorization could only be possible through careful organological evolution. Today's version of that school is generally industrial and technological, developing many devices as well as psychotechnological and cognitive networks leading to new kinds of behavior. But this careful evolution would require alteration of the entire knowledge-creation chain in this new instrumental instructional device for shaping the mind,[36] aiming at not only shaping *what is* but what is *to come*.[37]

In turn, that would mean providing the entire educational community (teachers and students) with a *genealogical intelligence* aware of its *hypomnesic base*, in the form of analyses of the grammatization process leading to the transindividuation process and leaving that base's most recent forms behind in order to return to an older one: a history of attention construction as the formation of disciplinary transindividuation circuits. Such instruction would have to teach strategies for *paying attention to psychotechniques of attention formation*, paying attention to technological reflectivity.

Only a genealogical thinking about knowledge revealing this originally technological (hypomnesic) dimension could lead to an understanding of *how* knowledge becomes technological in the modern sense (i.e., industrial); technoscientific knowledge is the central function of the current system of production and consumption. It then would become possible to critique this function and this system positively in terms of its future, of its *intelligence*. Foucault provides a major point of departure in his project of defining just such a genealogy. At nearly the same moment at which he declared that it was conceivable to "develop an analysis of power that would not simply be a juridical, negative conception of power, but a conception of a technology of power" (1981),[38] he opened the site for a study of hypomnesic knowledge techniques, analyzing psychotechnologies of attention in *Techniques de soi* (1982) and *Ecriture de soi* (1983), reintroducing the issues he had already sketched out in *The Order of Things*. We will come to see, however, that the biopolitical analysis dominating Foucault's last works is in some ways an obstacle to a possible psychopolitical thought, a critique of the to-come brought about by psychotechnologies.

Before coming to these issues, however, we must define the context in and through which psychopolitical thought is relevant to us today—to those of us attempting not to regress to minority status (to the status of *one*). Thus, we must further explore the current state of the attention for two reasons:

1. Because of the classification of an attention deficit as a disorder widely prevalent in the United States, attention has now been thematized there in a number of ways, not only in the areas of cognitive psychology, psychiatry, pediatrics, and pedopsychiatry, but equally in education science, which thinks and carries out its battle for intelligence across the Atlantic, and completely organologically.

2. Ergonomics and cognitive economics are currently engaged in research programs applied to marketing and to the conception of the services and interfaces of information and cognition technologies, whose ambition is to construct an *economy of attention*.

§ 5 The Therapeutics and Pharmacology of Attention

22. Deep attention, hyperattention, and attention deficit disorder: A generational mutation

The studies conducted by Dimitri Christakis, Frederic Zimmerman, and others on whom we will call here clearly show that psychotechnologies, as the weapons of the programming industry in its struggle against programming *institutions* for control of the referential individuation process by short-circuiting the process of primary psychic and collective individuation through attention capture, point to the destruction of attention as such through attention deficit disorder.

What parents and educators (when they are themselves mature) patiently, slowly, from infancy, year after year pass on as the most valuable things civilization has accumulated, the audiovisual industries systematically destroy, every day, with the most brutal and vulgar techniques, while accusing the family and the education system of this disaster. This care-less-ness is the primary cause of the extreme attenuation of educational institutions—as well as the family structure.

In order to be made available to marketing imperatives, the brain must early on be literally deprived of consciousness in the sense that the creation of synaptic circuits responsible for the attention formation resulting in "consciousness" is blocked by the channeling of attention toward the programming industry's objects. The young brain, having been treated in this way, *disaffected*[1]—and which takes all the more risk of incurring an attention deficit (and failure at school) if it has been exposed early on to television programming, such as Channel Y—is that much more available to the reconstruction of transindividual long circuits that have characterized knowledge throughout the course of human history.

This is precisely the knowledge that the education system and its intergenerational relations must transmit for a society as a system of care to form, and precisely what the programming industry, through its psychotechnologies, destroys. Yet it is only as a result of such psychotechnologies, activated by the programming industry and the cognitive technologies emerging from the recent numerization of communications, that one *must* think (and that it is *possible* to think) the future of teaching.

The organological mutation leading to psychotechnologies' appearance, particularly with the development of numeric media, has in turn led to what Katherine Hayles has analyzed as a cognitive change in the attention level, and thus to what she has described as a generational mutation: "we find ourselves in the midst of a generational mutation regarding cognitive behavior, one that poses serious challenges to every level of education, including universities."[2] This mutation occurs through what Hayles calls *hyperattention*, which she opposes to *deep attention*. She characterizes deep attention as the capturing of attention by a single object, sustained over a long period of time; her example is reading a Dickens novel. Hyperattention, on the contrary,

> is characterized by a rapid oscillation among different tasks, in the flux of multiple sources of information,[3] in search of a heightened level of stimulation, and having a weak tolerance for boredom. . . . [D]eveloped societies have for a long time been capable of creating the kind of environment in which deep attention is possible. . . . A generational mutation has taken place, transforming deep attention into hyperattention. (GD)

If hyperattention is actually a "generational shift," as Hayles points out, we must explore the possibility of achieving a synthesis between these two types of attention.

A report from the Kaiser Family Foundation entitled *Generation M: Media in the Lives of 8–18 Year-Olds*, indicates that "the average young American spends six-and-a-half hours with media each day, including schooldays. But given that this time can be spent with multiple media, the average total is eight-and-a-half hours, per day." The report also finds that the reading of printed books "is the least practiced form of media by young people in their spare time." When the young Americans observed by the Kaiser Foundation do work assigned and required by teachers, they do it while multitasking, remaining connected to various media, and as a result, their "desire for a higher stimulus level rises." But this research into stimulation, Katherine Hayles notes, is "also associated with Attention Deficit Disorder (ADD) and Attention Deficit Hyperactivity Disorder (ADHD)." Analyzing an attention deficit–hyperactivity disorder generation, Hayles also concludes that

> high school and university students are taking Ritalin, Dexedrine, and other equivalent drugs in order to prepare for important exams, . . . searching for cortical stimulants that will help them concentrate. . . . Such compensatory tactics have been developed in order to conserve the benefits of deep attention by means of chemical intervention into cortical functioning. (GD)

Hayles, like Zimmerman and Christakis, then refers to synaptogenesis:[4]

> Plasticity is a biological characteristic of the brain; humans are born with a nervous system ready to be re-configured as a function of their environment. . . . The cerebral system of a new-born goes through a pruning process by which the neuronal connections that are activated are reinforced and strengthened, just as those that are not activated wither and disappear. . . . Cerebral plasticity continues through infancy and adolescence, even in certain respects into adulthood. In contemporary developed societies, this plasticity means that the synaptic connections in the brain co-evolve with environments in which media consumption is a dominant factor. Children whose growth occurs in environments dominated by the media have brains that are wired differently from humans who have not reached maturity under these conditions. (GD)

That is to say, at least for certain among them, *adulthood.*

John Bruer, president of the James D. McDonnell Foundation, cites similar analyses in recommending a tight coordination among the neurosciences, the cognitive sciences, and education in further studies focusing on cerebral imagery, which can show "the correlations between observable actions that subjects are engaging in at the very moment the image is recorded, and, at the same time, the metabolic processes going on in the brain" (GD). Researchers at the Weill Medical College of Cornell University have thus observed, as a result of magnetic resonance imaging (MRI), that six-year-olds playing video games show significant differences from a group simply watching videos. As a result of this study, which concluded that it is the brain's *structure* that "changes through playing video games

at a suitable age," Katherine Hayles's hypothesis is that "stimulation by media, if it is structured appropriately, can actually contribute to a synergic combination of *hyperattention* and *deep attention*, which could have interesting implications for pedagogy."

23. Mature synaptogenesis

As Hayles reminds us, reading is itself a

powerful technique for reconfiguring the brain's active structures. When it is introduced at an early age, as is the case in developed societies, it is as though the process of learning to read—from beginner to experienced reader—contributed significantly to synaptogenesis. In environments dominated by the media, in which reading is a minor activity compared to other forms of media consumption, it might be expected that the synaptogenetic process would differ significantly from one resulting from environments in which reading is the primary activity. (GD)

Particularly clear here is the way in which synaptogenesis is a *translation*, at the psychic level, of the process of collective individuation supported by the technical process of individuation (especially psychotechniques) and a neurological process of individuation in the brain that itself, in turn, supports psychic individuation; as a translation and as this neuronal individuation, here synaptogenesis is Freud's sense of "conscience" as the construction of an attentional apparatus capable of developing into critical consciousness in the Kantian sense of "maturity," which is precisely the goal of the modern, democratic education system. But as Kant indicates, the condition here is that such a conscience can be "written" before, in, and through a public that reads, one that has developed a synaptogenesis forged by the specific psychotechnique that is always the basis of rational knowledge and that always "*câbla*" and "*connecta*" the central nervous systems of the intelligent *ancestral* generations.

As for the following generations, the Kaiser Foundation study found that they will read very little, and that at ever-earlier ages their attention will be splintered among many information streams with which they will "hook up" simultaneously. Thus, Katherine Hayles concludes that their synaptic circuitry could not possibly be the same as their ancestors'. And after having emphasized the fact that hyperattention can still be quite useful for numerous socialized activities (such as air traffic control), she develops the thesis that a coordination of *deep attention* and *hyperattention* is both possible and necessary to the education system's evolution. She begins her support of this contention in referring to another study, done at the University of Rochester, demonstrating that one of the principal motivations of the generation characterized by hyperattention and attention deficit hyperactivity disorder for playing video games is that the games provide *active and critical training* in which the player is *required* to learn.

At the conclusion of her study, Hayles provides a number of examples of possible connections between the two kinds of attention, mentioning in particular the University of Southern California experiments involving a class that had been organologically reconfigured on the Internet to switch the roles of teacher and students who, having been invited throughout the study to participate in it, thus individually and collectively exploited resources available in real time—always within a multitasking context and an attentional methodology that was distributed if not dispersed. Other experiments have explored the possibility of augmenting *deep attention*'s capacity, as opposed to *hyperattention*, to migrate toward objects of more traditional study, for example, in terms of what Katharine Hayles considers the proper work of teaching: creating the progressive links merging Facebook.com with *The Education of Henry Adams*, or going to the video game *Riven* through Faulkner's *Absalom, Absalom!*

Hayles argues that out of such examples a new conception of the devices supporting the educational environment can occur:

> Along with the tendency toward hyperattention that is already evident in the universities, these questions become urgent ones. The numeric media are offering the resources to face these challenges, both in permitting the reconfiguration of the space in which courses are offered, and through the opportunities they present for establishing bridges between *deep attention* and *hyperattention.* (GD)

These propositions, which question in particularly propitious terms any organological consideration of the conception of the psychic—as well as the education—system, however, present many problems and call up, if not objections, at least some preconditioned remarks—remarks that specifically anticipate the biases that might appear in Hayles's thesis:

1. Qualification, by the superlative *hyper*, of cognitive behavior that she sees as a generational mutation as not in fact being one.

2. The question of the symbolic industrial milieu dissociated—desymbolizing and deindividualizing (GD)—from its enormous influence, its legitimacy, and its objectives; of its regulation, and a fortiori of its prescription through public power; this question is never asked.

Yet it is incredible that the sole amelioration of the organological milieu as classroom suffices to fight against the programming industries for what remains, in every case, their principal motive: to take control of the process of referential individuation and, in order to do this, to short-circuit the education system and all intergenerational relations, be they familial or reconstituted through knowledge as *epistēmē*, in the Foucauldian sense, and as reason—particularly as the reason required to live together.

There is a great danger in suggesting an agreement between *deep attention* and *hyperattention* if this agreement does not consist essentially, structurally, and methodologically as a *critique* in the Kantian sense, an analysis of limits and of a regrounding of *hyperattention* as such. "In the Kantian sense" means not as denunciation but as thought, and through an attentive examination of all the evidence pertaining to the revelation of *deep attention*.

Were this not the case, the difference between the two types of attention, and insofar as only *deep attention* (produced through the necessary synaptogenesis) can lead to maturity, would not be rendered sensible or even thinkable for and through the "M generation" whose classroom, whatever its organological base, is charged with producing generational unity as a result of not being based on the consummation of objects and the flow of information but on the process of referential individuation (psychic and collective) from which knowledge is constructed; that is, on an intergenerational rapport underpinned by literary tertiary retentions.

24. Hypersolicitation of attention and attention deficit

To take these points further, we will have to go deeper into the question of knowledge itself and the point at which attention's mutation leads to the appearance of a *hyper*attention, since rather than as a hyperattention, what Katherine Hayles analyzes presents itself from the outset as an attention not only distributed but dispersed, disseminated, undisciplined. And in the example of air traffic control as a possible use for this form of attention, what is of primary utility is connected to vigilance, which is, strictly speaking, a form of attention without consciousness, a characteristic of wild animals.

The animal nervous system, whose priority is to provide a defense against predators in the fight for life and the instinct for survival,[5] also "multitasks," or, more precisely, as informatics would have it, must be capable of managing "background tasks." A grazing animal, for example, a stag (a forest herbivore who will return in the second volume of *Taking Care*), is vigilant at the same time that it grazes, first with regard to the possible proximity of predators; it can, moreover, even while grazing and protecting itself, also protect its young, as well as its grazing mate, who is herself protecting her young.[6]

What Katherine Hayles describes is obviously much more complex than a simple animal vigilance. But to address hyperattention is to use a superlative indicating that such cognitive behavior is concentrated on its object, if it is true that attention is always more or less a modality of concentration on an object. What Hayles calls hyperattention seems to me rather to suggest an intermediary situation between vigilance, as the nervous system's activity in aid of the survival instinct, and what is called, in psychoanalytic psychotechnics, floating listening.

These are the two forms almost paradoxically limiting concentration to the degree that the former (deep attention) is distributed between two centers, the one real (e.g., the grasses on which the stag grazes), the other possible (the feared predator), or perhaps the one real (the grass) or other "real"'s that are "ex-centered" rather than "con-centered" by attention (the mate and her young), the other still possible and all the more important if it is in fact actually *less* real (the ephemeral predator that can nonetheless become terrifyingly real at any moment). Two centers constructing a double-focused concentration and, in some sense, an equivocal, elliptical concentration. More than two centers make a network, and many attentional configurations are certainly possible there, since synaptogenesis interiorizes a technicity allowing them to be discerned and retaining them; this technicity is not available to the stag.

In floating listening, which is equipped with an interwoven symbolic medium structured "like a language," two signifying chains are in play (that of the analysand who speaks associationally and that of the analyst who associates in parallel), interacting and activating the unconscious—but through an *accidental* logic. Thus, this kind of listening is called "floating": its "logic" is like that of a dream and the *work* of a dream, and therefore perhaps connected with what Katherine Hayles describes as hyperattention, as the possibility of accidental connections.

In fact, there is a certain hesitation in these descriptions of hyperattention between, on the one hand, a solicitation of attention by many media, simultaneously, and, on the other, an absorption and nearly a drowning of attention in objects that are extremely captivating, indeed hyperstimulating. My suggestion of a cross between *Riven* with *Absalom, Absalom!* is a compound of these two situations: distribution of students' attention between the video game and the Faulkner text. But this distribution is not in itself what stimulates but, on the contrary, what creates distance. And perhaps in the end it is important to distinguish between two associative modalities, between *deep* and *hyper*attention:

1. the one *creating parallel circuits of transindividuation* and provoking connections, one of whose principal interests is its accidental nature or, more precisely, the formation of a new contextuality for the textual objects of *deep attention* (we will return to this later);

2. the other aiming at eliciting from the objects of *deep attention* structural homologies more easily accessed in the objects of *hyperattention*, thus "bootstrapping" to form *deep attention.*[7]

In her description of deep attention, Katherine Hayles does not mention concentration: she measures the force of this form of attention by its duration. It is true that duration can be ascribed to a single object, as the center of attention. Nonetheless, in Hayles's description, it is not concentration that stabilizes the object as object of *attention* but the duration of its perception. Yet one can imagine an extended attention that cannot be properly called concentrated since it is merely captive, channeled, and in that sense passive; this is precisely the case with television's channeling of attention—leading inevitably to channel surfing [*zapping*], already quite close to Hayles's hyperattention. This relative minoritization of concentration is clearly an effect induced into her argument by the antithesis needing to be established between *deep* and *hyper*attention, a term expressing intensity—which is finally an effect of its brevity, not its duration: it is a kind of flashing forth.

The source of stimulus for hyperattention as it "surfs" [*zappe*], leaping from one object to another, dispersed and unfocused (just as one might refer to an "unfocused" or "inattentive" child), is what *does not last*; such stimuli switch from one data stream to another. There is a multiplicity of tasks because of that multiplicity of streams: channels, networks, Web sites, and other programming industries that, like sharks, compete for attention; attention is, after all, merchandise and, as it happens, an audience, meaning that it is more "hyper*solicited*" than hyperattentive. And it is because of this hyperstimulation—but because it in turn produces *infra-attention*—that Hayles associates hyperattention and hyperactivity, as a complex form of attention deficit. But is it not paradoxical to associate hyperattention with attention deficit—even to what engenders this deficit?[8]

Attention's *depth* has less to do with duration than with *the length of the circuits of transindividuation* it activates, which can be very rapid even if duration is often a prerequisite, required precisely at the moment of learning, for this depth. Each circuit (and its length) consists of many connections that also form a network, as another constituent of depth, a kind of texture, and like some material, a resistant (even thick [*consistant*]) fabric. These connections operate according to rules that are also networks, forming "stitches" [*points*] in the sense of the word as it is used in knitting: when it is a matter of weaving a critical and rational attention, these stitches are the forms or motifs defining the rules of the transindividuation process that *construct the object* of attention, thus defining the rules of process by which this attention is constructed, but also that this attention constructs in return: by *paying attention*.[9]

25. Grammatization of the attentional context

Concentrated attention, in Western culture, is an attention whose object is not simply the word but "letters": it is constructed *literately*,[10] forming a text through this object as described, analyzed, and resynthesized— rationally grounded. This object, which is also grammatized, can be a definition, a theorem, a demonstration, or an experiment whose protocols and results are then written down. However, such a weaving together of the object, which in some way confers its rational materiality on it, through its textualization, is never done outside a context.

Today, this context is itself heavily grammatized, and in nonliterary—or not only literary—forms: forms activated by the programming industries' psychotechnologies that have become the instruments by which attention formation is entirely [*à la lettre*] liquidated, along with literary psychotechnologies and with the social machinery that has been constructed on them—and that have produced the deep attention that leads to maturity. These new nonliterary forms of grammatization are also the basis of the symbolic milieu in which the younger generations' synaptogenesis originates. A *text* can never be produced outside a *context* (i.e., "taking care": to take care of hypersolicited young people at risk to become infra-attentive is to activate this machinery into a new social machinery, which is what Katherine Hayles invites us to do).

As for the production of the connections that construct attention as the reactivation and perpetuation of a transindividuation circuit, distributed (hyper) attention creates a new milieu, and thus a new context, for deep attention. The Kaiser Foundation study of the habits of young Americans, such as being connected with more than one medium at a time—radio, television, Internet, and so on—seems to be cases of informational consumerism rather than configurations of distributed attention: they result in a *loss* of attention, that is, of individuation, an often hyperactive attentional *deficit* and, in the end, a desymbolization.

On the other hand, this situation becomes even more interesting if it is compared with that of Glenn Gould who, while playing a Mozart fugue, encountered the noise from a vacuum cleaner that interacted with his playing, producing accidental concurrences that filtered into his interpretation:

> Gould uses noise like a prism. This allows him to interpose a series of screens or filters between the work and his interpretation, filters that act as processes of material destabilization (elimination of a segment of the sound spectrum) and sensorial dissociation (disconnection of the tactile and the sonorous). The work in turn can "take off," to be projected ideally onto a purely mental surface: "what I learned in the fortuitous encounter of Mozart and the vacuum cleaner is that the internal ear of the imagination is a much more powerful stimulant than could come from exterior observation."[11]

In other words, the accidental filtering that initiates the transindividuation process, in this case performance as concentration on the score—and *via* this *organon*, the piano played by another organ: the hand directed by the eyes via synaptic brain circuitry, results from the concentration of attention on an object. One contextual element can emerge from another source and suddenly *compose a sign* by combining with the attentional process taking place.

I myself am often undisciplined in a time of distributed attention that basically leads, at least in part, to daydreaming. Something of this kind occurs when one thinks like a businessperson, and most powerfully of all when one takes a walk, like Walter Benjamin in Paris. Walking, which is also an ambulatory technique, allows for concentration on an object in an organic relationship with the repetitive motion of one's steps, in the same way that swimming and running or bicycling catalyzes many diverse effects, which are augmented during physical effort of any kind by the emission of dopamine in the brain; these effects combine with the accidental solicitation of, for example, the countryside, or some occurrence from the environment that suddenly causes one to think spontaneously, accidentally, which regular body movement, deambulation, like *deambulatio*, as an ego technique and the psychomotor organization of a distributed form of attention, makes necessary.

A similarly "necessary accident" occurs in the final part of Marcel Proust's *In Search of Lost Time, Time Found Again*, in the scene where Marcel's foot catches on a paving stone. Such accidents initiate another kind of anamnesia than the one Plato theorizes as the pathway to consistencies. And when Proust describes the marketplace criers he can hear from his bedroom who instigate his daydreaming, he is also describing disseminated attention—which is certainly constructed by this dissemination, but only to the degree that it coordinates with Proust's work in his writing chamber, where his sickbed is itself also an attentional device. It is no stretch of the imagination to think that engaging with the numeric media systematizes the possibility of this kind of anamnesis, or rather, in fact, of a third kind.[12] That, however, requires an analysis of organological characteristics each time it is implemented.

In *Technics and Time 2, Disorientation* (39–41), I try to show that textualization of an object of attention gives it a *différant identity*, thus provoking a chain of interpretations through the fact that the text, which is recontextualized with each new reading, necessarily engenders readings that are always different; this différance is then put into practice through the formation of circuits of transindividuation. Katherine Hayles describes a mutation of general contextuality for objects of deep attention—essentially, attention applied to literatized (textual) objects that are phenomenologically overdetermined by their context, attention being precisely the scene of phenomena.

This mutation is due to the fact that now, in all geographical and historical contexts, networks of the "classic" (audiovisual) or "new" (numeric) programming industries multiply or even confuse these contexts, then reground them in a fabric that has now become what we call "the Web," since all forms of grammatization converge in numeric technology and are then distributed through all possible means of telecommunications technology. These have now not only become virtually impossible to count but are also currently the means for all of the new conditions of deambulatory mobility.

Text, as the principal support for deep attention, has become a new kind of contextuality: a contextuality that is itself thoroughly grammatized, as a result of which deep attention's support is called upon to enter into relations with structured transindividuation well beyond the classroom, before and after schoolwork, and for all generations. But on the other hand, this process makes it possible to imagine new processes of transindividuation, and thus a new age of différance that must be both *thought* and *practiced* by the education system, since it confers—and we confer on it—nootechnical and nootechnological possibilities.

There are sedimented layers of grammatization that must be considered in any organological rethinking of the education system. Every kind of attentional device created by these varying grammatizational forms must be systematically indexed and defined in terms of its psychotechnical and psychotechnological effects, but also in terms of its possibilities for linkage with other older or more recent layers.[13] And most important of all would be to identify various forms of attention according to the kinds of retentional and protentional *flux* brought about in them by psychotechniques and psychotechnologies, each one of which is quite specific.

26. Organology of attention as stream of consciousness and as an element of politics

One of the central points in *The Time of Cinema* (TT3) is that the audiovisual object is the principal object with which the programming industry, transforming the minds of audiences deprived of consciousness through the flow of retentions and protentions, forms a kind of attention that captures this object (attention seen as the flow of channeled consciousness, concentrated on and captured by the flow of the temporal object); this audiovisual object and the efficacy of the attention capture it implements exist only because of the grammatization of the audiovisual, in which one no longer sees nor hears *the world* but rather its reproduction through various devices. These devices tightly control the flow of consciousness where the time of consciousness is subverted by the time of psychotechnology.

Yet with the book—which also reproduces the world, literally, through a grammatization of speech that becomes *logos* but does not require any apparatus, since the equipment required for reading has already been interiorized in the form of synaptic circuits in the brain itself, which require that the reader can write as well as read—the time of the text, which is a *spatial* object,[14] is controlled by the projection of the time of consciousness itself since text-time is *produced by* the time of consciousness that, without needing any mechanical control over the unfolding of a text or over consciousness itself, flows on throughout the course of a reading—which itself then forms deep consciousness.

With the eclipse of audiovisual temporal flux by numerization, which is nothing less than a new stage of grammatization and a major cause of the expansion of programming industries as well as of programming institutions—and which may open the era of their common future—today it is nonetheless possible to connect temporal objects with spatial ones, and thus to create new, organic functionality between the audiovisual temporal objects that in large part form the basis of hyperattention, in Katherine Hayles's sense, and literate objects that form the historical base of deep attention,[15] which is taught as such and engrammed into students' cerebral organs.

I count the musical score among the number of spatial objects, since it places music outside time: written (diasthematic) notation enables musical temporality and its vocal and instrumental flow to transform into linearity, that is, spatiality, through the Guido d'Arezzo notation that, strictly speaking, brings music (which is also a psychotechnique of the first order) into "the age of composition." But there are many other kinds of nonlinguistic textuality that are recognizable by their spatiality, such as the paintings registering the neoclassical episteme according to Foucault,[16] the language and formulae of mathematics according to Derrida, and so on.

The writing down of speech, originally a purely temporal object in the course of which discourse is formed, spatializes this spoken temporality just as a musical score spatializes the time of music. The reader then *retemporalizes* this spatiality, but this can take place only because it was *detemporalized*, that is, *materialized*, given the form of a tertiary retention. An audiovisual object, which is temporal and not spatial, is certainly also capable of being a tertiary retention, and in this sense it is also spatial (e.g., a reel of film, a cassette, a DVD, etc.). But the projector or player that reads it, and without which it is inaccessible, retemporalizes it *technologically*, by short-circuiting the temporality of attentional consciousness of which it is the object, then conferring on it a temporality that is not at all simple: it can only show itself audiovisually as the incessant flow of retentions.

Obviously, I do not mean that an audiovisual temporal object does not allow for the creation of deep attention. On the contrary, I mean that as a *pharmakon*, it has characteristics that have currently, within the context of the programming industries, been put to the service of a set of attention-capture devices that are fundamentally destructive, like the hypersolicitation of attention that gives rise to attention deficit, even though by all evidence the cinema is indeed an art and that like all art it solicits and constructs deep attention and is thereby both poison and remedy. Because it can anamnesically temporalize this temporal object, consciousness must understand it spatially, thus reconquering the motor machinery through which it is a function of time.

This is all a matter of *pharmaka*, and its basic issue is one of a therapeutics capable, with the aid of this *pharmacopoeia*, of treating its inherent poisons, since it is not prescribed by a care system that is also both an organized politico-industrial economy and yet care giving. In this regard, the situation Katherine Hayles describes is intrinsically ambiguous, which in turn imbues her own discourse with a certain ambiguity precisely in that she does not analyze this ambiguity.

The appearance of new, grammatized media, an unknown attentional context for objects of deep attention, within the organological history of humanity, is also an encounter at a veritable crossroads: newly grammatized symbolic media are a network of *pharmaka* that have become extremely toxic and whose toxicity is systematically exploited by the merchants of the time of brain-time divested of consciousness. But it is also the only first-aid kit that can possibly confront this care-less-ness, and it is full of remedies whose texts were, since the very origin of the city (and first for Plato), the prime example.

And this is not simply a question of the education system. It also concerns the *political milieu* constituted by *the state of minds* that are themselves nothing other than diversely structured attentional flux, more or less attentive and thoughtful, composing this milieu either as critical, rational consciousness (maturity) or as an agglomeration of gregarious behaviors and the immature brains of minors, artificial crowds whose consciousness has been enucleated by a regressive process of identification.[17] This means that the matter of the ecology of mind is also that of the ecology of the political milieu, and the transformations in the political *element*[18]—in the sense that water is the fish's element, just as the political element is integrally organological: there is no "natural element" of the political—"natural law" is a fiction.

One is tempted to ask whether the question is really one of knowledge if one wants to raise the general level of consciousness, and if that is possible; one is tempted to say to oneself that it is already too late and that it would be better to cultivate a difference between beings who are mature and thus organologically armed for the battle of intelligence, on the one hand, and the others, minors, under supervision and lost to this battle, on the other. Like beggars, just good enough to be cannon fodder, who can only march toward death (that of their consciousness) on the front line of this battle that will be won by others.

I absolutely do not believe in the truth of this second hypothesis (in fact, it seems intolerable to me). I do not believe that it is rational; I believe that it is *pseudo*reasoning that could be claimed only by an immature consciousness. I believe in the difference between maturity and immaturity, majority and minority, and that that difference will always be at the horizon of the humanity-to-come, since the pharmacological being that we have now become—and will increasingly become if we are really deprived of care, dignity, recognition, and the possibility of sublimation—will grow increasingly furious, thrown further and further into what I have called negative sublimation.[19] And given the current state of the world, in their fury humans could begin to descend into all sorts of widely disseminated, massively fatal actions (what Leroi-Gourhan called *megadeath*), themselves also *pharmaka*.

Humans could do this to themselves, in such an intoxicated state, to others (for example, students against classmates), as has recently so often happened in American schools, or to perceived enemies seen as hegemonic oligarchies of Evil belonging to an "Axis of Evil." It would thus be possible to pass from an economic war, in which a highly detrimental battle of intelligence against intelligence can already take place, to total war, having lost the battle for intelligence, believing that it might be possible to reserve intelligence for a few privileged individuals (still relying on the services of what in Great Britain is called *The Intelligence Service*, in the United States the *Central Intelligence Agency*); that is, in having rejected the need to take care of the young. To counteract this tendency would require the need to frame the problem *rationally* in terms of the generations; this shift in the problem of care for youth has already begun to take place, however, but *violently*, massively, and very dangerously, throughout the world.

Many obstacles still stand in the way of correcting our course: in the first place, a veritable *conspiracy of imbeciles* against which, moreover, none among us—we weak, pharmacological beings, weak and imperfect—can really escape: we can never become *completely* mature, such as we are ("God alone can enjoy such a privilege"[20]). This conspiracy of inattention, sloth, and cowardice is not solely the product of short-sighted economic and industrial interests: it is also the combining of political, intellectual, and artistic elements, plus those of corporations and public services, and, more generally, the generations that were formed in the era of the book—*they* (*we*) have also tended to become indolent.

27. The age of ostriches and "the hidden department of world culture"

For a wide variety of reasons, virtually all of that group (those of us who are supposedly mature) reject, in one way or another, the very idea of engaging in an organological revolution of the life of the mind—simply because it would be too complex and painful. They—that is, all of us—prefer to delude ourselves into believing (1) that things are not so serious, (2) that better times—things "as they used to be"—are at hand, (3) that nothing can be done about it (that *we* are simply not—at least not *all of us*—perfectible) and that we must try to sidestep it all and to protect ourselves, forgetting all the rest. These are, of course, all attitudes (other than a melancholic moping around hating everyone and everything) that *pay no attention to the world*, immature attitudes that are called, in the language of immaturity, "making like an ostrich," in the face of what in the final analysis is a looming colossal conflict between the generations. The irrefutable facts, however, are that the situation is now catastrophic, and that in the end all the ostriches know it. But we have interiorized the logic of TINA; *there is no alternative*,[21] because all of us are more or less under the influence of psychotechnologies that are destroying our maturity. In a study published in Quebec, Jacques Brodeur found that if

> after decades of struggle in civil society, governments have been forced to regulate air pollution, food, and water, . . . few governments have shown themselves capable of regulating marketing practices targeting children.
>
> This situation has left industry free to decide what children watch on television, what products they are offered in order to distract them, what strategies can be used to manipulate their wishes, desires, and values.[22]

And in order to explain how such care-less-ness has become possible, Brodeur cites George Gebner, dean of the Annenberg School of Communication: "[F]ewer than ten corporations control 85% of the world's media. They have become the hidden department of world culture." But the High Education Council of Quebec announced in February 2001 that "the number of children suffering from serious behavioral problems increased more than 300% between 1985 and 2000" (Brodeur). According to Brodeur, it is estimated that between 4% and 12% of American children suffer from either ADD or ADHD. The figures pertaining to juvenile delinquency in France are comparable: "in 2006, 23,200 minors were charged with aggravated assault, against 19,000 in 2005."[23] Christopher Soulez, head of the National Observatory on Delinquency at the National Institute of Advanced Studies in Security, has made the following comment:

> Previously, we observed small increases, but not much difference from the prior year. . . . The same thing was true for aggravated assault, which rose 23% [in 2006], against 9% for adults. This violence is notable because in the great majority of cases it was not motivated by robbery. Violent assaults by young women rose by 30%.[24]

In comments on State violence by the United States in Iraq, Al Gore cites Robert Byrd, senator from West Virginia, who stated to the U.S. Senate shortly before the start of military operations in Iraq that

> this chamber is almost totally silent—dangerously, terribly silent. There is no debate, no discussion, no attempt to share with the nation the arguments of those who are for and those who are against this war. There is nothing. We remain passively mute in the Senate of the United States.[25]

This could result, for better or for worse, in the kind of mutation Katherine Hayles identifies and analyzes in *media-rich* environments, in the context of the *new* war over the capturing of attention through hypersolicitation. In the course of just three generations, this mutation has become literally colossal, an almost unimaginable worldwide change.

We must remember that until 1939, 55% of the French, now grandfathers and grandmothers who might now want to short-circuit Channel Y but who were then still young children with no access to a radio or a telephone, certainly not a television and obviously not video games and the Internet—the current numeric technologies before which parents who might want to short-circuit Channel Y, no longer know whether they are still young children. Can we really understand that in 1920 there was no radio, in 1895 no cinema, in 1870 no phonograph, in 1830 no photographs or daily newspapers? And above all, are we capable of conceiving the extraordinary uniqueness of our age—and, perhaps, of imagining a future?

If we are not capable of any of this, we will have to become capable. If we must change our behavior with a view to reducing the production of carbon dioxide, this will be possible only on condition that we quite spectacularly reevaluate the formation of attention, most notably through drawing the consequences from the effects of the media environment on synaptogenesis. Since ancient Greece, and in our own industrial societies thanks to public instruction, scholarly education has formed the base and the best guarantee of the kind of attention that Katherine Hayles calls "deep," and that is a condition of the formation of critical attention through training in reading and writing, and of the likely synaptogenesis it creates in literate children, critical attention constituting the basis for maturity as responsibility.

Without any doubt, the new industrial model that will be needed in the fight against global warming will require immense investment in research and industrial innovation, as well as in fiscal politics, as Alain Juppé has suggested in his short tenure as the French prime minister.[26] But such measures could never replace the formation of a wider attention in a world, which is its precondition—including support of new markets for those new industries. They require a battle for intelligence in the form of the invention of a new way of living.

These measures also rest on our remembering that the programming industries have significantly evolved over the past thirty years, and that there is no reason to think that they will not continue to do so or that they will always evolve in the same direction—which, for the moment, is the worst direction. Elizabeth Baton-Hervé, in a study done by the office of Aid to Dependent Children,[27] recalls that in France, "after the dissolution of the ORTF in 1974, the three public channels were thrown into competition. It thus became necessary for each of them to attract an audience." Then came the law of 29 July 1982, passed by the new Socialist government, that created "audiovisual liberalization," meaning the first private channels, Canal +, La Cinq, entrusted by François Mitterrand to Silvio Berlusconi, and M6. This period saw "the first children's programs broadcast in the early morning." The year 1987 saw the privatization of TF1, the channel that then created youth programs that were finally exclusively commercial (e.g., *Le Club Dorothée*). Al Gore points out that the television viewer receives but never sends anything; he insists on the need to restore *participation* in participatory democratic life without which no true democracy can exist: political consumption—telecracy—is fundamentally incompatible with democracy: "it is not simply a question of better education but of the reconstitution of an authentic democratic discourse in which individuals can participate in significant ways." And in order for that to occur, Gore concludes that numerization (i.e., the Internet) constitutes a *new new deal* with "the power to revitalize the role played by the people within the framework of the Constitution. And just as the American Founding Fathers vehemently defended the freedom and independence of the press, we must now defend the freedom of the Internet." But this is a matter of defending against "*the hidden department of world culture*," the programming industries that *make* ostriches—producing ostrich behavior by putting their own heads in the ground and "autocretinizing." Their future is linked to that of the planet to which they are a key factor. The problem Al Gore proposes is that of a new political responsibility, a new way of sharing responsibility, first and foremost in giving back, in making citizens more organologically responsible, faced with what has deprived them of their responsibility, by depriving them of consciousness.

But this is not a question simply of responsibility as it defines politics in general—and democracy in particular—as the distribution of responsibilities among all those called citizens. It is also and indeed first of all a question of the responsibility of our political representatives, above all those who are not simply political representatives but who have executive power, and who today, in our care-less times, have really exceptional powers and obligations, new possibilities and constraints and thus also new *im*possibilities, both temporary and long term. In this regard, today it is not simply a question of being able to see where there might be "wiggle room"; now it is not a matter of evolving our conditions but of revolutionizing them, generating what French president Nicholas Sarkozy, when he was a candidate for the office, called a "rupture."

28. The therapeutics and pharmacology of attention

A "synaptic" analysis of attention construction clearly shows that pharmacology, which today means psychotechniques or psychotechnologies engaged in the human brain's synaptogenesis, is badly in need of therapeutic care. This would entail first an understanding of all physiological, cerebral, and psychological stages of development socially transforming immaturity into maturity. When we read the label of a medical prescription, we often find that this or that ingredient beneficial to adults can be deadly to "children under the age of three," for example, and we believe and respect this information, understanding that the prescription is part of system of care, a *pharmakon*, a therapeutics. We also know not to give alcohol to children—though we have not known this for very long; we know that giving alcohol to a child, let alone regularly, not only creates problems associated with various physical and mental deficiencies but can lead to dependence, abuse, and addiction as well.

These kinds of pharmacological and therapeutic issues must be faced at many levels and for all ages (since there are also medications that are bad for older people, other medications that are bad for adults suffering from various functional problems, etc.—and in fact, we all have physical and mental traits indicating that what may be good for others is not good for us, and conversely). These issues, addressed on behalf of physical and psychic criteria, must also be addressed to groups and societies, and for different localities in different eras: some eras are incapable of dealing with what might easily be handled in others, certain regions could be destroyed by what might make others quite productive, and so on.

But the pathogenesis of attention destruction across many forms, from the loss of adult responsibility to serious attentional disorders that are often seen in juvenile delinquents, does not result just from chemical pharmacology: counteracting it requires the regulating of psychotechnologies, and therefore a psychopolitics. Giving children Ritalin or Dexedrine in order to compensate for attention deficits, as Hayles shows, only adds more problems and the possibility of pharmaceutical dependence, which can then lead to other nonchemical forms of dependence that can be just as dangerous, that can in fact act directly, adversely, and irreversibly on brain structure.

Since October 2007, the American television channel Babyfirst, aimed at babies and young children aged six months to three years, has been broadcast in France on the Web at Canalsat.fr. On the Babyfirst Web site, in the section aimed at parents, the following statement appears, perfectly illustrating the rhetoric of psychopower:

> From the first hours of life, baby already has billions of neurons. But they are initially of little use to him since most of them are not yet inter-connected. In reality, to make these connections, the little one's brain must be stimu-lated. Stimulated by sounds, by colors. Because baby's daily environment is not always sufficiently rich to awaken the brain and to participate naturally in his development, television can be a powerful source of positive action for him. Pediatrician Lyonel Rossant emphasizes that "on the small screen, baby receives information one bit after another: one idea gives way to another, developing both the logical mind and the cortex's musculature." Through the small screen, baby comes to understand, for example, relationships among particular images, and little by little develops an understanding of the dif-ference between "before" and "after." This kind of stimulation leads him to be better structured mentally, better able to understand time and to give his memory more "muscle." Images in motion, . . . the colors they stimulate: full of life, television has everything to fascinate the child. Pediatrician Edwige Antier says that "as soon as baby can do so physically, she takes control of the remote, which quickly becomes her preferred rattle. Then touch leads to sounds, then to people, and that is truly magic! The human being is first and foremost a communicator. Everything that enhances communication charms us."[28]

Only the establishment of a psychopolitics can constrain the ravages of these kinds of "innovations" in a world of psychopower, which becomes the public's primary responsibility—notably in terms of the battle for in-telligence but first as a matter of public health. It must be a politics of *pharmaka*, of psychotechniques and psychotechnologies. As the battle for intelligence, this psychopolitics must then be translated into a noopoli-tics, not only through the limitation and regulation of these psychotech-nologies' use, especially for the young, but through a transformation of poison into remedy. Things that can lead to dependency must become things that bring about departure from dependence. These pertain to the

environment, industrial politics, educational politics, regulations governing mass media, and the politics of *new* media: all of this constitutes one
and the same challenge—the contemporary battle for intelligence, a battle
of *incomparable* importance in all of human history.

And this is not just a matter of ecology (of the mind and, as a result, via
natural environments in which we pharmacological beings are currently
living) but of hygiene, that is, of care in the truly classic sense. And as
such it is a matter that raises the issue of what Foucault calls biopolitics—
but that also extends it, introducing into it a dimension closer to philosophy's first questions as techniques of the self and the role of *hypomnēmata*
in individual and collective existence, that is, "the governing of the self
and others"; in Foucault's study of them he lays out the first genealogy of
psychotechnics, which will serve here as the basis for constructing a new
critical apparatus for thinking through evolution of the *epistēmē*. Foucault
will later call this apparatus an "archaeology"—mechanisms of tertiary
retention.

§ 6 Economy and Cognition of Attention, or the Confusion of Attention with Retention

29. Microeconomy of attention

We have now seen, from three different perspectives, how psychotechnologies' general spread provokes effects of attention destruction in a variety of ways, which are then combined and reinforced to create a collective pathology with many diverse, harmful consequences:

1. Psychotechnologies destroy intergenerational relations by short-circuiting the processes of primary psychic and collective identification (often through strengthening regressive identification processes).

2. When they construct children's day-to-day environment, psychotechnologies modify the synaptic organization of their developing brains, to the detriment of the structuring of the cerebral plasticity nurtured by the psychotechniques Katherine Hayles analyzes as "deep attention," critical consciousness, which education is responsible for inscribing as the basis of rational disciplines (regulated circuits of transindividuation).

3. Within the context of numerization, the appearance of so-called new media leads directly to the hypersolicitation of attention through increasing collaboration among the programming industries to capture audiences, to the detriment of deep attention and to the transindividuation circuitry underlying Kantian maturity, very probably correlating with attention deficit disorder and infantile hyperactivity—remembering that the combined daily time of attention capture in the United States has reached an *average* of eight and one-half hours per day, including school days.

To this list must be added another problem mentioned but not yet examined here, cognitive overflow syndrome, brought about through technologies of cognition. The convergence of audiovisual, informatic, and telecommunications techniques develops them in concert with cultural technologies through these new media, psychotechnologies initially designed and destined for professionals, but which have now also penetrated traditional cultural industries as well as service industries. But these technologies and the service industries that develop along with them are now the very ones confronted by what might be called a syndrome of hypersolicitation of attention through new media. The effect is that the cognitive sciences find themselves engaged in programs of research into the cognition of attention. And in a very similar way the microeconomy has made attention its new object, progressively abandoning the paradigm of the information microeconomy that, as management science applied to marketing, has led, in agribusiness, for example,[2] to "an information overload (a quantitative and qualitative proliferation) of agribusiness labels" now resulting in the fact that

> the rarest, most crucial resource is no longer information but individuals' attention. . . . Consumers and other [economic] agents spend less and less time and energy treating and analyzing the ever-growing flow of information. Individuals, having a *limited amount of attention*, must use it in differing areas according to those areas' use-value. Companies are thus not only required to *furnish information* and to ensure that it is correct, but also to *capture attention*.[3]

Businesses must now be attention-capture mechanisms for all their products and means of distribution, because only a "limited amount of attention is available"—as if attention were a fluid whose volume and pressure could somehow be measured; as if it were not the result of education as the formation of the individual as such, through the interiorizing of psychotechniques crossing an organological set of connections resulting in construction and expansion of consciousness (i.e., discernment) and the critical capacity to analyze; that is, *intelligence.*

Clearly, there are many different kinds of attention; equally clearly, the kind of attention discussed here, *deep* attention, is not something that can be bought in a supermarket. But to the degree that attention is the now a major focus of microeconomic theory, it must be modeled within the overall economy, then translated into technological mechanisms having an ever-greater effect on attentional behavior in general. Finally, as we will see in terms of the cognition of attention,[4] these will combine in order to constitute a new attentional system.

Moreover, it is not only possible but necessary to acknowledge that though it cannot be strictly measured, attention has limits. Yet at what point and in what way is it quantitative? It clearly is, just as the libido is a force of limited quantity. But the quantity of attention is initially *qualitative*, a function of the activation of psychic mechanisms—which Freud calls his primary topic. Above all else, it is contingent on the fact that *the object of the libido*, as *the object of attention par excellence*—and even the object of *all* attention—is an "object" that can only be constituted as *infinite*.

To *pay attention* is essentially *to wait* [*attendre*]. And what attention is attached to in all objects, what as attention it waits for/on, even if it forgets it is doing so, is the infinity of the object whose mirror image is projected back as infinite being, as a reflectivity that gives it the sense and the desire of an infinite whose hypothetical singularity is an immeasurable, incomparable, and incalculable image: it is through the singularity of its *object* that attention is attentive; it *attends* as the image of the infinite reflecting its infinite desire (as its to-come and as a future in which everything is possible).[5]

This is certainly not a question of a particular *kind of attention*'s producing a desire for items on the well-stocked shelves of a supermarket. But that is precisely the question: what conception of properly *human* attention must we employ to theorize an appropriate economy of attention? And how to model a human form of attention without saying how it is specifically human—*not inhuman*—most important in that it is at once psychic and social faculty, and thus constitutes (for example, as what Kant calls "maturity," which is the result of a victory) the very basis of care?

Either the economy of attention intrinsically generates the libidinal economy (my thesis) or it is a function of the (human) nervous system's vigilance, which is more or less the case for animals from mollusks to higher vertebrates (and including insects), distinguishing their nervous systems' level of <u>cerebral plasticity</u>; what distinguishes "the human" is

1. that this plasticity is endless, and

2. that humans interiorize the circuitry of what they can exteriorize initially, as artifacts.

In the second case—assuming that human attention is defined as *separate* from nervous-system vigilance, in configuring the technological economy of attention captured by <u>marketing systems</u> (acknowledging its usage as pharmacological, but letting it rely on the short-circuiting of a *therapeutic* synaptogenesis of this *pharmakon*), how can we decide the degree to which this is *not* a matter of folding libidinal economy back on itself—of a regression to instincts—always the result of short-circuiting?

And in fact we are faced with a situation today in which it has become normal to think that the functions previously located in the psychic realm must be transferred (abandoned) to psychotechnological or computational devices, from the pocket calculator to the software controlling financial, military, and medical decisions, without any subsequent interiorization and without any *structural coupling* between *pharmakon* and synaptic circuitry that would open the possibility of creating new transindividuation circuits,[6] the brain's thus limiting itself to information from only these mechanisms;[7] Al Gore has made the same claims regarding the telespectator.[8]

Yet it is possible to imagine an alternative model, combining various systems to assist in purchasing decisions, systems that could become tools required for a life in hyperindustrial societies but that would still depend on attracting the buyer's *deep* attention and intelligence, via an appropriate [adoptive] education system. This might be a utopian vision; if so, this utopia would be a politics understood as the struggle against care-lessness, a politics *taking care* of humanity, as opposed to the current politics, always working toward the expropriation of consumers' knowledge of how to live properly, confining them to habitual market-defined routines that train them to be proletarian;[9] in the final analysis, this would only be a matter of completing the process of what I have called generalized proletarization.[10]

A brief summary of this vital point: *to the extent that it is unfinished and open, the human brain's plasticity is the necessary ground for both the mind's and society's process of individuation, itself structurally unfinished,*[11] and the dual nature of this unfinishedness converges in both the psychic and social aspects of the object of attention. And "the object of attention" is contingent upon a *neotenic situation* that is exactly that of pharmacology,[12] in which technics and the brain form a transductive system.[13]

The training [*formation*] of attention required in this microeconomy for marketing the food industry is in reality a *de*forming of the kind of attention required in any democracy, a "rule by the mature."[14] This in turn requires the biological model of a human central nervous system technologically produced by technologies of control;[15] this kind of nervous system is an attribute of a gregarious, disindividuated mass whose brains have been stripped of consciousness, of their capacity to form long circuits of individuation incapable of critiquing extant circuits, a nervous system forever enclosed within strict neurological limits, significantly constraining both training and consciousness, both consciousness and maturity.

Gasmi and Golleau's findings, which merit extensive analysis, show how the psychotechnologies of attention capture evolve into a specialized sector of biopower, which in turn organizes society's food management and distribution such that attention is reduced to a function of a kind of consumption in which differential advantages ("the strategies of differentiation of the products of food-processing") are formed through a politics of the *consumer* rather than of the *product*. This results in the fact that the food industry itself enters the world of media, becoming systemically linked with the programming industries (as the commonplace "as seen on TV" has long shown) and psychopower, which just as surely rules over the financial world where "confidence," as the key element, becomes biopower's center of gravity.

30. Cognition of attention

What is true in the microeconomy of general distribution is all the more so in the area of cognitive technologies as applied to the essentially attentional devices forming numeric networks. Christophe Deschamps emphasizes that "the need to manage attention better, in a society in which information is omnipresent, is without any doubt the next threshold we must cross if we do not want to end up being drowned in the flood,"[16] by which he means "the flood of information." At this point we come face to face with COS, cognitive overflow syndrome, a pathology characteristic of adult populations, just as ADD and ADHD are principally problems of younger Americans, but that is well on its way to becoming a global problem. And it increasingly appears that COS is in fact a form of ADD—its adult form.

It would be necessary, for any program regarding the cognition of attention, to develop an *automatization* of attention, precisely in order to counteract attention's destruction—by automatization.[17] This would appear to conform to the central idea here: within the domain of pharmacology, which is not limited to chemico-therapies but actually concerns all techniques (of which psychotechnologies are but a single case), evil must be fought by evil to produce a benefit, a new stage of human development.

However, on the one hand, the only reason to think about the automatization of attention would be to eliminate immediately and without hesitation the *responsibility* that is *implicated* in attention insofar as it is also a social competence, as if the gains and losses resulting from uncoupling the psychic individual and the social group had been carefully weighed; and on the other, the manner in which attention itself is defined there, absent its being attentively thought, giving rise to the thought that the proposed therapy can only *kill* the pharmacological animal:

> "Attention" here means a bank of data recorded by a user who lists central interests (by keywords, for example) and their interactions (with evaluative criteria automatized by practice or simply declared by the user). The user's "attention profile" reflects areas of interest, activities, and values. It defines resources (keywords and sites or subjects of interest). (HG)

In reality, such a definition of attention used to remedy COS can in the end only aggravate it, to the degree that it is not seen as cultivating and thus developing attention, but as a technical system substituting for and short-circuiting it.

This is the result because in this case *attention* is confused with *retention*, or more precisely *reduced* to it (just as intergenerational confusion amounts to the reduction of adults through their infantilization). Moreover, retention is itself reduced to a form of tertiary retention *no longer internalized, shaped,* and *singularized* as a transindividuation circuit by *any primary or secondary psychic retention,* the goal clearly being the replacement of secondary psychic retentions—themselves singularly selected former primary retentions, and selected by a singular individual—by tertiary retentions that have been standardized and are thus particularizable, meaning that they are formalizable, calculable, and finally controllable, as we will see, by an "attention engine." In other words, what separates the psychic individual from the social group succeeds in destroying the psychic life of the individual; this completely conforms to the theory of psychic and collective individuation, which declares that the one cannot exist without the other and that the destruction of one is necessarily that of the other. Consequently, here, as in previous chapters' examinations, it is the psychic and social mechanisms that are being liquidated—through the *irresponsible* use of psychotechnological mechanisms.

What is at stake here is the effect of methods for automatically constructing secondary retentions through various means (initially through grammatizing such retentions, formalizing and standardizing them as algorithms, then through linking them to produce problem-solving programs consisting of rules—which are themselves derived from statistical data) but whose technology is conceived by systems experts. These quasitertiary retentions must be individualized to some extent, but they will tend to transmute back into calculable, collective secondary retentions— into behaviorally stereotypical "attractors,"[18] the activity of psychic individuals having been short-circuited, and individual psyches having been simultaneously somehow expelled from an individuation process that has become automatic.

To generate the perverse effects of psychotechnological automatization on attention, in the form of cognitive overload syndrome, transindividuation circuits are cut as short as possible, and the attention engine, taking the form of an attention automaton, replaces attention itself; that is, substitutes for the subject. What we have seen so far is that attention is the flow of consciousness of any object to which, precisely, this consciousness is like attentive flow, in that it singularly organizes retentions and protentions in order to construct its object, since it is itself singular. So we can see how a new short-circuit is produced, revealing what has long been called *user profiling*, one of the principal results of knowledge management but that here means the systematic development of an Attention Profiling Markup Language, a "standard language for describing attention profiles . . . in software . . . or online services . . . so that their use takes your preferences into account" (HG), a language facilitating the automatization of attention management by the motor-attention device named *Touchstone Live*, developed by Faraday Media.

31. Why not? The grammatization of the subject, by which psychopower becomes the central function of biopower

In such programs,[19] the social formation of attention must be replaced by its automatization and reduced to the most minimal human "subject" no longer somewhere between deep attention and hyperattention: "it" purely and simply delegates its attention to automata that then become its captors, meters, gauges, warning signals, alarms, and so on. Attention in this sense is precisely folded back on its automatizable behaviors of vigilance, the psychic having been reduced to pure biology, and is thus another aspect of the short-circuited nonhuman neurological apparatus.

I have already mentioned the user profile to show that it, like the personalized deindividuation of attention on the self and the construction of a self consisting of attention focused on an object, is a profiling system that destroys what could be called *observant attention* and replaces it with *conservant attention*,[20] a standardization of the subject induced by what is very clearly only an intermediate stage in its grammatization: the subject's "psychological profile" or "attentional profile" that in fact allows for deindividuation at its source, *as flux*, when as attention it was the basis for the system of care embodying the social.

Since attention catalyzes the psychic apparatus's *intimate* secondary retentions as a singular subject and as singular retentions that are incomparable with any other existent, whose "treasure" is an unconscious enriched by new retentions, objects from the world as material are primary retentions, objects of an attention constructing itself and taking form, in Simondon's sense of this expression,[21] *through* attention, then being interiorized as memories of the object, as secondary retentions.

Here it is essential to understand that because intimate secondary retentions, with and through which attention (i.e., the subject) arrives before its object, and with and through which it will select primary retentions in this object, and because these intimate secondary retentions already, before the appearance of the object of attention, contain *anticipation* [*d'attente*] (nearly always either preconscious or unconscious and thus intimate), when they become present, *producing*, literally, just what a lawyer "produces" as a piece of evidence before a tribunal that is *the horizon of anticipation* formed by the intimate shaping of secondary retentions: desire.

The object of *this* attention is always the object of desire (not vigilance), and the primary retentions woven into it become secondary while generating protentions (new anticipations) that both prepare for and accommodate the formation of new objects of attention, followed by a stream of objects that coalesce into an experience—an individuation, then a knowledge, understandings, and finally a consciousness functioning as the medium for tertiary retentions that can either support and intensify the experience by which they are interiorized and absorbed there, or short-circuited. In short, this object is the knowledge that Michel Foucault explores in *The Archaeology of Knowledge*.

Because attention's cognition confuses this process, requiring a singular, intimate period of waiting for retention to occur, it believes that it is possible to replace secondary retentions with an automatic system of tertiary retentions substituting for them, at the same time eliminating the work of the singular selection of primary retentions and the projection of protentions into the object, which enriches this object and the experience of which it is the ground. It also eliminates consciousness, but through the elimination of attention, not its capture.

A case could certainly be made here in favor of some motors of attention dispensing with the consciousness of vigilant cognitive tasks in favor of that of profound attention, which are basically search engines as attention automatization. And why not, in fact, develop some kind of computer-assisted attention, if attention is always assisted in some way? Why not?

In fact, from the beginning of this book—in fact from my earliest work on—I have been saying that attention is *always* not only assisted but in fact *formed* by a psychotechnique or a psychotechnology. But through addressing the question of care as a *mature* form of attention, I am suggesting that a system of care that augments attention is what persistently guards against the *pharmakon's* efforts to destroy the attention constructed precisely *as care*—as therapeutics. Yet in this regard, from the "therapeutic" point of view, computational psychotechnology always aims at *substituting* for attention, theorizing and modeling attention and its institutions, destroying them by seeming not even to imagine an attention beyond vigilance, let alone that this attention is consciousness constructing its objects.

But attention is always technically assisted by memory aids (since attention is fabricated from retentions), especially as the grammatizing of secondary retentions into tertiary retentions such as the book, agenda, PDA, GPS, and so on; yet none of these can be "attentive" in place of consciousness, which *is* attention: consciousness is a specific form of attention always assuming an a priori synaptic organization of the anticipatory body, in each instance to a greater or lesser degree interiorized through an education system that is not merely psychic but also a social mechanism forming the social body as a system of care.

Today we see the ubiquitous development of hypomnesic objects constructing the new, hypergrammatized attentional context we investigated in the previous chapter, but that also provides the opportunity for a new form of attention to emerge within the frame of a battle for intelligence. But in the texts addressing the "cognition of attention," such a grammatization of attention becomes destructive, since hypergrammatized cognition has no idea of either the pharmacological nature of attention or of the automata proposed to replace it, or of the therapeutic problem all of this initiates.

In this context, then, existence is reduced to subsistence, psychopower subjecting the psychic apparatus to the objectives of biopower. This process has evolved enormously since Foucault explored it: it is now almost entirely controlled by market forces, its psychotechnology now its central function. As a result, various disciplines have become societies of control in which psychotechnology is the primary organ, in the service of marketing. In terms of technological research, this has been translated into a cybernetic reductionism in which the microeconomy of attention has become a field of applications within agribusiness, in its pejorative sense.

In the struggle for control of the attention stream, marketing (as the sector of biopower charged with the symbol management of psychic apparatuses—non-inhuman consumers *as* attentive bodies) benefits from the results of analyses emphasizing the fact that attention is becoming increasingly rare,[22] analyses that wherever possible tend toward the control of attention. But marketing does not see that this seizure of control of attention, as a resource, is its destruction—and the market's as well, since it tends to replace attention with retentional systems aiming ultimately at the psyche's grammatization itself as, for example, *user profiling*.

Research into the microeconomy and the cognition of attention significantly contributes to a general grammatization of existence itself, with the effects we have already examined on the formation of attention in schools, but also in family life and, more globally, on the entirety of our systems of care. And this is occurring because the solicitation of attention has become the fundamental function of the economic system as a whole, meaning that biopower has become a psychopower. In this climate we must think about a revolution in the economic system, reversing the current situation by transforming this new stage of grammatization into the basis of a new form of noetic attention.

32. Three types of psychic secondary retentions

The process I have just laid out has major consequences in the battle for intelligence. Faced with the three limits confronted by contemporary capitalism, the battle for intelligence has become the primary element in the economic struggle. In the final analysis, the issue is not opposing grammatization—not even the grammatization of the psyche—but rather of asking the *new* pharmacological questions posed by the process and responding to them with a therapeutic plan that must then be transformed by the simultaneous invention of a new industrial model and a new era of education, training, and teaching: the formation of responsibility. At this point, approaching at least a provisional conclusion, it is appropriate to clarify once again just what it is in *re*tention that the cognitive sciences confuse with *at*tention.

*Re*tention is the basis of all care systems, which are always training systems for attention formation. To learn is to *retain*. Jean-Pierre Changeux's declaration is that "to learn is to eliminate" (NM), which precisely describes the conductance of neuronic flux in synaptogenesis. But to learn, in these neurological terms, insofar as it is organologically structured and already contains (and retains) what could be called secondary hyperretentions in the form of synaptic circuits (indications that the brain is living), is to retain constructed experiential objects as memories that could be designated as retentional *operations* that in turn build into disciplines that then both create and reactivate the circuitry of transindividuation,[23] which in turn relies on collective secondary retentions as they construct knowledges.

We must distinguish three broad categories of psychic secondary retentions:

1. *synaptic hyperretentions*, without which the other psychic retentions could not exist;

2. *retentional operations* and the *categories* of retention, which produce psychic "content";

3. *psychic content* itself, always products of the selections constituting the operation—and thus the products of an elimination.

If "retention" is the phenomenological label for what is generally retained by a consciousness, as such it is also a learning process clearly demonstrated, for example, in schoolroom recitation. This is how we learn mathematical operations and arithmetic tables, which are themselves retentional operations: moving from the ones column to the tens as one is learning the addition process is to learn to "carry" (eight plus two equals ten; I write zero and carry one [*je retiens un*]). Speaking and listening to speech is also to engage in an operation whose formal elements are grammar and semantics, born out of grammatization (and which generative grammar describes as a generation of rules).

All retentional processes, as attentional flux, rely on criteria in which *retentional operators* construct symbolic practices in which the broadest base is speech itself; it is on this practical base that disciplinary distinctions between knowledges are constructed. Any and every consciousness can be *instructed* through these disciplines, consciousness-as-attention imbuing the psychic apparatus with the *correct* retentional criteria: psychic secondary retentions, which then themselves become operators forming critical consciousness that in turn leads to maturity.

The very fact that consciousness can be *instructed* means that it has been reconfigured by a retentional *instrument* (an *organon*—as in Aristotle's *Logic*): the teaching profession. It is of course also possible to become a specialist *within* such a discipline—a mathematics, geography, or English teacher—in which case attention must be more deeply configured according to strict retentional criteria, and which will require developing a new attentional style over the base, creating transindividuational circuits that are not only innovative but that reactivate the already-extant circuits of the basic discipline.

All of this is possible only on the basis of an organology informing both the brain's synaptic circuitry and the material contents of various disciplines as they communicate among themselves and construct the unified structure of any disciplinary knowledge. To teach reading and writing [*alphabétiser*], as this infinitive so clearly indicates, is to transform the transformational capacities of the younger generations through the acquisition of a common retentional capacity, but only in that this capacity is also common to *all* the disciplines and knowledges that constitute knowledge *as such*, the body of collective secondary retentions. These are secondary because each one must be more or less *relived* (this is what Husserl calls reactivation[24]) and collective since they are made tertiary and shared organologically,[25] thus forming the *we* of any discipline.

The common denominator of knowledge's *taught* retentional capacity in the West is *letters*,[26] the basis of the "republic of letters" as the source of Kantian maturity and through which the young can accede specifically and thoroughly to what has been retentionally accumulated as works and well-constructed disciplinary knowledges. Further, this transmission is precisely the avenue through which knowledges can and must be enriched (transmission is the battle for intelligence) through renewal of the younger generations' being mnemotechnically shaped and formed *à la lettre*—to (and by) letters.

As the institutional interiorization of retentions, transmission of disciplinary knowledge via the operational body of retention (and as rules for rewriting) opens attentional anticipations through formation of protentional competency. The expanded horizons of anticipation underlying the attention projected by the *consistencies* of retentional groundings construct knowledge's infinite future, its to-come. Without these projected consistencies, in their entirety what Kant calls "reason," the rational attention underlying knowledge would be impossible.

These retentional groundings make up the preindividual medium (Foucault's "archaeo-logics") for individuation, the "statements"— "discursive formations" of knowledge, as Foucault calls them—that individualize scholars (in the Kantian sense: those with access to knowledge they can address to others with it). Disciplines-as-competencies are just such preindividual media for the individuation of scholars' *trans*individuation according to disciplinary rules. "Knowledge" is a *process of individuation* through a never-finished structure; individuation corresponds directly with *transindividuated* ("spiritual," in Simondon's sense) human individuation.

§ 7   What Is Philosophy?

33. Philosophy as teaching

> *Eudicos*—But you, Socrates, why are you silent, after Hippias has taught such an abundant lesson, and do not address yourself either to praise this or that point of his talk or to discuss with us what you judge to have been ill-said? All the more, in fact, since you remain apart, even among men who assert the privilege of practicing the exercise of philosophy![1]

So begins the *Lesser Hippias*, immediately following which the *Iliad*, the *Odyssey*, Homer, and other poets on whom Hippias has touched in his lesson are called into question. The *Lesser Hippias* is thought to be Plato's first written work.

The first question philosophy asks, at its origin, the initial and initiatory movement of thought and individuation, indeed of everything that is or could be asserted about rationality—this *first question*, which is perhaps not *philosophy*'s "first question," is not the question of being. Nor is it that of becoming, nor technics—not even in the form of this *hypomnesic* mnemotechnique. It is not about the law nor power, nor certainly about poetry. This first question that is not the first question (being generally made secondary) regards *teaching*.

And teaching is not simply the first question asked by philosophy; it is philosophy's *practice*, at least in the Academy, where Plato is following Socrates' teaching strategy, contrary to the methods of the Sophists, the age's common teachers, charged with training legislators—and where it really is a *battle* for intelligence:

The Academy, they say, immediately had the most spectacular success: from every corner of Greece and Hellenized Asia they came to be instructed there, or to have the honor of a private lesson. One of the reasons for its success perhaps resulted from Plato's program: his goal . . . seems in effect to have been to lay out a course of study such that the students capable of following him to the end were in a fit state thereafter to administer justice in their cities. (Robin, 10)

Teaching is not simply the transmission of knowledge but of understanding. And this can be reached only on the condition of its being publicly and explicitly transmissible: teaching and understanding are indissociable. Understanding must be teachable, or else it is not understanding. And teaching can only transmit understanding—even if it is often accompanied by an education and in that assumes the transmission of life knowledge. This is where understanding breaks with mystagogy: rational knowledge is no longer the fruits of an initiation but of an instruction.

This does not mean, however, that understanding no longer has *anything* to do with the mysteries. On the contrary, these remain within understanding as an experience of its limits, which confine mystery, like the bases and horizons of all understanding as it constructs *the proper object of philosophy* (and the kinds of quite specific attention formed into disciplines, which at philosophy's Platonic birth bring together the mystagogic *myths*). Greek philosophy, essentially the experience of this vestige whose first principle is the possibility of a nonmystagogic understanding, nonetheless still practices two kinds of teaching:

1. *exoteric*, available to all citizens already "formed" by *grammatistēs*, that is, by a teacher (rapidly to become the Sophist);

2. *esoteric*, available only to those with access to this mystagogic remainder's core issues, but who do not present themselves within philosophy as mystagogues, but in some fashion struggle against a *tendency* to revert to mystagogy by means of a teaching *practice*; these teachers are led, through various knowledge domains, to the *axioms* and *aporias* in all knowledge systems—that is, to the undemonstrable and, more amply, to the principles (*arkhaï*) forming what after Aristotle (but taken from his work) will be called *metaphysics*—as ontotheology, discourse on being as it projects beings on and from another plane: the *thēos*.

These principles, axioms, and aporias are not accessible as such, as objects of rational attention, not dogmatic in their cognition,[2] and thus sensitive to limits that remain the horizon of all expanding thought—an exoteric formation laying out what must be confronted there in order to consider them theoretically. But this "theoretical" is not, as it is today, simply what is formally consistent, but rather attention to what underlies and thus limits attention itself (as the primordial ground the Greeks called *hypokeímenon próton*) when it calls itself "thought," which reaches its pinnacle as what the Greeks called *aporia*.[3]

Aporia is clearly not (necessarily) a mystery: it is a limit, a cul-de-sac into which nonetheless thought *is logically, necessarily—and thus inescapably—led*. One of the most beautiful and celebrated of these aporia is in the *Meno*: a limit separates philosopher from mystagogue such that it projects the philosopher (the two are *separate*) *toward* the object from which he has been separated as, in fact, his most intimate object. In the *Meno*, the mystagogic object has the name of the goddess Persephone.[4] It is only when the philosopher is perplexed, in difficulty, embarrassed— when he has reached the *impasse*—that, according to Plato, he calls upon mythology.

But such an "object" is also, and persistently, philosophy *as desire*. And the figure of Diotima, who writes philosophy into the experience of this desire, is herself mystagogic. And this is also the sense of Aristotelian ontotheology: Aristotle posits that *theos* (θεος), which the philosopher thinks about through the specific form of attention called theory (θεορια), is all animate beings' desired object, the *object of all ontology*, all discourse, all thought regarding *what is*.

The philosopher loves (φιλει) wisdom (σοφια) precisely to the degree that it escapes and transcends him: wisdom is philosophy's object of desire in proportion—and disproportion—to its being chimerical,[5] persisting for the philosopher as an endlessly renewed interrogation. Within the experience of this thought process—whose path is always an *impasse*, a barricade [*embarrassé*]—Socrates evokes the divinatory power he calls his daimon (δαιμον). The predicament—the aporia—of philosophical teaching is, then, to mark the difference between the teaching of what *would be* philosophy and the object that can *never* be the telos of straightforward teaching (the simple interiorization of retentional operations), but that must become an experiment, indeed a way of life: an asceticism, a care, an *epimeleia* of a specific type (of which all Foucault's techniques of "self" are instances).

But this *impasse*, which puts philosophy perpetually in default, at the instant it opposes itself to mystagogy, becomes excessively mysterious (opening it to all kinds of reproach by even the very best intentioned), *as* a predicament, is at its origin a *pharmakon*: pharmacological being is originally mystagogic in that the *pharmakon*, by its very nature, endlessly returns to what Greek tragedy calls *enigma*. Enigma was for the Greeks a profane figure of mystery in a society in which divinities had withdrawn, and in which the most elevated objects of attention had been desacralized (this is my thesis) through grammatization. Mystagogy is at the very core of nonrational pharmacology, of which *magic* is only the most common form (common to all preliterate societies).

Understanding, on the other hand, appeared only with the advent of writing, which constructed its object as a *knowable* object, stripped of mystery. But the object of understanding, of knowledge, can never fully be reduced to this construction: there is an irreducible inadequacy between knowledge and its object; this inadequacy or incompleteness is inscribed at the very heart of the individuation process that is based on a conception of understanding *as desiring* its object: the object of knowledge is infinite *because* it is the object of desire.[6]

Plato and Aristotle declare that knowledge is not reducible to a technique, a simple *mode of production* of its object, since the object of knowledge—and of the philosophy that is its most radical and anxious form, going to its quasi-mystagogic limits—is also the object of love and desire.[7] It is object-as-affect. The true, the just, and the beautiful have an effect on me, transcending my understanding as such: they transform me. This intrinsic transcendence of the understanding by its object is what requires the individuation of "the one who knows" by *what* he knows (its object), where the knower is transformed even as the object being constructed is transformed in return.[8] Plato calls this individuation "anamnesis."

This difference between understanding and technics—which is also the *esoteric* difference between understanding and its object, which transcends it—directly refutes sophistry, which, according to Plato, is a simple technique, a cynicism-without-object (without desire), and finally a poison that [not only does not *affect*, but] *disaffects* young Athenians: the confusion of understanding and technics through which the difference between understanding and its object is also lost occurs when *grammatistēs* becomes sophist.

The literate *pharmakon*, with which the *grammatistēs* was charged with teaching young Athenians, begins to poison the city through what became sophistics as the psychotechnical power of grammatized language (as *pithanon*, the art of persuasion). The historicality of the *polis* thus quickly became a problem, and within this rapidly developing barrier the form of teaching describing itself as *philo-sophia* first appeared, claiming that its object always surpassed it, defining its teaching as, essentially, the "object-to-come" of desire; within the context of this aporia, philosophy is less knowledge and wisdom than the *love* of wisdom as the only true knowledge.

As teaching, *philo-sophia* presents a new form of attention and care: its intention is to configure a new system of care founded on anamnesis: philosophy is not simply *epistēmē*, but rather the ceaseless problematization and questioning of *epistēmē* such that, always tending toward the dogmatic, it risks being transformed into a technique that will finally be nothing but a hypersophisticated psychotechnique for the manipulation of "opinion." This process begins when philosophy starts down the path of sophistics.

As a result, philosophy is a system of care located between two dogmatic modalities: mystagogy, descended from the age of *muthos*, in which the philosopher calls to the *logos*; and a kind of knowledge that, having stopped questioning, has lost its object without knowing it, still believing more than ever that it *does* know. Plato calls this latter modality *polimatheia* (the knowledge of "Mister Know-It-All": the Sophist as seen by the philosopher).

The philosopher, who is fundamentally the Sophist's opposite and constructed through and through by this opposition, nonetheless cannot think what gives sophistics its power but only what *corrupts* that power: thus, philosophy as Plato invents it rests on the rejection and repression of a technics in which hypomnesia has only one form—psychotechnics. Thus, the anamnesis through which philosophy tests the need for a mind that understands how to transform itself *through* its understanding is thus a form of *epimēleia* and of attention revealed as *taking care of what is not oneself*, what will later be called an "object." As Foucault shows, philosophy (and what has become its academic system as a body of disciplines) has forgotten that understanding itself is *also and above all* a system of care, an *epimēleia* (which is very close to an *epimētheia*). And as we will see, philosophy *originates* in forgetting it.

As anamnesis, philosophy requires a hypomnesia that as a stage of grammatization makes it possible. But philosophy *denies* this. As *epimēleia*, it requires techniques of the self, but it also represses this *epimēleia* by submitting it to the anamnesis that denies its hypomnesic condition. There are also inevitable pharmacological conditions within this anamnesis as a new system of care, but philosophy denies these conditions at its very birth, by subjecting *epimētheia*—which is always mysterious, always containing a little magic, a little tradition, a little already-there—to *gnōsis*.

It is for this reason that although our entire academic heritage is constructed on the basis of a culture of letters [*la lettre*] as retentional technics, literate beings [*les lettrés*] transindividuating the disciplines that form the projections of knowledge (that remain always to come), this heritage, as metaphysics and epistemology, has since Plato's injunction against the Sophists' logographic *pharmakon*, systematically denied the *structurally* hypomnesic nature of the life of the mind.

34. Understanding and taking care

The *pharmakon*'s repression, bequeathed to us from Plato's Academy, which is the simultaneous repression of the pharmacological condition of and for the very origin of philosophy (and the repression of a/its *trauma* of origin), persists in *current* academic institutions. It has continued throughout modern times and on into us, we twenty-first-century latecomers, in our profound ignorance of (if not downright contempt for) the new forms of mnemotechnology that have produced first analogic, then numeric devices forming contemporary psychopower. But they must abruptly come to an end at the moment at which those initial questions return to us, along with contemporary figures of the *hypomnēmaton*, as they engage in a new battle for intelligence.

The general public's impotence in the face of the collapse of teaching institutions, a collapse that forms the academic context of the battle for intelligence, largely emerges from the *theoretical denial*, by the majority of the intellectual world, of the mnemotechnical and hypomnesic nature of all current forms of knowledge, even while the programming industries' domination of programming institutions moves toward its empirical mastery of the contemporary forms of psychotechnologies of hypomnesis.

These industries are currently formulating psychopower aimed at completing the biopower (with which Foucault is concerned but which he completely transforms): they instrumentalize psychotechnologies derived from psychotechniques, practically implementing the technics of self Foucault describes. In antiquity, the problem of attention-formation techniques was discussed primarily as one of attention to the *self* and of acquiring a technics *of* self, as *nootechnical* practices also producing academic instruction and training, initially as submission of attention to letters through the *grammatistēs*, opening access to *skholē* in the *skholeion* (σχολειον), the ancient Greek school.

And yet, the preceding chapters have shown us the following:

1. Techniques of attention control are at present in the service of the biopower of agribusiness, for example, as the economy of attention resting on the particular cognition of *at*tention that is mistaken for *re*tention, and that in the end entirely eliminates attention as care (this "biopower" often becoming pathogenic);[9] this is the mutation Deleuze describes as the formation of societies of control, beyond Foucault's disciplinary societies.

2. Toward this end, the programming industries—the armed wing of biopower become psychopower—enter into an agreement with the very programming institutions they want to supplant (by destroying the primary and secondary identification processes they replace with a regressive identification process) through their formative role in the process of referential individuation that since Kant, Condorcet, and Ferry has rested on attention formation called maturity.

The "battle of and for intelligence," then, presents a contemporary choice concerning the interaction of biopower and psychopower:

1. Either psychopower submits to biopower, in which case it *excludes* a politics of the mind, becoming a battle for intelligence against intelligence (this is what I have called industrial populism, or a capitalism of drives);

2. Or it distinguishes itself from biopower, in which case it becomes the object of *regulation* through the power of the public and in service to a psychopolitics that simultaneously becomes a noopolitics (for example, in developing a new "spirit of capitalism").

The question of care is as much that of care for the body as living flesh as for the mind, the psyche that after Plato Greek philosophy not only distinguished from the body but *opposed* to it. This opposition between psychic and somatic care, as the two species of the genre "care," is what is at stake in Plato's *Alcibiades*, to which Foucault gives special importance: what Plato plays out there, as Foucault tells us, is a turning in the philosophical question of care, which is also (since it occurs at philosophy's debut) philosophy's *original turn*. Socrates encourages Alcibiades to take care of himself by asking *himself* what it would be to "take care of himself":

> *Socrates*—Come on! Have confidence! If you were in fact fifty years old when you took stock of your condition, it would be difficult to take proper care of yourself (*epimēlesthai*). But this is the proper age for checking up on yourself.
>
> *Alcibiades*—But once one has done the check-up, what should one do, Socrates?
>
> *Socrates*—Answer the questions I ask you, Alcibiades! . . . Well! So let's see . . . what would it mean to take care of oneself?[10]

Foucault gives the *Alcibiades* exceptional status because it is possible to see in it the complex movement at play in philosophy between two distinct themes—themes that, as he tells us, are still indissociable today: that of understanding and that of care. Foucault shows that in the dialogue Plato subsumes the matter of care—of the *epimēlesthai*—as *taking* care, of *epimēleia* as the technics of the self, under that of the understanding (*gn ōsis, epistēmē*). This *new hierarchy of principles* leads to a progressive forgetting of care, especially as a *technique* of care, which has completely disappeared in the modern world.

The matter of care *as a technics of self* appears later on in Foucault (though it is central to his work on medical care[11]), and when it does appear, it is within the governing (which in Greek is also *epimēleia*) of human beings and of life, issues in high focus since the sixteenth century but that only became concrete with the rise of the bourgeoisie, as biopower. *Epimēleia* is as much a technics of self as the administration of public affairs in general. Consequently, Foucault conjoins these two issues into what he calls "governmentality."

Biopower is a form of care, a historic form of the system of care charged to the State, as governmentality. In the 1980s, Foucault declared that in order to think this, it would be necessary *also* to think the technics of self, for which the Greeks had a precept: "*epimēlesthai sautou*"—take care of yourself. Yet he shows that Platonism, and then Christianity, have progressively occluded this tradition, to the profit of the Delphic injunction laid out in the *Charmides* as well as in the *Alcibiades*: "*gnōthi seauton*"—know yourself.

35. *Epistēmē* and discipline (*epimēleia, melētē*)

We must pause for a moment to track Foucault's course from technologies of power to biopower, then to techniques of the self, and finally to the writing of the self.

The editors of *Dits et écrits* rightly present its various texts in the order of their original publication dates. But this does not correspond with the order in which Foucault addressed these issues. *L'Écriture de soi*, first published in *Corps écrit* in 1983, appears in the collected writings long before *Les Techniques de soi* and *La Technique politique des individus*, the results of courses Foucault taught at the University of Vermont in 1982. Yet in my view, *L'Écriture de soi* goes a step further than *Les Techniques de soi*—a step that allows us to derive the issues of psychopower and noopolitics from Foucault's analysis of biopower.

Rereading these texts in this order—first *Discipline and Punish* (1975), then *The Meshes of Power* (from a course taught in 1976)[12]—and reexamining Foucault's synthesis of biopower requires three preliminary remarks:[13]

1. At the beginning of the twenty-first century, what Foucault defined in the 1970s as biopower has fundamentally changed. Any analysis of the current age in the terms by which he defined biopower could lead to a misunderstanding of the specific elements of *our* situation.

2. Although Foucault thought through the psychotechnologies of attention within the context of what for him, at that time, constituted the techniques of the self, of care and caring for oneself, and then of the writing of the self (i.e., of individuation via the *hypomnēmata* constructing nootechniques), he inexplicably neglected the moment of nootechniques' socialization as techniques of the self becoming techniques of the *we*, through the secularization of the teaching process, and in the wake of what Sylvain Auroux calls the second revolution of grammatization—first by the Lutheran Church, then by the Jesuits. In other words, Foucault's study of disciplinary societies led him to efface the psychotechnical and nootechnical questions being asked of the religious, then the secular schools, at the same time erasing what differentiates religious forms of teaching from secular, public, and mandatory forms.

3. Foucault's analysis of the school as a disciplinary establishment, in which the discipline is that of the army, not of knowledge, and where normalization and individualization are produced through what Foucault

calls "the apparatus of writing"[14]—this analysis completely ignores the fact that writing, as a technology, and more precisely as a psychotechnology of attention, is also pharmacological and can *just as easily* construct an apparatus of disindividuation *through* individualization as the process of individuation in service to a self, as "the writing of the self," one of Foucault's last subjects shortly after his study of the techniques of self.

The status of writing is very ambiguous in Foucault's thought, sometimes foregrounded by the power of individuation, sometimes thought of unilaterally as a technological discipline, sometimes completely ignored. In "What Is Enlightenment?" published in 1984—that is, after *L'Écriture de soi*—he comes to a complete dead-end regarding the questions of reading and writing so central to Kant as the foundations of *Aufklärung* and maturity, defined by Kant as the results of a process of historical conquest.

Foucault does not even mention the perfectly technological nature of maturity defined as a mature consciousness *that writes* before a public of mature consciousnesses *able to read these writings*. This maturity is technological because it is inscribed within an *apparatus of writing* that is also a *society*. Foucault's scholarly reading of Kant's text, aimed at a public consisting of those of us who can read Foucault's text, in which he invites us to read Kant (to read Kant as *he* does: forgetting the very different scenes, the different worlds, of reading and writing) and what Kant *effaces* along with issues of reading and writing within the historical process Kant *does* address. But this effacement is a consequence of Foucault's general position during the 1970s regarding technologies of power: they are disciplinary and somatic, and the great question they address is that of the body. As a result, the forgetting of reading and writing, the mechanism for the production of maturity as an organological age of attention formation, is perfectly congruent with the fact that academia—as an institution Foucault addresses directly in *Discipline and Punish* through themes of "good upbringing" and surveillance (DP, 195), but that are still not analyzed as public instruction—has no other place in biopolitics than as one element of the disciplinary mechanism of child rearing and of *rationalization*, understood here exclusively as *normalization*—no relationship being established among school, techniques of self, and writing.

Yet Foucault's reference to schooling as a surveillance mechanism is based essentially, in *Discipline and Punish*, on texts dated between 1669 ("Instruction méthodique pour l'école paroissiale"; DP, 156ff.) and 1828 ("Conduite des écoles chrétiennes"; DP, 147), during which the only discussion topic was religious education and military training. There were simply no thematics for the mental origins of nootechniques in any teaching method nor for their nootechnical nature. Schools simply implemented disciplinary techniques copied from the army, the factory, and the prison. In "The Meshes of Power," Foucault writes that the tutor/teacher's place was the same as the head supervisor's and the prison guard's; the school employed the same panoptic logic: the students all sat facing the teacher, who could survey the entire class, making it as easy to "manage" students as prisoners.

In this section ("Panopticon"), Foucault makes no reference to Kant's concerns regarding the problem of managing (i.e., disciplining) a body forced to sit for long periods in the classroom.[15] Kant's concerns address the *organological* formation of bodily habits required for the particular kind of attention that can lead to maturity—as opposed to "tameness" and the laziness and cowardice that are its goals, in a simple process of subjugating individualization. Contrary to Kant, Foucault claims that the educational apparatus was essentially dedicated to just such a strategy: the formation of submissive beings.

In the kind of school Foucault analyzes as a surveillance mechanism, formation of attention is never the goal, nor the creating of physical conditions conducive to a technics of the *we*—of maturity, sought by Condorcet as well, but rather of finding a means by which to "classify individuals so as to ensure that each one is in his or her proper place" (Meshes, 158). But what Foucault completely neglects here is the role of the master/teacher who, through a discipline that is not *subj*ugation but *int*egration into transindividuation, builds circuits *regulated by concepts, not normatives*, forming a rational, intergenerational *we*, as mature attention accessible to the majority of students—through mandatory public education.

This *Foucauldian inattention* to what had made Foucault himself an individualized, mature writer and professor at the Collège de France translates into the fact that "The Meshes of Power" speaks of the supervisor replacing the tutor but not of the public schoolteachers, nor indeed of national education in general, or only to describe "normal schools" as those attempting to impose a "norm" (the professor described as a supervisor is not like a teacher but "reduced" to the status of a "pawn"), and into the fact that he offers no analysis of the motives nor the consequences of becoming literate [*alphabétisation*], as well as completely neglecting the school's historical transformations.

Though the question of writing does arise in *Discipline and Punish*, it is only through the question of a "writing apparatus" in service to a system of strict supervision and individualization (DP, 153); this is not in any sense similar to what could organize access to the self and to care constructed as *epimēleia*,[16] as the discipline and *melētē* intensifying self-sufficiency through the writing of the self, constituting the opposite of Foucault's description of a writing apparatus in service to a radically different kind of discipline, a surveillance mechanism for press-ganging students, starting with their subjugation, leading to control and isolation of students' bodies. Kant shows, however, that discipline's corporeal dimension is a condition of self-discipline (discipline *of self*) resting on maturity, which is simultaneous obeying of the law and critical consciousness.[17]

Foucault's exploration of how and why an academic or medical examination is a disciplinary technique for supervision takes place within this context: "the examination brings . . . individuality into a documentary framework; . . . placing individuals in a field of surveillance just as powerfully situates them in a network of writing: it engages them with a huge weight of documents that capture and paralyze [*fixent*] them" (DP, 189–90), but that also form a "capacity to write." What such an examination *tests*, according to Foucault, has nothing to do with the writing of the self. I remember very well, however, the exaltation I felt (rarely, I confess) when taking such tests—and I still remember how the feeling of scholarly *obligation* sometimes gave me a true feeling of euphoria.[18]

Such a writing power, which forms "an entire series of codes of disciplinary individuality" (DP, 189), as Foucault describes it—as surveillance—is obviously what makes up the standard, normal procedures [*l'ordinaire*] of academic life. The question is simply one of knowing whether to think about things in terms of the standard, the normal—or in terms of what, within the context of this standardization (and thanks to it), could be produced as *extra*ordinary, as excess serving that standard, a standard to which it would be necessary to reach out, for example, as the conquest of maturity in the struggle against laziness and cowardice.

36. The deceptive heuristic and the rhetoric of "only . . . [*ne . . . que . . .*]" in the face of the pharmacological strategy

It was in fact quite standard procedure, in the course of the dark 1970s, *to disappoint*, and to claim a *disappointing heuristic* in the name of the struggle against "received ideas" and "ideologies": it had become banal to pretend to demonstrate that what had appeared to be ideals in the eyes of philosophers had become nothing more than a relatively subtle kind of belief—in the political, economic, moral, and intellectual history of the West (chiefly Western Europe), a history that came to be seen as an illusion or series of illusions—even a fabric of illusions—not only as religion but as all that had pretended to be institutionally activated for the common as well as the individual good.

The entire problem was obviously the ideological struggle against ideology, which gradually lost all credibility as a philosophical concept inherited from Marx—the ideological being somehow eroded by an autoimmunizing, corrosive power (in the Derridean sense). Just as Marx demonstrates that the law masks and legitimizes the destruction of work, just as Nietzsche and Freud show how morality is in service to societal control and *ressentiment*,[19] it became simply good taste to reveal to the naïve world that all these beautiful discourses (on teaching methods, for example) are in fact doing service to a disciplinary State apparatus, and that the teacher who believes she is a teacher is actually a prison guard.

This view is sadly, profoundly false (any teacher who loves the job knows this—and there are still many such teachers, now so unhappily facing what may be an intolerable situation). But that view is also significantly performative, historically demoralizing: it installs a historical age of demoralization, a sort of economic depression of mind and spirit, and the libidinal energy composing it, energy ordinarily (and extraordinarily) sublimated within the social project and encouraging renunciation not just of the self, which Foucault frames as the Christian project of the forgetting of *epimētheia* and *epimēlesthai sautou*, but of *everything*.

This *disappointment* mind-set, evident in many famous figures newly graduated from, for example, the ENS in France,[20] and from top American universities and colleges—particularly after the hugely disappointing historicopolitical abortion called "1968"—has transformed its performative power from a discourse of *initiation* [*déniaisement*][21] based on the rhetoric of *only, ne . . . que . . .* [as in "it was *only* a dream"] into the future anterior: "school will have been *only* a disciplinary tool," or "political thought will have been *only* a big fiction": we are condemned to managing the economy; there is no longer a political economy. Such statements are attempts at universalizing and rationalizing the historical failures of a generation of thinkers, militants, and public figures. We are today paying the price: we live in what amounts to nothing more than a desert of nihilism in which such declarations are the subtlest versions—and thus in fact the most *revelatory*.

And yet, as for the normal or ordinary, it is certain that the "writing apparatus" Foucault describes as shaping the disciplinary academic establishment (in the same sense as "disciplinary battalion"), in which discipline is limited to surveillance paying no attention to what makes a discipline into knowledge, perfectly describes what is currently happening through technologies activated by attention cognition and the *economy* of attention in order to replace all forms of attention with an automatized retentional system *substituting for* literacy, for "the power of writing." Foucault explores this archaeology, but avoiding the vital element of knowledge: "these codes [of disciplinary individuality] were still quite rudimentary in both qualitative and quantitative form, but they mark the moment of the first formalization of the individual within power relations" (DP, 189). What will become for the Foucault of 1983 the basis for the writing of the self that *simultaneously* formed a "documentary field," a "writing network," and an "abundance of written documents" was for the Foucault of 1975 precisely the opposite: a "literacy," "the ability to read and write" implementing a field of surveillance and control of private individuals having been *des*ingularized and *dis*individuated by their "individualization," on the understanding that the "private individual" is the negation of the "singular person" (CE1, 46ff.; CE2, 99). Foucault says not a word here of the science of individuals as the origin of the human sciences nor of this question's Aristotelian origins.

In other words, what Foucault describes so brilliantly in 1975 and 1976 presents us with a pharmacology whose "literacy" is specific to the time. But Foucault subsequently erases this timeliness and, at the same time, the pharmacological nature of technologies of power in general; consequently, in the third part of *Discipline and Punish* (entitled "Discipline"), he claims that the school per se is just such a disciplinary system, even while effacing its organological dimension, since it always asks a phar-macological question—the *political question par excellence*—regarding the formation of a system of care in which biopower is but a historical stage, but which may not take *everything* at work in a given epoch into account—nor even, perhaps, only what is *essential* to it.

It is difficult, if not completely impossible, to take an entire epoch "into account": it is only possible to select those aspects of the epoch that support interpretations of it after the fact. The fact that there is not the slightest trace of Condorcet or Jules Ferry in Foucault's discourse on the school, nor of Kantian literacy, is the result of a skewed selection pro-cess—that, nonetheless, has its merits, as a kind of *epokhē* at the service of a new method and a new heuristic that, as disappointing as it might be, was and is remarkably fruitful.

But the fact that nowhere in Foucault does he question the possibility that what he describes, as he lays out the social consequences of gram-matization, is a *tendency* of the pharmacological field opened up by tech-nologies of power (and technologies of knowledge) in which the disci-plinary field, in Foucault's sense (that is, as the control and subjection of individuals), would only be one pole faced with another pole: the field of disciplines structuring knowledge—and as discursive relations based on techniques of self—is not simply a bias but an *incoherence* within its own methodology and its results: the fertile nature of *only* [*ne . . . que . . .*] is *only* fruitful on condition of its being critiqued—and the time of that critique has come.

Because he does not connect or question this *contradictory* multidimen-sionality of either disciplines or technologies (technologies as knowledge *and* as power), Foucault also completely neglects the *spiritual* origins of discipline in the religious schools, which nonetheless form the bridge to Christian techniques of self, in which Ignatius Loyola's *Spiritual Exer-cises* are canonical. Similarly (and correlatively), Foucault does not see the emergence of the conflict between programming institutions (of which the schools, the ENS, and the Collège de France—where he completed his professorial life—are the constituent elements) and programming in-dustries that reconfigure the question of biopower and biopolitics at the most profound levels, as the age of psychotechnologies. This conflict is actually what Foucault himself, in a section *against academic discipline* that seemed, after the fact, to be quite amazing, describes as the "power of the Norm."[22] As a result, this discourse shows itself to be extremely theoretical and indeed extremely standardized.

This is why, even if Foucault replies (as he does to a question from Michelle Perrot) that "the reformers of the 18th century who gave this opinion particular power . . . misunderstood the actual conditions of opinion, of the media: a materiality brought into the mechanisms of the economy and of power as the press, book-publishing, and then cinema and television,"[23] he nonetheless profoundly neglects these materializations and their organological and pharmacological effects on the body, as well as on the mind and its organization: its psychic, collective, and technical individuation. This is clearly manifest in Foucault's reading of Kant that, however, explicitly mentions the connection between writing and maturity, as does his analysis of disciplinary societies and of biopower in general. The fact is that for Foucault there is no pharmacological dilemma, a fundamental problem for a philosophy that in the end presents itself as a thinking through of care and of the self. The rhetoric of *only* is, as a rule, a renunciation of the *pharmakon*'s ambiguities. Doubtless, no one escapes from it: this is the eminently twisted nature of what Derrida calls "the logic of the supplement," in which I think he himself sometimes becomes lost.[24]

Foucault's analysis of academic institutions never addresses public instruction as a historic process passing through the Enlightenment—that is, through "modernity," in the sense that he gives this word in his treatment of Kant. Most important, and reciprocally, Foucault does not seem to see the developing power of marketing and the historical regression it represents as the identifying characteristic of our globalized age, exempting it from problematizing the programming industries' power and the marketing strategies that are those industries' manifestation. As a result, obviously he also cannot see the war that marketing, as the "science" of societies of control, is waging against programming institutions.

My case here is that on one side or another of these aspects of the disappointing context that "will inevitably have resulted" from what "will have been thought of" [future anterior . . .] as the "the end of philosophy" and the deconstruction of metaphysics, the potential objections to Foucault's best-known claims, *from a reading of his late texts*, are the results of both the premature death of this great inheritor of Canguilhem's thought and of a method of interpretation he introduces in *The Order o*

Things (1966) with the concept of the *epistēmē*, in the wake of *The Birth of the Clinic* (1963); then in *The Archaeology of Knowledge* (1969) he breaks with *The Order of Things*—but maintains the same blind spot, namely, a *total inattention to the process of grammatization*; the blind spot continues through *Discipline and Punish* and *The History of Sexuality*.[25]

§ 8 Biopower, Psychopower, and Grammatization

37. From production to consumption

Foucault's work on biopolitics and the techniques of the self constitute in their totality his reflections on sexuality and his discourse with psychoanalysis; it is this double goal that connects them, though problematically—and this is not just a matter of techniques. Or rather, Foucault addresses the question of sexuality-as-technics in a very specific sense, thinking through what, in the aftermath of Freud and Lacan, distinguishes instinct, drive, and desire from one another, but sidesteps any examination of matters directly and exclusively addressing the contents of the taboo, the law, and repression,[1] as they are traditionally treated in ethnology (HS1, 18ff.). Foucault thus takes on the challenge of thinking through the whole question of power, and not just of the law but of technology as well: what allows instinct to become drive is *power as technology*, through which Foucault makes technique part of desire.

Yet something remains unclear about the way his approach to technology is situated: Foucault never investigates the technologic nature of the law itself, for the same reason that he never explores the *specific* question of the school among the disciplinary institutions. Yet just as academic discipline in the *skholeion* is the initial discipline working to establish rational knowledge and therefore an introduction to *epiméleia, melété,* and the technics of self, as many diverse kinds of disciplines—that is, to the formation of attention—that also share with the law the fact of being techniques of letters, law literatizes and grammatizes existence by framing it within new sets of rules during the transindividuation process, and according to intergenerational mechanisms perfectly homogeneous with the circuits of transindividuation through which disciplines of rational thought are formed, circuits which then form laws as "discursive regularities."[2]

Technologies of power and the law have something else in common: they are both hypomnesic techniques forming the base for psychotechniques that in turn form *epimēleia.* These psychotechniques, as techniques of the self, are the very ones for which the school has been responsible since antiquity, passing through the church, then the secular school, aiming at a *self,* at least within *modernity,* that also becomes a *we*: the mature *we* (freed from religious dogma) of Kant and Condorcet. To neglect an interrogation of the *pharmakon's* essential duplicity appearing in this process is to close off the very possibility of thinking other kinds of *pharmaka* of, for example, the psychotechnologies mobilized by cinema and television, and by their effects on psychic and collective individuation—on the self.

There is no doubt that Foucault's process attempts a conjunction of all his themes into a single one, the self, with a theme of individuation insofar as it is indissociably psychic *and* collective, an individuation that Foucault calls "subjectivation": "I am more and more interested in the interactions of self and others" (DE4, 555). This interaction, as the essence of subjectivation, establishes the very foundation of government. But this conjunction had not taken place in Foucault's writing lifetime. This is true, I think, for one reason: after *The Order of Things* there was an absence of any problematizing of the general issue of letters and the republic of letters (as of the aftereffects of the print shop in the Renaissance and neoclassicism, then through the Enlightenment and beyond).

When Foucault's "What Is Enlightenment?" appears, a year after "The Writing of the Self," in which writing is seen as the grounding condition of a self-creation always already projected toward others,[3] connected through the *pharmakon* (which can also alienate and poison the self, though this is never addressed in "The Writing of the Self"), his previous work to some extent prevents him from marking the role that the techniques of writing play in forming the Kantian idea of maturity. In the end, Foucault does not ask the question of pharmacology—a question that is nonetheless essential to all therapeutics, all medicalization, and all questions of care and *epimēleia*: no medicine without pharmacopeia,[4] which is, perhaps, in the final analysis the true question of power.

It might be argued, contrarily, regarding writing's part in the formation of maturity as Kant's *Aufklärung*, that even Kant does not seem to
accord sufficient importance to what he writes on literacy, as if he did not
read what he wrote, as a scholar before other scholars, his readers. And
Foucault so precisely emphasizes the central importance of letters and of
writing that it is impossible not to wonder if Foucault's inattention to this
Kantian issue, to which Kant himself so strangely pays little attention, is
not part of a mechanism resembling denial, a denial that is inherently one
of metaphysics itself, as the organological stage in a succession of epochs
of the organon's (the *pharmakon*'s) concealment *by* the organon (by the
pharmakon), which translates in Kant into a theory of schematism that
makes one wonder about the point at which it undoubtedly influences
Foucauldian archaeology.[5]

In "The Meshes of Power" Foucault echoes Marx's rejection of legalism
as a theory of power, claiming that there is not *one* power but many: the
workshop, the army, slavery, servitude, and so on (DE4, 183). It is necessary to think of *powers*, and "to attempt to localize them in their historical and geographical specificities" (185). But Foucault's biopower, which
he himself describes (and so powerfully) historically and geographically
by localizing it in Europe, is no longer the force behind *our* age: without significant modifications it cannot account for the specifics of *psychotechnological* psychopower, nor of the new situation of biopower that
results from it—nor of a "biopolitics" that has become a psychopolitics
no longer emerging from the nation-state (and its programming institutions) but from deterritorialized economic forces (and their programming
industries); these forces construct new discursive and nondiscursive relationships, that is, new apparatuses.

At the same time as technologies of power, efficiency analysis [*performance*] is born: its goal, according to Foucault, is no longer to "prevent"—as the interdictive power of the law does, and out of which psychoanalysis theorizes the transformation of instincts into drives that are
themselves linked through the libido's role as a mechanism of censure—
but to "optimize" (187), which Max Weber describes as a process of rationalization and disenchantment.[6] It is also important, however, to interrogate everything specifically designated as obligatory under the law (for
example, the law establishing mandatory public education), and specifically by initiating a right to know by legal measures that are not reduced
to interdiction but instead institute a positive power of sublimation as a

disciplinary transindividuation that in turn fosters political maturity, the essence of *Aufklärung*.

Efficiency analysis, systematically and technologically researched through the science of power since the Renaissance, leads to disciplinary societies as organological assemblages. The rifle, as a technical organ,[7] creates the need for a new form for the army, a new disciplinary social organization structuring the development of capabilities through which individuals (soldiers, factory workers, schoolchildren, etc.) acquire a value, through interiorization within their psychic and somatic organization, of their technical organs' functions, that functionality being their individualization in and through the efficient "machine of production."

Individualization, however, as opposed to individuation, is a particularization, a disindividuation (as Marx shows, and Simondon out of Marx[8]): individualization does not interiorize, and the discipline of its technicity does not contribute to self-construction. Individualization leads to automatization, depriving individuals of knowledge per se. Like all technologies of power, and like grammatization, it inevitably moves toward the *ex*teriorization of knowledge into machines with no other pseudo-interiorization than that by which the individual "serves" the system (the canon, the machine, the apparatus)—all within the pharmaco-logic and within the context of a biopower in which attention is *liquidated*, creating an *immature social body* that is exploitable as a pure, living resource of production or, as Marx calls it, the workforce. In the twentieth century, this pharmaco-logic extends to the consumer—though this is exactly what Foucault's theory of biopower does not allow to be thought.

Simultaneous with the development of this disciplinary political technology of and in the army, the factory, the school, and government, a police force—in its largest sense—also forms "to control the smallest elements within the social body, by which we reach the 'social atoms' themselves, that is, individuals" (193), in order to best exploit the "value" of a population formulated in this way, and in order to confer a new, fundamentally functional role on technical training, and more generally on education. According to Foucault, the army, factory, and school open to and implement an individualizing—disindividu*ating*—technology in service to a politics "basically targeting individuals in their bodies, in their behavior, . . . while anatomizing them" (193). This power technique, a "political anatomy," is, however, not still biopower, properly speaking, because it is exercised not on subjects but on populations, "living beings composed, commanded, ruled by processes, by biological laws" (194) and who, once mastered, become a population of "production machines."

But *today* the question of biopower is less one of "utilizing the population" for *production* than of establishing markets for *consumption*. This is where Foucault's analyses are insufficient for us. His claims regarding the genesis of the State leading to the Industrial Revolution, with the bourgeoisie's taking power, set up the formative conditions for nineteenth-century capitalism as Marx describes it, in which production is the first preoccupation. But the twentieth century devolves entirely different issues. The greatest of these is the revolution in which human ways of living evolve into ways of consuming, through progressively liquidated life skills in an industrial-service economy based on programming industries.[9] The destruction of associative (symbolic) media is the inevitable outcome of this evolution, as they are replaced by *dis*sociative (cybernetic) media (TCD, 29; RM, 50–55) whose "science" is less cybernetics itself (as Heidegger believed[10]) as a stage of grammatization, than marketing that determines, *prescribes* this pharmacology, making youth the central influence on—the prescribers of—their parents, transforming parents into "large children";[11] marketing is revealed to be *a prescription against all systems of care*, most important, against all intergenerational circuits.

This scenario, in which the State's biopower is transformed into market psychopower, is currently still less in evidence in Europe than in the United States. Only making its appearance in Europe after World War II, its significant invasion began in the early 1970s, shortly after 1968 and at the same time as the gasoline crisis and shocks to the welfare state. In the early twenty-first century, we in an industrialized world now mired in the resultant colossal financial and systemic failures, a world in which all biopolitics (which for Foucault are always State created) have been wiped away but where the psychotechnologies of the psychopower that has ravaged the mental and physical health of the entire population—chiefly of children—as well as the very future of the world economy, these psychotechnologies have conjoined, forming a common system with this disastrous financial reality.

This is a system that has destroyed investment, replacing it with speculation as it systematically plays the short term against the long term. Since the summer of 2007, it has been clear that this recklessness and lack of care are now grounding principles of the world economy, which should give us some initial idea of the immense dangers they pose to humanity and the world.[12]

38. The other discipline: the power of writing and the writing of knowledge

In a course Foucault taught at the University of Vermont in 1982 (a year after the publication of "The Writing of the Self"),[13] he makes frequent reference to economist Johann von Justi:[14] "the police govern not through law but by intervening in very specific, permanent, and positive ways in the conduct of individuals" (DE4, 825). But today the market, much more than the State, "intervenes" "in very specific, permanent, and positive ways in the conduct of individuals." And although this was clearly already the case in 1982, it seems that Foucault saw nothing of it (on the other hand, this new intervention is precisely what Deleuze emphasizes in 1990). The concept of "the population" appears for the first time in von Justi's writing, along with other thinkers of "State reason," then the police and the "science of the State" addressed by thinkers such as Bottero, Turquet, and Lamare, setting up the concept of biopower. In the spirit of von Justi, Foucault writes that

> the physical and economic aspects of the State, taken as a whole, constitute a milieu to which the population is a contributor, but which reciprocally depends on the population. Before all else, the State must care for men as population, exercising its power over living beings as living beings, and consequently its politics must necessarily be a biopolitics. (826)

Moreover, as Kant would interject here, this living being is noetic, endowed with consciousness, capable of passing from minority to maturity, a maturity without which no politics worthy of the name is truly possible. For Kant, Frederick II's greatness did not reside in his not having reduced Prussian politics by handing it over to the police—Prussia being the exemplary country of von Justi's (and Foucault's) "science of the State."[15] Even if a "good Prussian" must obey, in the sense of observing a discipline, Kant says—as he thanks Frederick II for making "the century of Frederick" possible (and surpassing the century, Prussia, and the good Prussian, for embodying the image of the mature human being who arrives "cosmo-politically" with the *Aufklärung* and defines it in his very arrival)—a good Prussian must also critique, and one must *ob*serve (as one observes a rule), not merely *con*serve.

To *ob*serve here is to observe the *other discipline*: the formation of maturity as the kind of attention called rational consciousness, inscribing itself in the space of "the power of writing" whose advent Foucault sees in von Justi, Bentham, and others as *also* and *still* and *always* being a *knowledge* of writing, in turn opening a political space as the *critical* space of writing before the entire literate world. The fact that the power of writing can be deployed as a sophistic or disciplinary individualization can certainly mask the fact that there is a mature form of the knowledge of writing that can be masked only for the immature. Writing as a critical space is obviously and simultaneously duplicitous, pharmacological—and thus "critical" in *that* sense.

This is the exact condition, Kant tells us, for the writing of knowledge as the pursuit of individuation. In more contemporary language, we might confront von Justi with the objection that the pharmaconoetic being is symbolic because he desires, and that in desiring he transforms his drives, which as an action forming a law are thus not simply instincts—to that extent he is symbolically noetic. His noesis is, moreover, his will to know, to have access to consistencies as ideal objects. Biopower attempts to reduce the pharmaconoetic being to the condition of subsistence, what Marx calls the renewal of the workforce. But biopower is also the object of a *struggle* with political, institutional, and material effects, most notably as public instruction; Foucault, despite paying a great deal of attention to material institutions, as we will continue to see, very strangely erases them from his historical descriptions.

Biopower's struggle posits that beyond it there is a psychopower—a power over minds—that the philosophy of a Hippias, Alcibiades, Meno, Phaedrus, or many other young Athenians critique; they oppose the sophistic practice of a logographic *pharmakon* and transform psychopower into the noopower that Plato calls dialectic and anamnesis. This follows a historical, organological process leading to what Kant, Mendelssohn, and *Aufklärung* call the maturity (*Bildung*) of literacy. Condorcet places the school at the heart of any social struggle for precisely this reason,[16] and Jules Ferry's work is its French social concretization less than a century after Kant's response to the question of the Enlightenment in the *Berlinische Monatsschrift*.

When Deleuze declares that disciplinary societies have taken the place of societies of control, he means that now psychopower guarantees control of behavior, since police-science and State-science have ceded their place and their power to management and marketing, their discipline to modulation.[17] With Edward Bernays (Freud's nephew), then Ernest Dichter and Louis Cheskin, early twentieth-century marketing presents itself for the first time as the technology of *public* relations,[18] whose goal is no longer to form and exploit producers (of things) but to control the behavior of consumers (as such) through the rapid development of psychotechnologies finally liquidating the noopolitics that since Jules Ferry had been governed by programming institutions. In the face of these forces, disciplinary industrial society encounters its limit: overproduction, first in Bernays's time (the 1920s and 1930s), then after World War II.

39. The state of the market

An article by the publishing house McGraw-Hill appeared in *Advertising Age* on 24 October 1955, addressed to American producers:

> As a Nation, we are already so rich that consumers have no need to buy the better part—perhaps 40%—of what we produce, and this will necessitate progressively decreasing it in the course of the next years. Yet if consumers choose not to buy a large percentage of our production, a powerful economic depression is not far away.[19]

This warning is in fact a concrete consequence of the inevitable trend in cyclical, "free-market" capitalism, toward the eventual lowering of profits, the corollaries of which are unemployment and poverty. The trend is of course something against which capitalism continuously pushes back through incessantly intensified innovation, but which itself inevitably leads to further production excesses and the chronic obsolescence of products, resulting (again inevitably) in the increasing need to support consumption artificially. As Packard says, "[S]ince 1950, with over-production threatening on a number of fronts, the preoccupation of the managers of industrial societies has undergone a fundamental modification. For them, production has become secondary. Instead of thinking about making things, they think of selling them" (HP, 24). It is no longer a question, then—and today less than ever—of controlling the population as a producing machine, but rather as a *consuming machine*; and the danger is no longer biopower but psychopower as both control *and* production—production of motivations: "in industrial and commercial gatherings the discussion is of the 'market revolution,' and much reflection is devoted to the means of 'stimulating' buyers, creating 'needs' in them that they did not know existed" (HP, 24). This is the context in which *Motivational Research*, of which Ernest Dichter is the principal representative, first appeared in the United States. Dichter proposed that what must be found was "the means of pre-conditioning the client to buy through 'engraving certain characteristics in the brain'" (HP, 28; Packard is citing *The New York World-Telegram and Sun*).

This is a thought process that has led directly, in terms of our central theme here, to the destruction of the juvenile psychic apparatus and the liquidation of intergenerational relations. In order to accomplish this, following Bernays's first work (but also after, for example, the cybernetics used to train the crews of Flying Fortresses during World War II), Dichter and Cheskin adapted psychoanalysis to the systematic analysis of markets. They suggest that industry distinguish among three dimensions of their "clients'" psychology:

1. consciousness (not manipulable)

2. the preconscious (manipulable; Dichter and Cheskin generally call it the subconscious)

3. the unconscious (manipulable)

In this context, Packard could write in 1958 that "the exploration of our attitudes regarding products, at levels 2 and 3, is now known in the new science as Motivational Analysis or Research" (HP, F28). Could a statement more clearly capture what we saw at the beginning of Packard's text?: how now, early in the twenty-first century, the central question for the media world is that of control of youth's psychic and social apparatuses from the youngest age, despite its destruction of the intergenerational circuitry.

But we must not lose sight of the fact that this intergenerational circuitry also forms the circuits of biological reproduction of "the population"—circuits of sexuality in which biopolitical and technical questions of the self, both somatic and psychic, interact. And it is on this central question of sexuality in its largest sense (as the socialization of desire, and socialization *as* desire, giving rise to the pleasure principle and the reality principle) that all of Foucault's works converge. He writes in 1976 that "sex is the hinge between the anatomico-political and the bio-political; sex is at the crossroads of all disciplines and regulations and, as such, became by the end of the 19th century a *political* element of first importance in making society into a machine of production" (DE4, 194). But in addition to this, "regulations" must be understood in a very narrow sense, not at all the sense in which Keynes, for example, uses the word (particularly given that we are faced with the dangers of overproduction that this problematic of biopower seems to completely ignore): the sexuality Foucault is determined to connect with desire, libidinal energy, has became the basis of our current consumer culture's economy: it is required if society is to be a consumption machine (i.e., an industrial machine engaging in ever-increasing production, then reduced profits and rising unemployment, to which capitalism then reacts by intensifying the race to innovation and obsolescence—and psychic controls, then increasing production, etc.), a new kind of libidinal economy.

But today's fundamental challenge is more serious: it has become the autodestruction of this capitalist/consumerist libidinal economy, since a *durable* libidinal economy [a libidinal economy in the proper sense] always rests on primary identification and secondary psychic and collective identification,[20] through formation of a superego and the capacity for sublimation. But at the same moment that Packard was describing "MR" (Motivational Research), Herbert Marcuse demonstrated that the development of televisual marketing, as a behavioral programming industry, simultaneously created what he called an "automatic superego" and a process of "*de*-sublimation."[21] And this is perfectly congruent with the fact that if biopower leads to "the replacement of law by government" (786), national education is a unique instance of "management" as a behavioral-programming industry (for Foucault, this means "disciplinary," in the same way as those disciplines dedicated to mature attention formation through the acquisition of knowledge, and of knowledge-forming disciplines) through which, however, this management structure-become-education evolves from a *right to public education* that is also an *obligation*, as much for the citizenry as for the State.

It is this right, this mutual obligation, as a system of care (and management as the governing of the *epiměleia* of self and others) that must be replaced in the new American capitalism, which is less a biopower than a psychopower (a "soft power"), through the formation of behaviors determined by "MR" psychotechniques applied through psychotechnologies and implemented through marketing—and now, today, through the microeconomy of macrodistribution and the cognition of attention. Thus, in a service society that has come into existence since the second half of the twentieth century, the goal is to replace management, as academic programming institutions, by programming industries, thereby to replace public administrations generally (and biopolitical ones in particular), by consulting firms, private agencies, and oversight boards.

This strategy has devolved to what Anthony Giddens calls "expertise," resulting from the development of "abstract systems" induced by "spatio-temporal distanciation" (AG, 21ff.),[22] another name for deterritorialization, and by the fact that our existences are now deeply implicated in networks of specialized technological information of which we are largely (unavoidably?) ignorant, yet which force us to delegate our futures to the firms and agencies that then delegate them to markets. This is the context in which the service economy "produces" dissociation—the destruction of associational media through development of psychotechnologies eradicating psychic and social faculties (particularly attention), replacing them with automata stripped of any reinteriorization process; that is, without *critique*, and thus without *responsibility*.

The inevitable result is attention deficit, hyperactivity, cognitive and affective saturation, the infantilization of adults, the premature "maturation" (a double oxymoron) of minors, and, in the end, disaffection and disaffectation of what leads to the formation of either human wastelands or communal groups who react by throwing themselves, sometimes very violently, into the most archaic regression: the Iran Foucault visited in 1979, for example, where he wrote very troubling (though quite beautiful) pages—while still completely misunderstanding the situation there, seeing nothing other than a society rising up against the State.[23]

The development of this "expertise" through which the State's biopower recedes before market psychopower is also the origin of what Giddens believes must be described as a reflexive integration of the social sciences into society as a whole:

> One could apply the discoveries of the social sciences to an inert subject: they will only be able to be imposed through their being comprehended by social agents. . . . There is a give-and-take between the universe of social life and sociological knowledge, and in this process sociological knowledge is re-molded by and remolds the social universe. (AG, 15–16)

But it is not at all obvious that one should actually speak of "reflexivity" here; if it is true that *comprehension* is *critique*, and thus *mature*, forming the very condition of an associational milieu that has become a critical space, then the problem here is one of *adaptation without comprehension* of behaviors into rules that have been socialized as norms (which is a very specific modality of the adoption process) within a dissociative context.

Whatever it may be, the social science discourse Giddens addresses emanates from the development of technologies of power over individuals, as Foucault tells us, and this is what results in a science of individuals whose aim is a political technology: "it is impossible to isolate the appearance of the social sciences from the new political rationality, or from the new political technology" (DE4, 784). At the Vermont conference in 1982 Foucault also specified that an analysis of the techniques of the self needed to be added to his 1970s analysis of biopower, and that his final objective (encompassing, as we have seen, his discussion of the history of sexuality) is focused on what he calls "governmentality," governing forces distinguishable as "four kinds of technics: production, sign systems, power, and the self," which are only rarely separated. For Foucault, governmentality is the "encounter between techniques of domination and techniques of the self" (785). It might seem obvious that psychotechnologies are precisely this encounter's outcome, yet such a supposition entirely ignores the fact that therapeutics cannot be reduced to biopolitics[24]—and it would be to misunderstand why Foucault returns, at just this time, to the *other question of discipline, epiméleia,* whose radical form, *meléte,* later meant *meditatio*—Bailly has taught us that *meléte* originally meant "discipline," though not to be understood in the sense of "disciplinary societies."

40. *Epiméleia* and *pharmakon*

Meléte (μελετη) derives from *melētaô* (μελεταω). This polysemic verb's first meaning is "to take care of something" but also means "to exercise" in general, to prepare oneself for something, and thus a kind of training. Socrates, waiting to drink his hemlock, prepared himself for death disciplinarily, by his *meléte. Melētēma* (μελετημα), then, means "practical exercise" and, by extension, "study": clearly, then, *meléte* becomes *meditatio*.

Foucault's return to a consideration of the techniques of the self through techniques of domination or power that, along with the rise of the bourgeoisie to power, form a biopower, lead him to a reexamination of this matter of training (*gumnasia*), now no longer as the formation of a social body individualized by anatomo-political controls but as the individuation of a self whose very nature is in excess of such controls. Clearly, then, near the end of his life, and at the very heart of the issue, Foucault launched an examination of the other meaning of the word *discipline*—its ancient meaning, the origin of the radical sense of *epimēleia*, as management, administration, governmentality.

The question, and the history, of *epimēleia* must be examined in two different contexts: that of Greco-Roman philosophy and that of Christian spirituality:

> In ancient Greece, these practices, as techniques of the self, took the form of a precept: *epimelēsthai sautou*, "take care of yourself," "have a care for the self," "be concerned, care-ful about yourself."
>
>   This precept of "self-care" was one of the great principles of the ancient Greek cities. . . . It is an idea that for us today has lost its force and has become obscure. When one asks "what moral principle dominated all philosophy in antiquity?" the immediate answer is not "take care of yourself" but the Delphic principle, *gnôthi seauton*, "know thyself." (DE4, 786)

Moreover, this Delphic principle transformed itself immediately into a practice, "a rule to observe when consulting the oracle. 'Know thyself' meant 'do not imagine that you are a god.'" But as Foucault tells us, philosophy forgot the first principle of *epimelēsthai sautou*, of which the Delphic principle was a special case.

In Greek and Roman texts, the injunction to know oneself is always associated with this other principle, to care for oneself. But its being forgotten begins with philosophy's very birth: as the *Alcibiades* attests, Socrates' declaring that in teaching human beings to "have a care" for themselves, he is teaching them to have a care for the *polis* (783).

It must be emphasized, however, that in the *Alcibiades*, Plato argues (through Socrates' mouth) in favor of *dialectic and anamnesia*, of the thought that *thinks by itself*, not by receiving lessons from others. Plato argues, in other words, against sophistic psychotechnology as a technology of power. This *Platonic* injunction to have a care for oneself in order to learn to have a care for the city rather than to go and listen to the Sophists teaching against retribution and in favor of logographia and the *pithanon* (the art of persuasion) goes against the psychotechnical usage of the *pharmakon* and agrees with the condemnation of *tekhnē* and finally with *tekhnē*'s denial (i.e., with the denial of its constitutive role in all anamnesia as hypomnesia), as the origin of the denial by which philosophy creates itself, finally, as metaphysics.

This is why if there are historical reasons "explaining that *know thyself* eclipsed *take care of yourself*" (784), and in particular the fact that with the Christian morality of renunciation (chiefly renunciation of *self* under the weight of a morality of guilt) (787), "the moral principles of Western society underwent a profound transformation" (789), in which the initial orientation of philosophy as repression of the question of the *pharmakon* (especially of writing) activated, in Platonism, the mechanism of initiatory occultation of the principle of *epimelēsthai sautou* as *taking care, technically*. Foucault himself emphasizes this: "to take care of oneself consists [in the *Alcibiades*] of knowing oneself. . . . The dialogue concludes when Alcibiades understands that he must take care of himself through examining his mind [*âme*]" (791). Thus, after Plato, *epimēleia* becomes synonymous with *gnôsis*. If then "there is an inversion in the hierarchization of the two principles of Antiquity" (792), if the Stoics and Epicureans revalorize the techniques and writing of the self, as we will see, then Plato's first question, subjugating *epimēleia* to *gnôsis* (just as he subjugates *tekhnē* to *epistēmē*) must be that of the *technicity* of techniques of the self: *gnôthi seauton* means that he does not need to work through the Sophists' techniques, any more than through those of *epimēleia* when it is not founded on anamnesia and a dialectic opening to the question *ti esti? (what?)*, in turn opening to the question of what *is*: to ontology.

Here what Plato specifically denies is the need to pass through writing—through the *pharmakon*—as the Sophists did, and as the Epicureans and Stoics will. Foucault shows all of this clearly in "The Writing of the Self" published, we remember, one year after the Vermont course articulating biopower and political technologies as technologies of the self, all within the question of governmentality (793). In *Techniques of the Self*, Foucault had already underlined the fact that the Hellenic period saw a renaissance of the culture of self-care, in which writing had new importance:

> To take notes on oneself, notes one could re-read . . . to re-activate for oneself the verities one had needed, . . . the development of administrative structures under the empire will augment the number of writings and the importance of

writing in the political sphere. [After Plato and] with the arrival of the Hellenistic era, . . . this dialectic finds its expression in correspondence. To take
care of oneself becomes co-existent with writing as a constant activity. The
self is something on which there is a great deal to write. The act of writing
intensifies and deepens the experience of the self. (810ff.)

These psychotechniques—techniques of the *mind* [*âme*] accompanied
by somatotechniques, these cases of bodily techniques (in the sense in
which Mauss addresses them), for example, as *de-ambulatio* and *gumnasia*—these psychotechnologies that, as *melētē* understood as *meditatio*, are
processes for concentrating on an object of contemplation,[25] prefiguring
confession (800) as the art of listening—given that "listening to oneself"
foreshadows the examination of consciousness (802). The examination
of consciousness will soon be anticipated, even dictated, by a "director
of consciousness," which Kant's definition of *Aufklärung*, in the wake of
Martin Luther and Ignatius Loyola, will condemn as the producer of immaturity as he affirms that reading and writing form the historical process
by which maturity is constructed as rational consciousness, as critique.

41. Psychopower, grammatization, and Christendom

Anachorēsis, askēsis, melētē, all underscored by the practice of *hypomnēsia*, mnemotechnics in general, and *gumnasia* itself, defined as the struggle against temptation in the Stoic sense with the advent of Christianity,
all these techniques of the self are reinscribed within the framework of a
religious institutionalization of psychotechnical practices (DE4, 803) in
which *askēsis* is redefined as penitence, and "what was private for Stoics
becomes public for Christians" (804). Since Cassien,[26] Christianity has
made use of verbalization techniques that, after the eighteenth century
(and then with the human sciences and psychoanalysis), are no longer
"the instrument of renunciation of the subject . . . but . . . the positive
instrument for constituting a new subject" (798). In this ecclesiastical
Western history of the techniques of the self, an "inherited conglomer-
ate" through which Loyola will write his *Spiritual Exercises*,[27] Foucault
remains silent regarding what has taken place through Erasmus, Luther,
and Loyola, who are nonetheless at the very origin of the establishments
(or at least the prescriptions of the lessons) that will interest Foucault in

Discipline and Punish. Nonetheless, he says nothing of printing, without which Protestantism, the precondition of the Counter-Reformation, would never have been possible. Port-Royal's logic and grammar, even in 1966 (i.e., for Foucault),[28] were at the heart of the analyses of the classic *epistēmē* in *The Order of Things*. In the classical age, "commentary makes a place in critique opposed to commentary as analysis of a visible form, relative to the discovery of hidden content" (OT, 94). This eventuality rests on an analysis of language itself, and aims at "constituting the treasure of a perfectly analytical language. It is also manifest in grammatical order as a representative analysis of syntax, of word order, of sentence construction. . . . The critique also takes place in the examination of rhetorical forms" (94).

This new experience of language addresses representation, where "language can never represent thought in its totality; it must address it bit by bit, in linear order" (96). This is how General Grammar comes to condition the formation of classical thought: "General Grammar, the study of verbal order within its rapport *with the simultaneity it is charged with representing*. As for the object itself, it has neither thought nor language but *discourse* understood as a group of verbal signs" (Foucault's emphasis). General Grammar also forms the classic question of universality: "Grammar, as reflection on language in general, manifests language's connection with universality. . . . Universal language does not re-establish the order of bygone days; it invents signs" (91–92). But despite everything Foucault says about the place of writing, and reflection on it, through the theory of derivation in *The Order of Things* (110ff.), the formation of these "discursive regularities" was not, in Foucault's view, related to the constantly intensifying grammatization Sylvain Auroux claims takes place, after the end of the Roman Empire, an intensification that underlies and conditions "the development of European linguistic knowledge,"[29] and that in the end leads to the industrial printing of newspapers, then to what Auroux calls a *third* technological revolution of grammatization: informatics and the development of "language industries." Auroux brilliantly demonstrates the development of linguistic *knowledge* as linguistic *technologies* through which linguistic *capacity* forms. Without such technologies, and most notably their mobility, initiating orthographic normalization and syntax, but also translation and semantics, the questions of linear discourse, grammar in general, and universal language have never been able to form, and certainly not to result in mandatory public instruction. And Auroux further shows that these are essentially techniques of power rather than of knowledge.[30]

Printing as grammatization completes a process that began at the end of the Roman Empire, as we have seen; in 1982 Foucault himself remarks on the importance of writing in the administrative structures of imperial antiquity. According to Auroux,

> from late antiquity (the fifth century CE) to the beginning of the 19th century, . . . we can see a unique process developing: the *massive grammatization of world languages* emerging from a single initial linguistic (Greco-Latin) tradition. This grammatization constitutes, following only the advent of writing itself in pre-history and deep antiquity, the second techno-linguistic revolution. Even if the activity of grammatization is in fact virtually infinite, . . . it could be considered to be practically complete today. (RTG, 71)

The activity of grammatization, as an operation, is mentally and technologically indissociable from the linguistic formulation of idioms.[31] Auroux shows that the arrival of the print shop is intrinsically linked to colonization, as the exporting of Christianity through the technology of the printed book. Martin Luther began his struggle against Vatican domination via the spiritual practices of Ignatius Loyola who, in the *Spiritual Exercises*,[32] founded the Company of Jesus *and* the scholarly institution created through its missions; then via Reformation, Counter-Reformation, and Enlightenment critiques of the minority imposing "spiritual advisers" on the population, the *space of critical and scholarly writing* for a literate world took form.

But this was accompanied by a grammatological theory and practice that depend on what Auroux calls "extended Latin grammar," the historical basis for what Foucault analyzes in 1966 as General Grammar, the classical thought of representation and its underlying orders of *mathesis* and taxonomy (OT, 91). The development of extended Latin grammar, quite similar to what Derrida calls "globalatinization,"[33] is linked to a transformation of the scholarly environment:

> Greek or Roman children who attended the school of the grammarian already knew their language; grammar study was only a stage in their accession to written culture. For 19th century Europeans, Latin was at best a second

language they were forced to learn. Latin grammar exists: it will become, primarily, a training technique for language. (RTG, 81)

It is on this basis, accruing over a long period of vernacular grammatization beginning in the fifth century CE, that extended Latin grammar generalizes, "globalizes," and undertakes the grammatization of all the idioms that the new technologies of *l'esprit* (here, *Le Saint-Esprit*, the Holy Spirit) have made possible through printing, constructing such linguistic tools as grammar books, manuals, and dictionaries (RTG, 109) by which the Bible becomes accessible to all colonized peoples—and along with it the system of care called Christianity, which simultaneously transforms (and institutionalizes) the techniques of the self as *epimēleia*.

This is all only possible because of the "basal Latin" of our linguistic culture of letters; but it is also what creates the possibility of the General Grammar at the heart of the theory of the classical *epistēmē* Foucault describes in *The Order of Things*:

> Basal Latin is a factor of theoretical unification without equal in the history of the language sciences. It alone explains the conceptual homogeneity of all disciplines, such that one might consider it their metalanguage. (RTG, 84)
>
> Without the Latin grammatical tradition (essentially that of Donat, Saint Jerome's teacher and the translator of the Bible into Latin, and Priscien, who is much more complex), there quite simply would not have been what today we call linguistics. (85)

General Grammar, which though it is not yet linguistics is certainly a step toward it, is constituted by three fundamentally historical elements: "The recasting of Latin Grammar, printing, and the Age of Discovery."

> Grammatization and printing are part of the same techno-linguistic revolution. . . . Medieval manuscript production provides for . . . in each copy, great variability, most notably orthographically. With printing, not only the multiplication of an unavoidable sameness, but the normalization of vernaculars becomes standard business. Spelling, punctuation, and the regularization of morphology become the concern of typographic printers. The wide diffusion of the printed book, then, imposes the construction of an unlimited space in which each idiom, freed from geographic variations, has become an isotope. (95, 97)

"Normalization," which since Georges Canguilhem has evoked a great deal of thought and which is especially important in Foucault's work, is a fundamental result of grammatization. And literacy clearly must lead to considerable consequences in all technolinguistic disciplines, and thus on the formation of linguistic, literary, and logical attention, as the capacity to discern the various parts of a discourse within the flux of idiomatically[34]—that is, singularly—symbolized consciousness, and as mature consciousness.

Formatting and controlling these discursive disciplines become the object of a virtual concurrence among a wide variety of spiritual powers, within which General Grammar develops. The limitless space formed by grammatization, in which each idiom tends to become an isotope, is a space of both critique and combat.[35] The Enlightenment theme is a singularly dynamic and decisive version of this combat: the formation of critical, mature consciousness requires the logical attention produced by the grammatization of discourse. Yet there is no trace of this combat in Foucault's theory of the technologies of power that are *also* technologies of knowledge: for Foucault the question is how technology, always the base of any "battle for intelligence," *contradictorily* ties knowledge to power, and reciprocally.

For anyone focusing on the history of printing, and before that on *scriptoria* (or even the library at Alexandria[36]), the sections of the *Archaeology of Knowledge* devoted to the book are disappointing: as an indispensable retentional device, the book is not clearly thought through, not in its material nor in its intellectual *technicity of production*, such that it is specifically and narrowly linked to the construction of what Auroux calls "linguistic tools" (AK, 33–34). This might, retrospectively, surprise the reader who knows the kind of attention Foucault pays to the importance of literacy associated with the techniques of the self. Moreover, and this is still more striking, the *Archaeology*'s insistence on documentary materiality (AK, 14–15) should have led directly to the thought that this *material history of the book* must be the object of very specific attention.

But there is nothing more in the *Archaeology* on the place of the "republic of letters" in the advent of the bourgeoisie, an advent that nonetheless parallels the development of a kind of writing that for a very long time has no longer been that of the Hellenistic and Roman empires but that leads to industrial society. Yet this will be a new stage of grammatization that is itself far beyond the discursive formations of the Enlightenment, and without which James Watt would never have encountered Matthew Boulton.[37] Grammatization becomes a connector, unique in human history, between *logos* and its other—but of which the *Archaeology* says nothing, despite the fact that the issue of the link between discursive and non-discursive is its principal object.

§ 9   Disciplines and Pharmacologies of Knowledge

42. Disciplines and knowledges

Foucault's inattention to what Auroux describes as a major episode in the history of grammatization—the advent of linguistic technologies through printing and its effects on the very concept of language as well as on its usage—is especially striking when, three years after *The Order of Things*, Foucault asks in *The Archaeology of Knowledge* how and why it is possible to say that "analysis of judgment by the Port-Royal grammarians belongs to the same domain as the discovery of vowel gradations in the Indo-European languages" (AK, 31). Studying the substructure of such domains—insofar as they are reducible, he says, to disciplines—leads him to the development of his concept of archaeology, through which he is able to go beyond that of the *epistēmē*. Foucault's archaeology investigates the conditions contributing to the diachronicity of a kind of knowledge that *cannot* be reduced to disciplines,[1] in which the documents' and the archive's very materiality are fundamental elements.[2]

Moreover, Foucault makes no reference to the materialities grammatization implements nor to the processes it supports since they are ostensibly essential to the formation of "discursive regularities" as the objects of archaeology, and of which General Grammar is a specific case of particular concern to grammatization since it must now be connected to the constitutive materiality of discourses, as Foucault rightly insists.

Nothing can be formed discursively, *Archaeology* effectively claims, that does not go through a materialization, no matter how ephemeral or abstract it may seem to be as discourse:

Could one speak of a statement if a voice had not articulated it, if a surface did not bear its signs, if it had not become embodied in a sense-perceptible element, and if it had not left some trace—if only for an instant—in someone's memory or in some space? . . . The statement is always given through some material medium. . . . [I]ts materiality is not given to it, in addition, once all its determinations have been fixed: it is partly made up of this materiality. (100)

Foucault's example of this constitutive discourse is grammar, and "the relations of materiality and language—the role of writing and the alphabet. . . . Materiality . . . is constitutive of the statement itself: a statement must have substance, a support, a place, and a date" (101). A statement presupposes a regime of materiality in which it is formed and inscribed and that defines "all these various forms, repetitions, and transcriptions" more than its spatio-temporal individuality (101). But grammatization is the material spatialization of discourse's temporality; that is, its material formulation,[3] most clearly in the form of grammar books and dictionaries, the linguistic tools of which Diderot's *Encyclopédie* is an unparalleled exemplar as an *instrument* of knowledge—suddenly consisting of what Barthes likes to call "planks"—and as tertiary retention.

As for possibilities of "reinscription and transformation," these are what in the vocabulary of psychosocial individuation I would call the process of transindividuation that in fact establishes, and as metastable mechanisms,[4] the possibilities for reinscription and transformation as rules for rewriting, for translation (which is linguistically conditioned by grammatization), for transmission, and so on. As the grounding of tertiary retentions, transindividuation requires material support.

Archaeology is more interested in the discursive formations produced through these processes than in "disciplines," in the usual sense of the term, and less as groupings of signs than as "practices systematically forming the objects about which these discourses speak" (38), since there are materialities (the technical developments of the materiality of discourse) that must be considered essential discourses as practices.

However, these materialities are the products of a *materialization*: they do not fall from the sky. And this materali*zation* is precisely, within the domain of general discourse, the effective reification of grammati*zation*. In the emergence of knowledge(s), the grammatization process is this materiality's genesis, the very materialization of discourse about which Foucault says not a word, and its principal institutional translation.

Discursive materiality is exactly, for Foucault, what is concretized into material institutions: the institutional dimension of materiality is a central theme of *Archaeology*, which posits that the materiality of discursive formations rests on "a complex regime of material institutions" (AK, 104). No doubt, learning to read and write is a unique "moment" within the material institution. Yet, just as grammatization is absent from this materiality, and *because* it is absent from it, literacy (literally a *monumental* moment of grammatization,[5] as well as of documentation[6]) never becomes the object of a larger thematization by Foucault; as a result it will be reduced six years later, in *Discipline and Punish*, to a disciplinary organization, in the sense of a discipline that will still not accede to disciplines as they might be taught in the school as a system of care ("the school" as formulator of rational, intergenerational relations); or, rather, that reduces these disciplines to the quite different "ability to write," leading to the disindividuating individualization of students of all ages, in public schools or not.

But in the case of the school, this materialization is a function of mature material and an institutional mechanism specifically activating the school's disciplines in three senses that constitute knowledge acquisition:

1. as construction of a system of care regulating the connections of the individual to self and others, intergenerationally, containing the techniques of the self through which the objects of a *skholē* or *otium* are formed;

2. as transindividuation of a transmissible knowledge to "ordinary scholars," citizens with rights (Kant's and Condorcet's subjects) who attain such knowledge in the form of a discipline formalizing consciousnesses, and that can be taught as such;

3. as apparatus of surveillance, control, and individualization, and thus to disindividuation.

For Foucault, to think through and describe the genesis of discursive practices, a genesis that implements materialities coming from materialization, is to think through and describe their relationships with nondiscursive practices, which are themselves based on materialities. But since the nineteenth century, *all* knowledge, including nondiscursive practices, has increasingly been subjected to a generalized grammatization that has gone beyond the *logos* (i.e., discourse[7]). Biopower results directly from this development, and it is also why grammatization as a process of materialization increasingly includes *and overdetermines* all other social processes, thus contributing to the individuation of disciplines that must be understood here in the widest sense, far beyond that of the teaching establishment, particularly in the factory and the other workplaces of the Industrial Age, wherever they are. Grammatization affects every form of knowledge: those resulting in discursive practices but also those resulting from nondiscursive practices—for example, "know-how" and "lifestyle" as social disciplines, manners, dress, laws and policing (in all their various forms), civility, techniques of the self, the governing of others, and so on. The grammatization process has been radically transformed since the end of the eighteenth century through analysis, reproduction, and transformation of formalized machinic processes, as well as by devices recording and manipulating the information stream. This has been before all else a matter of production, but then also of all the human streams that contribute to human being (in an age not of production but of consumption); the apparatuses of grammatization—analog and numeric—have established psychotechnologies as image and sound notation, and through them, a grammatized stream of consciousness.

The archive, Foucault's term for tertiary retentions, epiphylogenesis, hypomnesia, psychotechnics, and psychotechnologies *as* techniques of the self and of care in general, has as its consequence the fact that the individuation process is metastabilized by a *trans*individuation process in which opposing and imposing pharmacological elements in which knowledge formation is a battlefield, as a process of grammatized transindividuation—forming knowledge's critical space and time. And because it does not take this pharmacology into consideration, I believe that Foucault's archaeological theory cannot apprehend knowledge and its diachronization in all of its dimensions—dimensions that are always and indissociably not simply archaeological but architectonic. In the final analysis, this pharmacology always invokes an arbitrator in the form of an architectonic that locally (and as *domain*) supports (as dogma, or as a problematic axiomatic *corpus*) a *referential* individuation process.

This referential individuation constructs a field of transindividuation supported, at the same time, by the Foucauldian archive. An archaeological field understood in this sense then generates the establishment of

> the measures according to which Buffon and Linnaeus . . . were talking about the same thing . . . in laying out "the same conceptual field," facing each other on "the same field of battle"; thus it became apparent, on the other

hand, why it cannot be said that Darwin was talking about the same thing as Diderot. (AK, 126)

Foucault is interested in just this archaeology, one that establishes referential individuation as a domain (for a historically and geographically situated group), but all of whose possibilities have been undermined by grammatization; this is why Foucault is not interested in discipline as transmissible, teachable knowledge in the form of constructed understanding, but rather in the field on or in which it could appear. Yet such a field is structured by disciplines in an even larger sense, from taking care (of self and others) at the most elementary levels, to the least careful control systems;[8] all mental activity is more or less a subset of such disciplines as the simultaneous fabrication of psychic and collective individuation and that, *as this "simultaneous,"* produces fields of transindividuation.

Buffon and Linnaeus transindividuate a field of significations (discursive formations) by co-individuating them within the same milieu in which the same discursive and nondiscursive practices forming the system are metastabilized far beyond this field itself; this co-individuation (unity) is at once itself a system of care *and* the horizon of an *epimēleia* at whose core what Foucault calls *singular events*, that is, "spoken things," can be formed and produced. But these "spoken things" are the results of "a mixed system of discursivity, possibilities, and . . . enunciative impossibilities. The archive is first of all the law of what can be said, the system that regulates the appearance of statements as singular events" (130–31). Foucault claims that "discipline" is merely an impoverished dimension of this process.

But he makes this claim only because he understands the process in a very impoverished way himself, particularly with regard to his comments on the *melētē* and the *epimēleia*, on the one hand, and on disciplinary societies, on the other.

43. Pharmacology of the archive

The individuation of knowledge in the widest sense, as it affects all forms of knowledge, consists of its general diachronization *as* metastabilization and transindividuation, as achieved through what *Archaeology* calls "relations." But to the degree that it conditions *all* discursive regimes as their *pre*condition (and therefore that of their relations, such as the relations between discursive and nondiscursive, especially from the moment when nondiscursive realities are grammatized by analogic and numeric technologies), the grammatization process *is* the process of individuation in the West, as well as the process of psychic individuation that in its collective, technical,[9] and scientific forms also transforms the stream of consciousness to the point of possibly destroying it (as attention) and threatening the psychic apparatus itself.[10]

Archaeology says nothing of any of this, since Foucault declares that these processes are the life of a "documentary materiality" in which history "is a particular way for society to give itself status and to develop a documentary mass from which it cannot be separated" (AK, 10). This materiality has now become numeric, virtual, and automatically downloadable—which is not to say immaterial (as one might naïvely think), and here Foucault is quite precise. This new materiality, of which the handwritten (then printed) book[11] is the chief epistemic manifestation as a fabric of tertiary retentions, the hypomnesia produced by grammatization—and as noetic technology, but also, and primarily, *psycho*technical (we will return to this); this virtual materiality produces *objects* that are not *things*. Archaeology's program, contrary to the phenomenology of the "ante-predicative," in effect wants

> indeed, to do without "things," to "de-presence" them, . . . to substitute for the enigmatic treasure of "things" prior to speech, the regular formation of objects that are only to be designated as defining objects without any fundamental reference to things, but connecting them to the aggregate of rules permitting their formation as the objects of a discourse. (65)

But these rules of discourse, given their objects, are part of a regulated process of connections between psychic, collective, and material retentions—which only the later Husserl's post-phenomenology allows us to think, as Derrida clearly understands in reversing his initial analysis of *Origin of Geometry*.[12]

Central here is the *rematerialization* of what *The Order of Things* calls "the *epistēmē*" conceived across numerous disciplines (botany, grammar, biology, economy, etc.):

> [T]he domain of these articulated statements . . . no longer has the allure of a monotonous and indefinitely extended plain I gave it at first, when I spoke of "the surface of discourse." . . . One is now dealing with something more

complex. . . . Instead of seeing, superimposed on the great, mythic book of History, words that translate into visible characters thoughts previously constituted elsewhere, one has in the heavy volume of discursive practices systems that inscribe statements as events . . . and things. All of these systems of statements (events in one sense, things in another) I propose to call *the archive*. (AK, 187)

Thus, the question of the archive supplants that of the *epistēmē*. What Foucault calls the archive is in general terms a material tool for retentions through which discourse can be fabricated—as event as well as thing, which I have analyzed here as a stream of primary and secondary retentions and protentions forming *attention projected as an object*, through tertiary retentions.

In this sense,

> despite its immediate flight, the archive is not what safeguards the statement's event-ness and conserves it in its guise as an escapee, for future memoirs; this is what, at the very root of the statement-event, and in the bodily form it gives itself, defines from the outset the system of its enunciability. (128)

The archive, for Foucault, is "a generalized system for the formation and transformation of statements" (129)—for their transformation. And the archive is made possible by the grammatization process as the engramming of statements and of discursive as well as nondiscursive material (and myriad other kinds of) flux,[13] and by the deployment of a technics that becomes technologies, which in turn produce the apparatus for all of the processes of delegation through which it becomes possible to short-circuit psychic mechanisms and institutions—to the advantage of programming and service industries: the archive is the fruit of grammatization's becoming machinic. But once again Foucault says nothing of this technologization, despite the central place he gives to technologies of power,[14] and because he thinks the machine within the framework of a very conventional Marxist model.

Grammatization increasingly undermines the entire archive, all the more in that the very concept of the archive has now been extended to many kinds of intracategorical distinctions. But "history," including industrial history—and a fortiori hyperindustrial history—is the history *of grammatization*. Discourse is only "analytic" to the extent that grammatization is, but even this is increasingly concerned only with the producer's and the work's "scientific" work (i.e., its discipline), by operational cognitive sequences formalized within the service industries, such as genome sequencing, the possible connections between IPv6,[15] and the nanometric indexing of matter,[16] and so on. Grammatization is, in other words, the necessary condition for the constitution of both the biopower and the psychopower of hypermatter.[17]

Grammatization is the origin of Western rationality and its archaeology as the process for forming *hypomnēmata*—the successive ages of psychotechnical *pharmaka*. But that means that it simultaneously confronts the very *construction* of rationality's critical space (since in this context reason is the highest form of care) *and* what *poisons* this critical space. The archaeological process is fundamentally pharmacological, which has resulted in the current crisis in the face of which Prime Minister Fillon launched "the battle for intelligence" in 2007 and President Sarkozy published his "Letter to Educators," which was addressed (in the Kantian sense) to *all* of us. And yet literacy, as the basis of *deep attention*, and the consequences of numeric grammatization, the basis of *hyperattention*,[18] should not be ignored in any consideration of the way in which the archive, over time, transmits the social bit by bit, transforming it technologically and becoming its key stimulus for evolution and industrial revolution.

And again, Foucault is silent. The entirety of the Foucauldian enterprise undergoes a kind of stutter regarding the connections between three types of discipline: as *techniques of the self* and *the writing of the self*, as *melētē*, and as *epimēleia* (*hypomnēmata* being its documentary and material base). These become the objects of thought only late on for Foucault, when it finally appears that connectivity (as *epimēleia*) is the origin of discipline itself, as the body of constituted and transmissible knowledges based on a *gnôthi seauton* that is itself based on (the discipline of) geometry—which is always in danger of being degraded into a control discipline of both individual and collective behavior, aiming at establishing a society of control rather than a mature form of attention as the basis of another kind of (democratic) society.

The problem is that the archive's *field* is a disciplinary one structuring pharmacological tensions that could become a disciplinary field. But in a Foucauldian archaeology giving thickness and depth to the *epistēmē*'s two-dimensionality, no such conflict exists: Foucault's archaeology is not dynamic; its archive remains inert, stationary, without *process*.

44. The archaeology of conflicts

In the *Archaeology of Knowledge*, knowledge is much more than a discipline or a group of disciplines; it is "the field of coordination and subordination of all statements in which concepts appear and are defined,
applied, and transformed" (AK, 207). But the real question has to do
with this transformation. My thesis is that it is a psychic, collective, technical, and scientific process of individuation forming a system of care
through the materialization of various streams or flows, leading directly
to today's surrender to machines and to a short-circuiting of psychosocial
transindividuation—of the generations as well as the social classes and
territory: this grammatization has produced, and even more important,
transformed into, a hyperpharmacological archive. The *pharmakon*, in
the same motion, relinks and delinks, just as the process of psychic and
collective individuation is thoroughly inculcated with technical tendencies and theoretical problems (which are all critical statements formed by
mature consciousnesses) whose job it is to upset the "stable" *pharmakon*.
A conjunction such as this can exist only as a group, despite its many
internal tensions, through a common *epiméleia*.

I make these points emphatically not just to launch a polemic within
Foucault studies but because the concept of biopower, as presented at the
beginning of the twenty-first century in the face of psychotechnologies
and the liquidation of systems of (cultural) care, in addition to psychosocial attention (i.e., the psychic and social apparatuses that make up the
material institutions), will no longer allow us to avoid these questions or
to leave them hidden in the present-day's archaeological opacity, rushing
along to celebrate its great thinkers' postmortem. Grammatization runs
across and disrupts *all* the ages preceding it, during which it grew into a
process integrating (now far beyond any particular actions) the recognition of genes and neurotransmitters, synaptic circuit analysis and their
cerebral activation, and the formalization of individual behavior, in an
attempt to particularize them via the technologies of *social engineering* and
the cognition of attention.

On the basis of an ancient archaeology, much more ancient than what
Foucault refers to as the first codes of individuality,[19] the current grammatization process forms in all its layers (psychological, technical, technological, and social). This is the archive's real technologization in the
Foucauldian sense—a sense Foucault does not consider—and ignorance

of this process, in its historic and geographic specificity, poses a major problem for the methodology of *The Archaeology of Knowledge*, which is already within the horizon of Dominique Lecourt's 1970 critique. Having emphasized that for Foucault "the apparent need to think the history of discursive events as being structured by material connections is incarnated in institutions" (118), institutions forming the base on which scientific knowledge is built, Lecourt focuses on the tacit nature of the discursive/ nondiscursive distinction and asks about the *formation* of practical and theoretical ideologies:[20] "[P]ractical ideologies give their *forms* and their *limits* to theoretical ideologies. . . . But through what specific processes do practical ideologies intervene in the construction and functioning of theoretical ideologies?" (CET, 130). Such processes, says Lecourt, are built on class contradictions (133), which might seem today to be a dated critique, but he is right: if the question is no longer asked simply in terms of class or work/capital opposition, it still has to do with the place given to opposing tendencies within a field transductively characterized by poles, but one that *com*poses,[21] and in which capital (which is only the opposite of work by being composed with it) and *work* form a dyad manifesting this conflictual *dynamic*.

On the other hand, the dynamic polarity within the individuation process is today, perhaps, less one in which work and capital (a polarity that has both not disappeared and grown more brutal than ever) stand in opposition to each other, than to one where within a complex grouping of polarities dominated by marketing and consumption,[22] joining with an increasingly speculative idea of finance that no longer invests, *long-term attention* and *inattention exhausted short term* oppose each other—and *com*pose: compose the care, on one side, and on the other, the care-lessness that arises when short-term speculation short-circuits all transindividuation—which is too long term, too slow for speculative markets, compromising all long-term projection and all future intelligence. From this new polarity emerges another: *curious* (which takes care) and *incurious* (which pays no attention; does not care).

Though it is generally true of Foucauldian thought that technologies of power and knowledge, that is, of *epimēleia* in its widest sense, range from the techniques of the self to government (passing through disciplinary sciences). Lecourt, on the other hand, shows how archaeological analysis simply erases the entire problem of the conflicts, contradictions, and struggles pervading the archaeological field, constituting its principal dynamic. This dynamic, which is obviously far too complex to describe here but which includes everything from the *internal* tensions in all psychic systems to the *axiomatic* limits of knowledge in general, including class and generational conflicts, is stimulated above all else by the pressures of technical tendencies and by the contradictory effects they provoke in producing the *pharmaka* that are hidden away to compensate for the unexpected effects caused by other *pharmaka.*

Yet this pressure produced by technical tendencies is itself what since the Neolithic Age (and in what becomes "civilization" understood as urban life regulated by secure management of foodstocks—*subsistence*—but also separating out *surplus* production that could lead to new forms of *existence*) has brought about the formation of hypomnesic, protohistorical, or historical techniques that deployed the grammatization process from the start, essentially as *comput* and discursive order,[23] separate from subsistence production, then today as the total reconfiguration of subsistence consumption—at the risk of destroying existence itself. Though mitigated somewhat, in that it has been managed according to predeterminations controlled by a therapeutic that can never be reduced to a simple biopower, in these circumstances the *pharmakon* becomes essentially poison, while the most important question remains that of psychopower (and the battle for intelligence).

45. Literal individuation[24]

In *L'Écriture de soi* (DE4, 415ff.), Foucault intrinsically associates *hypomnēmata*, as tertiary retentions and archives, with the "exercise of thought" (416) in the sort of writing in which grammatization begins to emerge as a discipline, and primarily a solitary discipline—but also as the source of a new dialectic, a new kind of transindividuation process, at once anamnesic and hypomnesic as a result of the grammatization of life during the empire, as Foucault pointed out in his course at the University of Vermont.[25] Commenting on Seneca's *Letters to Lucilius*, Foucault describes the culture of the written self as "material memory of things read, understood, or thought" (418), in which techniques of the self begin in the hypomnesic interiorization of discourses, whether they have been bequeathed and inherited or conceived and produced, the condition being that they are in the form of tertiary retentions—which also constitutes, under the direction of a teacher, the principle of all education.

Hypomnēmata are "a material and a framework for frequently-used exercises: for reading, re-reading, meditating, conversing with oneself and with others" (419).

> These archives and their practices as exercises (as disciplines) form a *logos bioethikos*, and it is important that they are not simply stored as though they were a trunkful of memories, but profoundly implanted in the soul, "filed in it," says Seneca, and that they thus become a part of ourselves: in short, that the soul made them not only one's own, but oneself. (419)

The passage from "one's own" to "oneself" means that what was *mine* becomes *me*, what Foucault calls subjectivation, which is to become subject to the object, its interiorization.[26] But what is most important is that this subjectivation, here strictly psychic, also presents itself as the individuation of a *we*, not just an *I*: through the *I*, as what *one* could understand and read, which was not *mine* and was thus preindividual, then being individuated and becoming transindividual, that is, *we*. In this process, the *ego* [*moi*] becomes itself a *self* that is always already supraegoic, "spiritual."[27]

The documents Foucault addresses in 1969 in the *Archaeology of Knowledge* appear in 1983, in *L'Écriture de soi*, as what, having passed through "the apparatus of writing" in *Discipline and Punish*, create the preindividual milieu of psychic individuation that reconnects it with collective individuation. The goal of *hypomnēmata* is thus to

> fabricate out of the recollection of a fragmentary *logos* transmitted through teaching, listening, or reading a means for establishing a rapport with the self as adequate and complete as possible. . . . How is it possible to be brought into one's own presence with the aid of discourse that is both ageless and coming from anywhere? . . . Seneca insists: self-practice means reading, since we could not know how to draw it all from our own experience. (420)

Individuation presupposes the preindividual, just as it requires what I have previously called an "associated techno-symbolic milieu," in which "reading and writing cannot be separated" (420). The individuation of the preindividual is a function of the "disparate" (422) that must be unified, which Seneca compares to the gathering of nectar by bees, to digestion, and to the arithmetic operation of addition (which I have analyzed here as an operation of retention): "reading's role is to construct, using everything that reading has constructed, a body" (422). This tendency toward unification is individuation. But how does it move toward (or not) transindividuation? First, as intergenerational relations: "it is one's own soul that must be fabricated in one's writing; but just as a man's face shows his natural resemblance to his ancestors, so it is good to be able to perceive in what he writes his filiation with the thoughts that have been engraved in his soul" (422–23). The archive here sits atop an intergenerational, spiritual genealogy of *hypomnēmata* forming circuits of epistolary transindividuation: "writing that helps the recipient arms the writer—and eventually the others who read it" (423). Foucault describes the way in which, according to Seneca writing to Lucilius, writing forms an associated medium producing a psychic and collective individuation that is already a grammatization of the psyche, as a discipline (though in the service of its individuation). Since it is clear in this correspondence that the practice of *hypomnēmata* is "something more than an apprenticeship of the self by writing . . . it is also a particular way of manifesting oneself to oneself and others" (424), this means that "others" are *already* contained within self-fabrication, as Derrida underlines in his emphasis on the essentially epistolary structure of geometry.[28] Yet as reciprocity, and to some degree as *literal dialogism*, correspondence is a reciprocity of the gaze and of examination, and a sociating through an associated double medium in which "the letter that . . . works toward the subjectivation of true discourse [the result of intergenerational transmission], toward its assimilation and elaboration as a 'good' that also and at the same time constitutes an objectification of the soul" (426), its *tertiarization*, which literally says that interiorization *is* exteriorization, occurring only on condition of being itself exteriorized, and only subjectivized in that it is an objectification of the subject in what Simondon calls a transductive relationship: what is appropriated must also be expropriated, or expropriated by itself [*s'ex-approprier*[29]], must be projected beyond itself, transindividuated, in order to form a circuit that is also a circle, or rather a whorl; Seneca expresses this as "we must regulate our life as if the entire world were looking at it" (426). This is what will be transformed, Foucault tells us, in Christianity's becoming a public institution, renouncing the self through confession and guilt.

§ 10 *Oikonomia* in the Object of All Attentions

46. The attentive life of the care-ful being

Léon Robin asserts that Plato created the Academy in order to form philosophers capable of administering the *polis*. And he adds that in ancient Greece it was an obvious goal for any philosopher to become a legislator in the pre-Socratic tradition:

> For a long time, in the eyes of the Greeks, one of the highest aspirations of the philosopher was to be a legislator or a government head. Heraclitus had this ambition, without success, at Ephesus; . . . Parmenides was an Eliesian legislator. How could such an important task be abandoned to the arbitrary individual without well-defined principles and universal values, without proper methodology to offer guidance on the road to truth? (10)

Plato's Academy is a *school of administration*, if it is true that to administer the city means precisely to implement *epimēleia*, care, and this is just how Plato's *Alcibiades* must be interpreted. As Robin insists, it is necessary to form legislatures, but in such a way that they take care of the city, and to correctly interpret the precept *epimēlesthai sautou*, as Socrates says to Alcibiades, by this precept, which is also absolutely traditional: *gnôthi sauton, know yourself.*

In this context legislation, knowledge, and administration are hardly separable. Yet Foucault, referring to the historic corpus of "modernity" (which will lead to the bourgeois conquest of power), asserts that in order to understand this development properly, it is necessary to renounce all thoughts of power—of administration, and thus of *epimēleia*—that are associated with the law and right: power must be thought of as techniques and technologies of power. This means three things:

1. *Care* must be rethought, says Foucault, invoking Marx, not simply from the point of view of *right* but from technologies of power that began to form the basis for a theory of the State (and the *reason for* the State), in the sixteenth century when these theories were first sketched out, but which were first significantly implemented in the nineteenth century, by the bourgeoisie.

2. But this also addresses the question of *knowledge*, which Foucault poses in the *Archaeology of Knowledge* and *The Order of Things.* Yet as we have seen, Foucault addresses them without asking the question of teaching as an aspect of disciplinary society and a technique of domination—thus neutralizing the question of knowledge and overvaluing that of administration as a discipline, even though knowledge is not thinkable independently of its teaching.

3. Further, it is then necessary to interrogate knowledge's *organization*, since it is the necessary condition for the training of administrators/teachers as the formulators of attention. This is what philosophy has taught since Plato, but as Foucault finally says (quite late on, in the context of the techniques of the self, i.e., for individuals; he has nothing to say about teaching in schools), it is equally important to take account of the technologic nature of self-constitution, distinguishing the *self* from the *ego* not so much because of its reflexivity, as the ego looking at itself, as because *the self is indissociable from care*: from its inception it has a double dimension, psychic and collective/social, such that taking care of *oneself* is always already taking care of *the other and of others*.

Techniques of the self are ineluctably transformed into techniques of the other and others, techniques for governing the self and others. And for us, we pharmacological beings of the twenty-first century, this means that biopower, ineluctably becoming a psychopower, mandates the sublimation of psychopolitics—and of the psychotechnologies of psychopower that destroy the *I* and the *we* by confusing them with the impersonal, the *one* or *it*, very much including as generational confusion—confusing the *one* as noopolitical or, more precisely, as an *industrial politics of technologies of the mind* (or, as in Simondon, of the *spirit*) that are actually nothing more, momentarily, than psychotechnologies of the programming industries hegemonically controlled by a power that is no longer the State but care-less-ness itself, short-term hegemony and the destruction of investment (i.e., of motivation), where "the State," though more real than ever, is now just one aspect of the delinquency resulting from such confusion.

The techniques of the self and others create tertiary retentions as *spatializations of time that are both retentional* (archives) *and protentional* (images, icons, underpinnings of *phantasia* in general, and infinitely varied representations of objects of desire). These are the very tertiary spatializations that create the *attentional* (and intentional) *stabilization* of a present, for example, as geometric figures, but also as Seneca's letters to Lucilius or Lucilius's own letters. Tertiary retentions (such as Foucault's "archive") are the grounding condition for the creation of objects of knowledge; this is precisely the sense of the *coup de théâtre* in Husserl's *Origin of Geometry*, where hypomnesia transforms into anamnesia. And this spatialization is also the catalyst for *operations*, in which mental exercises and techniques of the self are sublime analogs, as the reference to Seneca indicates.

Today, an "economy of attention" impinges on a "cognition of attention," constructing a technology of attention that I suggest destroys attention, initiating an age of generalized organology. This is the environment for what Aristotle calls "the noetic sensitivity," the "attentive life" as distinct from the sensitivity of the oversensitive mind [*l'âme sensitive*]. In *De la misère symbolique*,[1] I try to demonstrate that this noetic life is engendered in the course of an incessant process of organic defunctionalizations and refunctionalizations in which the noeme, the process of mental formation (as the formation of νουσ) is originally a technesis, a becoming-pharmacological requiring a kind of care grounded in techniques of the self.

Plato finds that this anamnesis/hypomnesia opposition renders impossible any thought of noesis as the technesis from which Foucault's techniques of the self emerge. Nonetheless, Plato opposes anamnesis and hypomnesia in his struggle against sophistry because insofar as it employs "logographia" (grammatization of the *logos*), it creates a dissociation within all associated milieus, short-circuiting all transindividuation. But it is never enough simply to face Plato with the problem of the *trace* that is always already the *phonē*: we must make this deconstructive projection, as a pharmacology, the very basis of a therapeutic.

But we must depart from a deconstruction of Plato's pharmacy in order to address the problem of an ecology and economy of the mind in the age of psychotechnologies, a *general pharmacology* for the forming of a system of care that places limitations on the apparatuses of attentional control that have been and are being implemented by the service industries.[2] Giorgio Agamben has described this economy as the *oikonomia* of what he calls "apparatuses"[3]—borrowing the term from Foucault.

47. The *oikonomia* of apparatuses

Agamben develops a theory of apparatuses in direct reference to Foucault's concept with regard to the question of governmentality,[4] which Foucault lays out in the 1977 interview "The Confession of the Flesh," explaining that the apparatus is a formation that

> has as its major function at a given historical moment that of responding to an *urgent need* [and that] has a dominant strategic function. . . . It is a matter of a manipulation of relations of forces. . . . The apparatus is thus always inscribed in a play of power, but it is also always linked to certain coordinates of knowledge which issue from it but, to an equal degree, condition it.[5]

The apparatus is "a strategy of connected forces supporting many kinds of knowledge, and is supported by them" (CF, 196). As Agamben points out, what Foucault in the 1977 interview calls an apparatus is designated in the *Archaeology of Knowledge* as "positivity" (WA, 3). For Agamben, Foucault owes this term to Hegel and to Jean Hyppolite, Foucault's professor at the Lycée Henri-IV, then at the École Normale Supérieure. Hegel's "positivity," according to Agamben, is "the historical element . . . loaded with rules, rites, and institutions that are imposed on the individual by an external power" (5). This "element" is only "historical," however, in that it is "internalized in the systems of beliefs and feelings" (5); thus, what is at stake is "the relation between individuals as living beings and the historical element" (6). Even in the language Agamben is developing here, one would have to say that this "element" is the third organological level, and that as *the element of noetic life* it forms the symbolic milieu of individuation resulting from the transindividuation of both individuals *and* their milieu. Referring to Foucault's idea of the apparatus, and further emphasizing that Foucault's "*dispositif*" is a translation of Heidegger's *Gestell* (via the *oikonomia* of the theology of the Trinity),[6] Agamben suggests "a general and massive partitioning of existence into two large groups or classes: on the one hand, living beings (or substances), and on the other, apparatuses in which the living beings are incessantly captured" (13). It might be possible to think that this reference would lead to a discussion of an *oikonomia* of apparatuses. But this question is problematic for Agamben: in a certain sense, as we will see, he will come to think that *it is not asked at all*—that in fact it is not a question but a factual state *with no alternative*.

Before launching into any examination of this point, I must emphasize that all of these terms can be translated into a general organology that here, within a history as much of humanity as of apparatuses, amount to what Deleuze could have called "apparatuses of capture," or "of control," or "of modulation"; Agamben calls the *dispositif* "anything that has in some way the capacity to capture, orient, determine, intercept, model, control, or secure the gestures, behaviors, opinions, or discourses of living beings" (14). This is Agamben's name for all apparatuses, though he speaks about contemporary apparatuses as being typical of an age that is nothing other than an impasse.

But it is also a matter of the apparatuses of grammatization and of notation, a process that plays a very specific role in the apparatus's future of the apparatus, especially with regard to the general framework of institutions: the apparatuses Agamben speaks of are not just buildings and institutions, nor institutional practices, "not only, therefore, prisons, madhouses, the panopticon, schools, the confessional, factories, disciplines, juridical measures, and so forth (whose connection with power is in a certain sense evident)" (14). And it is not just a question of these terms, which are so often identified with place, concentrations, and constructions, with the fundamental architectural and control gestures of living beings through their submission to spatially formed, anchored, and localized logics. But this is also a matter of what finally rises up from a set of *pharmaka*, of which language itself is a part. Not only spaces and institutions, "but also the pen, writing, literature, philosophy, agriculture, cigarettes, navigation [Web browsing[7]], computers, cellular phones, and—why not—language itself" (14). *All of this* is pharmacological—and this is why the list includes the *cigarette*, which adds the most volatile energy to this series of *pharmaka*: their *poisonous* dimension, leading directly, for example, to sickness through dependence and addiction, which is significantly more than a simple alienation and gives the term "capture" its urgency.

"And—why not—language itself." Why not, in fact? but this means that language is inherently pharmacological, which is also to say that it is "always already writing," as Derrida so often writes. Why "agriculture"

here, however, and why "Web browsing"? Is this latter an echo of what
Heidegger means regarding the marine in his comments on the chorus
in the *Antigone*?[8] We will return to this question in the second volume of
Taking Care, in which agriculture and navigation are central. Navigation
could in fact be expanded and clarified here, it seems to me, as *transport*
(by water, land, or air—at the very least in that it also includes "orientation" and "circulation" ["browsing"?] in virtual numeric space), a concept
of transport that raises many questions of pharmacology, pollution, addiction, and so on.

Whatever the rationale behind Agamben's list, which is certainly not
a simple rhapsody, between prisons, the panopticon, and factories as the
first series of apparatuses, and the pen, writing, the cigarette, cell phones
[*téléphones portables*], and means of transportation as the second series—
there is a sense of a *double materiality* about power apparatuses that are
also knowledge apparatuses: structures for erecting buildings inhabited by
human bodies and that already frame them, and those of archives housed
there as well. Yet this archival materiality is inseparable, particularly in
psychotechnical times, from devices and operations by which it can be
extended, via external apparatuses, beyond buildings and institutions,
and formed into networks, either by carriers or by waves and "binary
streams,"[9] forming into a meta-apparatus—of precisely the kind Heidegger calls *Gestell.* Archives that can circulate on such networks are the
products of grammatization; their grouping together allows for control
over the body in the space to which they have been consigned, and over
the mind in the time thus captured.

Minds, after all, *are time;* that is, individuation.

48. Capitalism as the empoisoning of apparatuses

What Agamben calls "the subject"—and this is undoubtedly quite
close to what I am here calling "individuation"—forms in the tensions
between living beings and the apparatuses that "capture" them: "I call
a subject that which results from the relation and, so to speak, from the
hand-to-hand combat between living beings and apparatuses" (WA, 14).
This is indeed a matter of a psychic individuation process insofar as it is
always already in the process of collective individuation, itself inscribed in
a process of technical (since all archives are technical) or technoscientific
individuation.

Agamben inquires into the very *nature of capitalism* as the linking of such apparatuses to living beings, forming a "massive accumulation and proliferation of apparatuses" (15) tending toward permanent control of the attention (or inattention) of beings who are subjectivized (and therefore disindividuated) by this very (in)attention: "today there is not even a single instant in which the life of individuals is not modeled, contaminated, or controlled by some apparatus" (WA, 15). But why is this the case if not because, on the one hand, the *tendency toward a reduction in profits* mandates, at the same time, a condition of ever-more restrained innovation and total control of the libidinal energy aimed at organizing consumption, and because, on the other hand, this results in a *tendency toward a reduction of libidinal energy* itself, which is broken up into drives that then must be captured as such, *at the risk of demolishing even more attention* when these drives are linked in a libidinal *economy*—that is, in a limiting of the one tendency by its countertendency, and vice versa, and where these apparatuses allow for their connection and prevent or defer their disconnection?

Agamben does not interrogate this *oikonomia* of the *libido*—the *oikonomia* of objects of desire, a desire diverted, for example, toward cell phones,[10] and perhaps he does not ask because the answer would be *incompatible* with Foucault's thinking about apparatuses—with the exception, of course, of what he will say about techniques of self and the writing of the self. But Foucault never theorizes these energetically or pharmacologically, and Agamben makes no reference to them. But pharmacology, engendering *all* apparatuses in Agamben's sense of them, after Foucault and beyond, is not thinkable outside the economy of drives that it simultaneously connects and disconnects, and of which it can be the remedy (the support) and the poison (the ruin).

In not considering this *oikonomia* of the *pharmakon*, Agamben leaves this poison without remedy. And because he cannot ask the salient questions, Agamben can only describe the *empoisoning of apparatuses* as a fatality with no other possible outcome than submission and loss of self, on the one hand, and retreat into something resembling *Gelassenheit* on the other. Agamben writes, in effect, that even if it is not possible to destroy these devices, it is also no longer possible "as some naively suggest, to use them in the correct way" (16). This declaration does not mean what one might want to understand by it—knowing that it is not enough to define a "correct use" for the *pharmakon* as a *reduction* of its pharmacological (and thus *poisonous*) nature, since that is absolutely *irreducible*. And Agamben does not mean that the *pharmakon* must be dealt with *as pharmakon*, to think through and to practice a therapeutics without pretending to *care*, finally, for all human beings captured by this capture (the very idea of tragic culture) without pretending to *save* them, as they could be saved by a savior, a Good Shepherd, leading them to paradise.

But in Agamben's declaration there is a great deal else: he declares that the *pharmakon* is a poison, pure and simple, even if as we shall see, it is the human being's original and originary condition, seemingly meaning that humanity is destined for hell, not for some promised paradise, and this is a hell with no possibility of remission, since God is dead and the *oikonomia* of the Trinity no longer exists, nor that of the Holy Spirit. Apparatuses [*dispositifs*] are, in effect, the *disposition* (what in Greek could be called the *kosmos*[11]) of the human as such, since they "are rooted in the very process of 'humanization' that made 'humans' out of the animals" (16) that we are. Here, Agamben returns to and follows up on a train of thought he initiated in *Profanations* on the role of apparatuses in the formation of the sacred, defined as separation, and in profanation "that restores to common use what sacrifice had separated and divided" (19). Agamben's analysis of capitalism (for him, of disciplinary society) leads him to describe it as *that which makes profanation particularly difficult*— compared to "traditional apparatuses":

> Every apparatus implies a process of subjectivization without which the apparatus cannot function as an apparatus of governance. . . . In a disciplinary society, apparatuses aim to create . . . docile, yet free, bodies that assume their identity and their "freedom" as subjects in the very process of their desubjectification. (19–20)

Simondon's theory of individuation, laying out the formation of a metastable equilibrium (metastable in that it is formed across contradictory forces—about which one could say, along with Canguilhem, that they are at once entropic and neguentropic,[12] and that the play of their composition constructs the dynamic of individuation that can always be blocked by a historical impasse) appearing as disciplinary society to lead inevitably to *the end of history*. Or, to speak differently, the "subject" and "subjectivation" are the interaction of inseparable and irreducible synchronizing and diachronizing logics, forming what Simondon calls a transductive relationship, but which disciplinary societies—and I am speaking here precisely of societies of *control*—have brought to the point of their own decomposition, and, as I have said, *without remission.*

49. To intervene and to profane: societal caretakers and I-don't-give-a-damn-ers before the "Ungovernable"[13]

Agamben claims that the apparatus is "first of all a machine that produces subjectifications, and only as such is it also a machine of governance" (WA, 20). But is not this *duplicitous* dimension of subjectivization the real history of its primordial and originally pharmacological nature? This is not a matter of a reduction but of law itself: *the law of technics,* underlying individuation *and* disindividuation. If so, Agamben's thesis is mine here (as in *Mécréance et discrédit* and *De la misère symbolique*): "what defines the apparatuses that we have to deal with in the current phase of capitalism is that they no longer act as much through the production of a subject, as through the processes of what can be called desubjectification" (21). Agamben is here describing disindividuation, in fact, though without connecting it to the generalized proletarization of the loss of job skills and life skills that are not themselves apparatuses but their *implementation* through a nullified and exhausted industrial organization (and through a political economy). In the "current phase of capitalism," apparatuses empty "subjects" out, since they can no longer engender anything but desubjectivization, with an immense risk of exploding.

In fact, Agamben claims that *in principle* this impasse is irreversible: "Here lies the vanity of the well-meaning discourse on technology. . . . If a resolute process of subjectification (or, in this case, desubjectification) corresponds to every apparatus, then it is impossible for the one subjected to an apparatus to use it 'in the right way'" (21–22). But *who* asks what this "right way" is? And if in fact there must be someone to ask it, does not that very designation require serious discussion—if only to eliminate a completely different way of thinking, as a result of this contrasting claim? And is not *this* very question really one of a *practice,* obviously not a "utilization:" there is never a *certain* way (a "correct" or "right" one), nor even *a* way, correct or not, to put an apparatus into *practice,* but rather a *spectrum* [*spectre*[14]] of possibilities the institutions of *power* (and the knowledge engendered in and by them) perpetually occlude in order to protect their positions of power?

To claim that *a* "process of subjectivation (or, in this case, desubjectivation) corresponds to every apparatus" is to ignore the totality of subjectivation's intrinsically pharmacological condition, where on the contrary *many* possible processes always exist; and further, it is to renounce any thinking in terms of a political economy, in which desubjectivation equals proletarization. In Agamben's reference here to capitalism there is no analysis of a logic of investment and speculation, or of the reality of a division between work and the distribution of roles, for example, between public institutions and private organizations, or between the operators of circuits of production and mass consumers, and so on. It is as if [Foucauldian] biopolitics simply dispensed with any thought of the political economy, as well as the many battles that have taken place there.

This is why Agamben asserts that in this situation, "the eclipse of politics" (22) and the "triumph of the *oikonomia*" are outcomes in which "the Right and the Left" become the two poles of the same "governmental machine." But even if one can but agree with Agamben's facts, and if it seems obvious that this right/left bipolarity accounts for all consumers making it impossible to think through any other future, I must object

1. that this eclipse results as much and perhaps primarily in an incapacity to think, to critique, and to conceptualize an absolutely new situation, particularly regarding Foucault's biopower, whose roots, as Agamben himself says, are ancient but whose possibilities of being thought, or of thinking *with* them (let alone *acting* on them), are concealed by a process of originary repression and denial that neither Foucault nor Agamben—nor anyone else—can escape, but that must and can be thought through, and carefully; that is, acted upon as and through the dynamics of this very repression, requiring a return to Freud—certainly not to repeat him but to *confront* the question that he himself never finally addresses as such;

2. that if this right/left polarity is seen as less important, it is because the initial question is formulated by a different, and contradictory, polarity: the short- and long-term dynamics that are the modalities of Heidegger's *Besorgen*, but in which the difference is a matter of *Sorge*; in other words, here it is a matter of *thinking time completely differently*, through a situation in which the care-less-ness of a political economy that has become purely speculative structurally conflicts with the now universally felt need to *take care*, to invent *systems* of care on new terms and through a new therapeutics of apparatuses, in which biopower and biopolitics are no longer the issue, right/left polarity having been redistributed and

overdetermined by another polarity: curious / incurious, caretaking / I-don't-give-a-damn;[15]

3. that the matter at hand is precisely the rethinking of care, not being satisfied with reducing the disciplines and institutions to apparatuses of subjectivation that lead ineluctably to *de*subjectivation: this would mean *rethinking the contemporary archive* through new philosophical, historical, and political concepts in which new forms of *hypomnēmata* can be studied as *pharmaka* at once poisoning and simultaneously furnishing the only possible pharmacopoeia for sociotherapies that are always the source of political ideas and actions.

In the face of these needs for action, the weakness of current thought is as unprecedented as it is immense, in that it must "search for new weapons" and rearm itself; this is the result of a fundamental disorganization of thought; and thought is not a faculty of the intellect localized in the brain any more than the heart or the liver: it is the product of social organization and works properly, when it does, through apparatuses in which *disciplines* are the conditions sine qua non, understood in terms of the three senses we have just examined.

Thought has all the more rejected thinking these apparatuses in that it has itself become just such an apparatus: an institution, different from any it has ever been, the producer of works of the mind, tertiary retentions (archives), a *pharmakon* in service to a kind of attention that can at any moment transform into a diversion of attention into its *abyssal* objects, themselves apparatuses (and the most fascinating ones)—gambling that thought-as-apparatus, within the meta-apparatus of the *Gestell,* can only make the "liberal" logic of TINA (*there is no alternative*[16]) its most refined concept, as *Gelassenheit.*[17]

Profanation is certainly not of this order, and on this issue the last paragraph of *What Is an Apparatus?* remains quite enigmatic, seeming to open or half-open a mysterious possibility:

> The problem of the profanation of apparatuses . . . cannot be properly raised as long as those who are concerned with it are unable to intervene in their own process of subjectification, any more than in their own apparatuses, in order to then bring to light the Ungovernable, which is the beginning and, at the same time, the vanishing point of every politics. (24)

What does Agamben mean, "to intervene"? Who are *those who are concerned* with this problem? What is this "*Ungovernable*" lurking in the shadows? And, I might add, from what *mystagogy* does all of this come? These are the questions we must address to Giorgio Agamben.[18]

50. The idealization of the sovereign

God is dead. And thus the logic of apparatuses is revealed as an enormously rich moment of thought that, after Derrida, is a pharmacologic. Another of its results has been what I have called a "rhetoric of *only . . .* " [*ne . . . que . . .*], which I take to be a distant result of "*being only intermittently*" [*n'être que par intermittance*], which I investigate at the end of the first volume of *Mécréance et discrédit.*[19] This "*being only intermittently*" claims that (1) the human being is not a god (this also means a *gnôthi seautou,* as Foucault reminds us) and cannot attain what in modern metaphysics is called mastery, and (2) the human being is *obliged to* act,[20] and that this action, *always a form of profanation,*[21] is a passage to the noetic plane: a passage (a *breakthrough*) to the plane of ideas, a *leap* to the plane of consistencies.

Through discipline, this leap intermittently but also regularly allows for techniques of the self. Generally presented in the history of the West as a religious, spiritual practice, the leap quickly becomes a profane and even tragic practice: tragic in its very origins, in that it is dedicated to the finite nature of humans as pharmacological beings, even if that does *not* mean that the Stoics or the Epicureans think of humanity *as* pharmacological. The practices producing this leap, emerging from knowledge as being-only-intermittently, have a complex history during which they undergo a transformation (through the Jesuits) leading to a rhetoric of the "*only . . .* " as a version of being-only-intermittently after the death of God, through the mourning and melancholy that often result across many forms of denial.

But this rhetoric is quite dangerous: it tends to turn *being-only-intermittently* into a justification for abandoning all actions other than purely destructive transgression (which can also be profanation); from this perspective it also justifies a certain care-less-ness or indifference, to the extent that it declares that since it will always fail, the impetus for action is finally in vain, and since care-less-ness is inscribed in all care, like a law against which one is powerless. This discourse results in the renunciation of all therapeutics other than administration—*governance* (by the right or the left) of a finity no longer knowing how to address infinity—and indeed of the infinite nature of *the object of desire.*

The only valuable object is the one attesting to the consistency of all the others, and it consists of the object of all attentions: the *unconditional object.* The object of all attentions is imposed on all other objects of attention, sometimes replacing or displacing them, vampirizing, ventriloquizing, or substituting themselves for those objects in myriad ways, haunting them as their "spirit," as "the object of all objects," the *meaning* [*sens*] of all objects.

From this perspective, the *unconditional object* tends to become unconditioned—absolute, omnipotent, eternal. It appears as an object of idealization in the sense that it presents itself as without condition, independent, absolutely sovereign relative to all other objects—especially the other object that is the subject of attention: consciousness of the object of desire and all of its attentions. Thus, the transformed object rises up toward the horizons of sublimation, producing durability (in Arendt's sense) and the attachment that, as *philia*, structures the social (for example, a family), if this object is a husband, a wife, a child, or a parent; but also all sorts of other structures, such as knowledge as the scholar's *libido sciendi*, the nation, the church, and so on.

Here the mystagogic structure of consciousness as γνοσις becomes the gnosis of an absolutely sovereign object—Plato calls this the Sovereign Good—which will become God for the entire remaining history of monotheism, up to the present day. But this theology begins *theoretically, before* monotheism, with Aristotle, and completely free of the guilt complex Freud sees concretizing itself in the monotheism of the Eternal Father as the object of all his children's desires and all their covetousness.

The theory of attention, and of systems of care, that I am attempting to elaborate here, suggest in an Aristotelian way (as a thinking of motion and emotion) that all systems of care project just this mystagogic object and that there is no care that could be completely protected from mystagogy. But what needs being cared for always reverts to being an object of *all possible desires*, as their *unity:* an object of unlimited collective individuation—which in the lay world is called the *universal.*

This does not mean, however, that the mysterious *object* is miraculous or supernatural; it means that the object *makes* mystery, produces mystery, and in order to become accessible, requires initiatory, mystagogic, or esoteric discourse—a discipline involving practices of the self.

In twentieth-century philosophy this access becomes a conversion, for example, that of the gaze with phenomenology (deriving eidetically from "natural demeanor"), or listening for the psychoanalyst (who searches for the unconscious behind all consciousness). As the product of an idealization without which there can be no desire nor *libido sciendi*, the object of all attentions is nonetheless *originally* on the plane of consistencies and has required, since antiquity, the practices of the *otium* or the *skholē* by which objects of contemplation become accessible. These necessary practices are *theory*, whose perfect place is the *skholeion*, the school as it has been conceived since the Greeks.

The noetic mind, the one capable of taking spiritual action "intermittently," and in this sense profanely, thus becoming diachronic and individuating, is less "human" (and as a result always too human) than *non-inhuman. We*, because we *are* pharmacological, are less human than *not-inhuman*, always a little *too* human in always being a little too close to taking ourselves for gods. But we are only *not-inhuman* when we take noetic action in the knowledge of *not-being-a-god*, meaning first of all the *gnôthi seauton*, and in understanding *being-only-intermittently*—which is not, therefore, an abandonment of the "*only. . . .*"

Yet most of the time we tend not to be not-inhuman-*in-action*: we *tend* toward not-humanity, understanding "humanity" as what is taught in what we call "the humanities"; most of the time, in other words, we tend toward being (not-inhuman) minors, if not an inhumanity that could always become just such a minority. This is the "tragic condition" of being-only-intermittently. And in more contemporary language, this means that we are always interwoven with drives we are responsible for linking in order to elevate them to the level of objects of desire, directly and permanently exposing us to the shame of being human; thus, we never cease seeing and confronting stupidity—which is from the outset in us, not just against us.

To think is to act, and to act with dignity: to exist between these two. Agamben speaks of the market as it seizes control of libidinal energy, breaking it up into drives. But by not critiquing Freud and not reinterrogating the political economy (and biopolitics), he comes to an impasse—as does Hans Jonas, as we will see[22]—with regard to the question of desire, and thus of sublimation within the capitalist economy.[23] But perhaps this is not without its effects on desire as such: what Jonas describes as the process of subjectivization leading to the subject's submission could be applied here to him—and not only to him but to Foucault as well.

Kant's thought of maturity as humanity's sovereignty, extended by Condorcet as popular sovereignty—this Kantian thought that thinks itself, if not *as* apparatus, at least from and through an apparatus (since Kant speaks of the adult—mature—apparatus of reading and writing), written in this medium that he reads in order to be able to write it, this thought of maturity as an *idealization device*, requires the measuring (but also in some sense the *infinite expanding*) of the effects of the pharmacological nature of the very apparatus Kant fails to problematize (though he sees it) and thus fails to make the core of his thought. Only by retracing these steps can we avoid renouncing the thought of "maturity" in an age of psychotechnologies.

§ 11 From the Twentieth Century to Our Own Times—If We Have Time

51. Population as noetic potential

Philosophy has posed an *oikonomia* of noetic apparatuses as its first question, and if not as its primary issue, at least as a teaching practice. Plato's theory of anamnesis is the basis of all instruction as the dialectic transmission of apodictic or formal knowledge, and anamnesis as recollection, contrary to the Sophists, requires a kind of attention the learner *forms itself as a knowledge* by inscribing it on long circuits of transindividuation—by *individuating* it, then individuating knowledge itself according to the logic of associated symbolic media.

Whereas Plato sees *hypo*mnesia as opposing the formation of *ana*mnesic attention, the later Foucault—significantly complicating the sense of his early works—shows that *hypomnēmata* operating as supports for techniques of the self (i.e., the writing of the self) are the technical condition for this dialogic life as *self-attention*, as care. But the techniques of the self, for Foucault inscribed within sexuality and desire, are also techniques of sublimation, which means that thinking through them can occur only as a function of apparatuses that form, deform, and transform the libidinal economies constituting organological eras and the *pharmaka* they employ as apparatuses.

For Foucault, as for Plato after the *Symposium*, knowledge must be seen as a genre of desire. The object of desire par excellence is the object of attention, and vice versa: there can be an object of attention for a desiring being only if attention is originally and irreducibly *both* psychic (as concentration, "attention span") and social (as kindness and solicitude). Thus, the question of attention is also one of care—*therapeuma, epimēleia, cura.* Such a theory of attention can account for the generating of systems of care constituting the social appropriation of tertiary retentions as pharmacological constraints that are unique to them, and for the interiorization through which individual and collective attention can initiate retentions and protentions individually and collectively, for example, in a school teaching the governmentality of the self and others.

Attention formed in the play of retentions and protentions creates a politics of attention, which in turn becomes the heart of economic and military, not just political, power, through retentional apparatuses—the material institutions of archaeology—as they create tertiary retentions. This "psychopolitics" is the object and the goal of integrated economic, military, and political strategies as *soft power.*[1]

The generation of evolving systems of care could not produce the economy of Foucault's fundamental works on this subject. But their mobilization can be productive only if it also attempts to understand its limits— limits obviously induced by the archaeology and pharmacology within which Foucault's discursive formulations themselves take place without his seeing them clearly. My claim here is that Foucault, who formulates these limits, does not address the issue of sublimation, which is that of education as metacare: his work does not have a true libidinal economy.

Foucault shows how with the transformation from monarchy to bourgeoisie a biopolitical State administration is formed, a governmentality whose goal is to optimize economic development by investing in caring for a population seen as a living organism demographically and statistically managed through intermediary technologies of rationalized power: a population constructed through biopower (technologies that I claim proceed from grammatization). Care, which until that transformation had been inscribed in a spiritual and subliminatory social apparatus, thus becomes administrative management. The "bourgeois State" is essentially biopower instituting a politics of governmental management of the future and of population growth, for example, as a politics of birth or public hygiene: biopolitics.

Biopower as Foucault describes it is always a function of the State, specifically of the nation-state, resulting from the bourgeoisie's acquisition of power. This "modern" biopower manifests itself within the context of a generalized rationalization and secularization, the central traits of Max Weber's description of capitalism as "disenchantment,"[2] leading to what Marcuse calls desublimation experienced as progress: the century of Pasteur. It is only in the twentieth century, however, that this social rationalization comes to its full fruition when, borne along by a modernization project that doubtless benefits the great majority of the population, it solidifies into the Welfare State within a generalized Keynesianism throughout "the West." According to Foucault, the Welfare State's central mission is care understood as management of a population seen as a "potential being," through economic development conceived as a virtuous circle, its biopolitics, however, obviously not having been stripped of its inclination to dominate: care, says Foucault, can and finally must always mutate into a constraining, even alienating, discipline, into norms, standards, and regulations in which individuals are embedded, dominated by a mass technocracy through which the State suffocates "society."

I suggest, however, that Foucault here significantly neglects (1) the fact that the twentieth century is also and above all else the century of market growth, as we saw in Section 39, dominated by a previously unknown technology of power (marketing), and (2) the fact that the mission to form mature consciousness that since the nineteenth century has been the purview of the State has become a mission not only to emancipate minds (laicization), and thus the adoption of modern ideas, but also the formation and solicitation of the population's intellectual talents; the "population" is thus no longer viewed biologically but *noetically*—and already engaged in a new battle for intelligence. This has become an economic factor of much greater importance than support for production workers, meaning that the *otium* and the *negotium* have entered into a completely new[3]—and very problematic—relationship.[4]

52. Noopolitiques, cultural industries, and "the younger generation"

Throughout the nineteenth century in France, in the same movement that made hygiene a central public preoccupation, the State instituted mandatory public education as part of the systematic laicization of public life. But just as the biopolitics of care seized on the conditions vital to the population's development, demographically seen through a global economic politics, by the twentieth century this had become a politics of public health and social welfare in partnership with and paralleling the growth of the pharmaceutical industry, on orders of the State that the population itself has delegated to it—the Welfare State, which then plans out industrial development politically (for example, as life sciences in service to the biochemical industries), makes public instruction a *politics* of, simultaneously, mandatory national education, higher education, and scientific and technological research, by forming, acculturating, and transforming of the public's minds, including the best among them, mobilizing them to serve a new age of intelligence.[5]

National education based on mandatory public instruction as it developed during the nineteenth century laid the groundwork for the potentially noetic mind of scientific research that then became, in the twentieth century—chiefly after World War II and decolonization—the key to the global economic war, first between States, then among transnational groups to the detriment of both States and of regions. National education has become the other pillar of industrial democracy—something Foucault completely ignores. The system of education and scientific and technological research is a noopolitics: a politics of minds [*esprits*] aimed at developing and managing a national spirit [*esprit*] serving a national economy and a national industry, guaranteeing the possibility of individual social advancement through the ever-expanding knowledge that the nation-state both requires and brings about through industrial development.

The example par excellence of just such a politics in France is Gaullism, which adds a public mission of the democratization of what has begun to be called "culture" to public instruction, national education, and scientific research. Previously, a concept such as this would have been seen as a privilege exclusively available to the bourgeoisie created in the nineteenth century, along with a taste for serious music (that one played as an amateur), frequent visits to theater and opera, knowledge of art history and practice (chiefly through museums), love of reading, and so on. The politics of a democratization of culture was the desire of the Popular Front in the 1930s but was only implemented, finally, by André Malraux in the 1960s (inspired equally by Jean Vilar and the supporters of what in France could be called "popular education," whose chief promoters were Jean Zay, minister of national education for the Popular Front, and Léo Lagrange).[6]

But this political culture, as an element of a noopolitics,[7] began in the (Gaullist) Fifth Republic in 1958, at the very moment when the cultural industries were first deployed on a massive scale in France as elsewhere. These industries—then, most recognizably, in such technologies as "transistor" radios, the word indicating metonymically the first portable electronic devices—advertised to (and targeted to) the young *as a market with purchasing power*, frequently locating itself in what was then the "counterculture." Even more significantly, the advent of the Fifth Republic coincided with the development of television, which, in 1958, was in only 10% of French households but which quickly became the principal organ of political life (initially as "the General's television"), then of economic life (13.1% of French households owned a television in 1960; 70.3% in 1970).[8]

With the growth of the audiovisual companies making up the programming industry, noopolitics confronts its *other* and in many respects its *opposite*, but nonetheless also its *complement*: the development of analogic *hypomnēmata* creating media psychopower that is then progressively deployed by marketing, destroying attention formation as consciousness. This progression has significant ramifications: the generational crisis that led to the 1968 actions in large part resulted from the fact that starting in the 1960s, principally through the arrival of portable media starting with the transistor radio, which have played an extremely important role in youth's transindividuation and development into a discrete market,[9] young people captured by television and numerous other technomedia have progressively, irresistibly become the primary market predictor for adult behavior. This formula simultaneously raises youth to the ranks of a generational political and economic power, and at the same time revolts them: they live through this process in a profound malaise.[10]

As a consequence, the "Younger Generation" senses that it is in the process of being molded into an extremely problematic position, which then launches the *second* malaise in twentieth-century culture, surpassing what Freud explored in his writings on the telephone and other psychotechnological apparatuses: with the simultaneous appearance of the transistor radio and television a new stage in technology opened. But now, at the beginning of the twenty-first century, cell phones, networked computers, and the many other devices in (and since) Agamben's critique work through cognitive numerization and cultural technologies whose linking psychotechnological connections compound their effects on intergenerational relations; they also catalyze ruptures in the juvenile psychic apparatus's synaptic circuitry, to the advantage of *hyperattention* and the detriment of *deep attention*, creating an intergenerational fracture on the cerebral level, that is, within the organology of the central nervous system itself.

Moreover, young people's current malaise results directly from the crisis the previous generation experienced when it was younger (*grosso modo*, the generation of "68") who, now adults approaching retirement age, have not yet fully absorbed the fact that its adolescent crisis was no less than a crisis of civilization: 1968, which cannot be reduced simply to a generational conflict,[11] since it was also a social conflict felt by the working class, was in fact not an uprising of *all* French youth but rather largely of students (that is, of universities, including professors). The movement of 1968 was a *student* movement among youth because if it is true that biopolitics is the system of care charged with the population's vitality,[12] tending to become the avenue of access to modern amenities for all—in other words, to become the consumer society initially called the "petite bourgeoisie"—education is an *other* form of care.

53. Care and the shame of being human

Truthfully, education is an *entirely other* form of care: it is in fact a *meta-care*, not care of the body nor even of numbers of bodies but of what have for centuries been called "souls," whose collectivity constitutes *a* spirit. The increasing disuse of such a vocabulary is largely the result of the rapid expansion throughout modern society in the era of 1968 as the rejection of diametric oppositions—body/soul and spirit/matter, most notably: we discovered through Europe No. 1 that the soul somatizes [*l'âme somatise*] and that there is a somatopsyche.[13] Most of the time it is in the name of a more or less badly assimilated historico-libidinal materialism that the generation politicized in 1968 opposes any power identified as synonymous with the State-as-repressive-superego, a power the French Communist Party a little later called "monopolistic State capitalism." Consequently, this generation's historico-libidinous materialism is reacting against the dominance of calculation and "output principles" as aspects of a desublimation they learned largely through the ideas of Herbert Marcuse.

If, as Georges Pompidou thought in conceiving the institution that after his death would be called the Pompidou Centre, 1968 was a crisis of modernity and, again according to him, a rejection of modernization in France, it is because "modernity" as experienced by French youth was no longer the achievement of maturity vanquishing "laziness and cowardice" but exactly the opposite: as what leads directly to the sacrifice of noopolitics in favor of biopolitics by way of a State power of which General de

Gaulle was the very incarnation. In other words, the State's biopower, as it modernizes, reduces existences to subsistences, to mere producers or consumers: to the diminished status of proletarized beings condemned to inhumanity and inexistence; this is the sense in which Marcuse's thought was referenced in the movement called "68."

The movement itself formed in the universities (in France and, in fact, worldwide) because education (familial or collective, private or public) constituted care in the strictest sense, if "care" here can be understood as *constituting the social* as that in which all human beings worthy of the name find themselves originarily and ethically charged, and charged precisely as existence itself—it is not by chance that the "68" movement immediately follows the reign of Sartrean existentialism. All human beings worthy of the name are charged with their own existences in order not to become inhuman, and in order to inspire shame of being human in all other human beings worthy of the name. This is the care Primo Levi speaks of at the conclusion of *If This Is a Man*, and he speaks of it as what *saved* him, not by transporting him to paradise but in allowing him to *return* to Auschwitz. He committed suicide on 11 April 1987.

This care cannot be seen as the basic conditions for survival, as subsistence. Care, "strictly speaking," always works through the care one takes *of oneself through* the care one takes of others, in that they are constituent elements of that "self" as the transformation of individuation. Throughout virtually all of protohistory and *non-inhuman* history, and doubtless for a significant part of prehistory, the *non-inhuman* pharmacological being that we were and are never ate without offering a sacrifice—I will explore this fully in the next volume of *Taking Care*. And that sacrifice was offered because beyond the fact that it was necessary in order to gain the power to transgress, to profane,[14] and thus to take action, that early being was capable of feeling shame, and before all else the shame of having the tendency to eat like an animal—which thus had *nothing to do* with a feeling of guilt.

For this reason Zeus makes *aidôs* (shame) mortals' fundamental condition in the Prometheus/Epimetheus myth, as Pythagoras tells it: taking care, *stricto senso*, means to *cultivate what it means to take care*, to make it productive, and in that sense to transform it in order to improve it through the effort of taking action intermittently, which Aristotle calls *noēsis*. To take care, to cultivate, is to dedicate oneself to a cult, to believe there is something better: the *non-inhuman* par excellence, both in its projection to the level of ideas (consistencies) and in that this "better" *must* come. This is exactly the *ēthos* for which techniques of the self are required; to take care is to know that since there is a "better," there is a "worse," and that it *must* be combated, without cowardice, since it endlessly returns through the window of those who, whether naïve or presumptuous, believe they have shut it out, or that they can "not give a damn."

In the strict sense that the truly educated learn to take care *of themselves* and thus of others, in taking care of objects *of knowledge* they have been given, knowledge by which they can and must take care of *the world*, this politics of care called "national education," brought to the population's minds by the laic State through free, mandatory public instruction (in which a population *becomes* a people and not merely a population)—this politics of care-through-instruction, evolving in the twentieth century into higher education and the politics of research, the pillar of modern democratic, industrial society, is in fact a *meta*care that, as it were, *shapes* care in modern society in the strongest sense—as the taking of noetic action that is *politically and economically organized*. It is thus on a completely different plane from the biopolitics emerging as the administration of what Foucault describes as biopower.

In the current world, this metacare must become a psychopolitics, an industrial politics of techniques of the mind, even before it struggles against the disastrous effects of the savage use of psychotechnologies by the programming industries as they destroy attention and consciousness, disseminating a global attention deficit disorder at the very moment when the development of a planetary consciousness is appearing to be the single hope for the survival of we non-inhuman beings.[15]

To take care also means to pay attention, first paying attention to taking and maintaining care of oneself, then of those close to us, then of their friends—and thus, by projection, of *everyone*: of others whatever they may be, and of the world we share with them; formation of this kind of attention creates a *universal consciousness* grounded on (and profaned by) a consciousness of singularity. As attention, this care cannot be reduced to caring for a large mass of human beings: it is, rather, the basis of *sociability* as well as the psychic health of the non-inhuman being living in a society in perpetual evolution, radically distinguishing the non-inhuman being's psychic health from the health of the animal central nervous system: the non-inhuman psyche is formed by desire supported by will.

To take care means caring for an equilibrium always at the limit of disequilibrium, even "far from equilibrium," and it is also caring for a disequilibrium always at the limit of equilibrium: it is taking care of *movement*. Such metastability requires something entirely different from a biopolitics, since it is founded on a pharmacology that creates this equilibrium at the limit of disequilibrium. This is what Foucault could not see. And he thus did not see that sublimation is the very economy of this pharmacology (sublimation makes a "poison," for example, a *hypomnēmaton*, its "remedy"). But our early twentieth-century metastability, which is extremely close to disequilibrium and instability as a result of the psychotechnologies and infantilizing hegemonies of various psychopowers, calls for a sociotherapy that is nothing less than the conceiving of a new age of the formation of care and attention for facing the care-less-ness of a global consumer society that we know is condemned to vanish given that it entails the autodestruction of the non-inhuman precisely in that it is reduced by biopower to its demographic characteristics, managed solely through its solvency [*solvability*].

54. Non-inhuman societies, I-don't-give-a-damn-ism, and the inhuman

It is difficult to know how to speak simply about psychopower with regard to the politics of attention formation, as in the final analysis it (psychopower) fabricates all forms of non-inhuman societies: it is, rather, a nootechnique in the sense of a technique for the formation and development of the psyche *as* noetic (that is, spiritual) and not simply sensory or nutritive (that is, reactive). Nootechniques exist in *all* non-inhuman societies in that they are all spiritual—inhabited by spirits that become, with the Greek *pneuma* and *noûs*, the Jewish *ruah*, and the Christian Eucharist, *one* spirit—and this spirit, as unity, in turn in Protestantism—becomes the spirit of capitalism (whose "spirit," today, has been lost).

Non-inhuman societies develop nootechnologies through rituals as magic practices and cults as religious practices, but also through the regulated life of the *skholē* and the *otium*, through ascetic philosophy and the culture of the self, or through monastic life founded on confession in the true "catholic" sense laid out by Martin Luther—which Ignatius Loyola responded to through the Jesuit mission of subjecting actions to the order of the *Spiritual Exercises*. It is difficult to know how to speak simply here about psychopower, since it always transcends simple powers, even the power of testing the fact that there is always a "beyond" of power, and through the formation of knowledges in which the knower's singularity is so constructed that it cannot be reduced to a particular unit within a homogeneous whole.

We can and we must, on the other hand, address a psychopower from which techniques emerge that lead to control of the mental activities of individuals' becoming increasingly *calculable*, and as *audiences*, with the appearance of the cultural industries, first cinema, then the audiovisual (i.e., "broadcasting") starting in the 1920s with radio, then television in the late 1940s, and so on. When capitalism (both economic and "cultural") employs these programming industries, it begins to produce *temporal industrial objects*, and these are the key elements in what Deleuze calls societies of control in that they work toward the capturing of consumer attention, causing them to adopt new psychomotor behaviors through which they help form the perpetual markets required by industrial innovation. Societies of control systematically implement the most recent iterations of grammatization, opening new possibilities for control of central nervous system functions through the powerful stimulation of retentions and protentions. The problem is that this control is antithetical to the very life of the *esprit*, since it mortgages the formation of juvenile synaptic circuits normally belonging to the kind of attention characterized by reason. Some kind of psychopolitics must redefine these psychotechniques as nootechniques: a psychopolitics elevated to the level of a noopolitics, not simply a translation onto the noetic plane of biopower and biopolitics—this is "the State." But psychopower is now held prisoner by various economic agents under the pressure of their clients, who have become structurally incurious I-don't-give-a-damn-ers, while psychopolitics must be implemented as a noopolitics in order to reverse and sublimate the mental pharmacology that develops essentially as a toxic agent destructive of all forms of attention.

At the end of the twentieth century, it was not the United Nations and the "bourgeois" public powers desiring the psychic control of populations but corporations eyeing global markets (the bourgeoisie having disappeared, increasingly displaced by various mafias). By 1997, there were over a billion televisions in the world, as Craig Mundie (vice president of Microsoft) exalts, which explains why Microsoft wants to become the principal partner of all audiovisual programming companies. The market for these audiovisual programs is expanding internationally and exponentially, and even became the object of fierce negotiations at the Uruguay Round and the General Agreement on Tariff and Trade negotiations that led to the creation of the World Trade Organization—the cultural exception (before "cultural diversity") defining the object of these negotiations on conceptual, political, economic, and philosophical bases that are much weaker today.

Now it is financial capitalism that knows how to conceive, to adopt, and to make vanish at will the media products of a psychopower whose singular goal is the global mastery of behaviors (including finances—chiefly through the fabrication of beliefs productive of autorealistic prophesies within the financial world, in which the world banking system has sadly but very predictably been confronting great dangers since at least 2007[16]) according to immediate needs and as quickly as possible, in the shortest possible term, and as functions of extremely rapid rotation cycles imposed by the global economic war and by global hedge funds.

This is the deterritorialized capitalism, freed of all its links to the nation-state and orchestrating the behavioral changes in world culture, whatever their seeming singularities that must be eliminated by a global audiovisual, psychotechological industry—to which the telecommunications and numeric industries added themselves at the end of the twentieth century. But this new implementation of apparatuses is also a hope for the reconstitution of the politics of attention, as new forms of noopolitics grounded in the psychopolitical regulation of economic psychopower.

Because industrial temporal objects are able to capture, monopolize, and penetrate attention in ways unequalled in history, in the twentieth century they become industry's principal products; their mediation fashions certain ways of life in which biopower and biopolitics become secondary matters, no longer any more than aspects of psychopower (its somatic aspects). Industrial objects' *economic* power short-circuits the *political* power of the State, taking massive control of behaviors. If it is psychopower that is deployed throughout the twentieth century, at least the last two decades have seen the total globalization of all modes of production and consumption that began in Renaissance Italy, Portugal, and Spain but that then migrated, combining with Gutenberg's technical inventions, throughout all of (Christian) Western Europe, through violent religious conflicts. Now, at the beginning of the twenty-first century, Asia has clearly adopted the most advanced forms of grammatization (in the face of which Europe is so dramatically behind) and begun a modernization process racing ahead at a literally vertiginous speed that would have been unimaginable just a few years ago. This modernization results from importation of industrial technologies and methods of production and a radical transformation of individual and collective ways of life.

However, we know that the way of life in industrial societies, based on the constant growth of consumption first established in Europe, then transferred to North America, and now known as *the American way of life*, cannot last. We know that the challenge, in the face of this emergency, is even to put an end as quickly as possible to this way of life that we ourselves, Europeans, have adopted in return: it has already become, in terms of the conditions we are living in today, "unsustainable," and will become massively and irreversibly deadly if adopted by the three billion human beings now "modernizing," who appear to be driven by an ultra-speculative and completely insane logic, taking care of *nothing*, frequently criminal, spreading care-less-ness everywhere.

The great question of the twenty-first century will be finding the way to abandon this way of life and to invent new modalities of non-inhuman existence within societies that have become thoroughly technological— modalities that are less toxic, more useful to a non-inhumanity that has become a global community in which isolation is impossible, as Ulrich Beck wrote just before Chernobyl (in 1985), and more desirable for the world's population as a whole (particularly the younger generations who will *themselves* have to invent and solidify these new ways of life: this will be *their* work since we, having left them such a heavy heritage, will have to discover both how to have confidence in them and to give way to them).

Today, the consequences of the conflict between programming *institutions* and programming *industries* is blindingly clear: teaching institutions are crumbling, and a systematic symbolic misery reigns instead and in the place of culture, despite the fact that these institutions and this culture exist precisely in order to form new generations of non-inhuman beings. The result is a psychological and social disaster whose overriding consequence is the liquidation of our cognitive faculty itself, and its replacement by informational dexterity.

The cognitive faculty—what we call reason—is the only solid link between the psychic and the social, in that it is passed through the succession of generations transformed and sublimated by disciplinary learning;

this process constitutes knowledge. Informational saturation, on the other hand, desocializes the consumer of that information. Knowledge and understanding must be psychically assimilated and made one's own (one's own *self*), while information is merchandise made to be consumed—and is therefore "disposable."

Knowledge individuates and transforms the learner, interiorizing the history of individual and collective transformations; this history *is* knowledge. The information diffused by the programming industries disindividuates its consumer. Information cannot become the substance of thinking nor the object of a knowledge capable of being the object of transformations, operated according to disciplinary regulations that are themselves knowledges, and that can be produced only as and in the transformation of the one who transforms this information.[17]

Education, conceived of as instruction in knowledges created in this way (as transmission of knowledge by programming institutions), is what learns *along with the educated* to effect such transformations, the result of which is then individuation as non-inhuman being. The programming industries, on the contrary, cause what has been learned in programming institutions to be *unlearned*: the process of learning discipline(s) in programming institutions requires the forming of an attention that is always specific to the objects of those disciplines; programming industries capture this attention and divert it from the disciplinary objects that are also the objects of knowledge, destroying attention as a faculty of understanding and an experience of knowledge—as reason. And they aim directly at *inhumanbeing* [*l'êtrinhumain*] by liquidating what Jacques Lacan calls speakingbeing [*parlêtre*].

This destruction of attention is disindividuation, and this in turn is precisely a *deformation*: a destruction of the formation of the individual that education has constructed. The work of forming attention undertaken by the family, the school, the totality of teaching and cultural institutions, and all the apparatuses of "spiritual value" (beginning with academic apparatuses) is systematically undone in the effort to produce a consumer stripped of the ability to be autonomous either morally or cognitively—to have conscience as free will, without which there can be no "science" that is not ruinous.

55. The time of responsibility, before infinite generations still to come

Responsibility is *shared* through attention formation, and this sharing is the grounding condition for solidarity: among contemporaries and their social linkages, and among the generations of ancestors and descendants, without whom such linkages (what Aristotle calls *philia*) could only be imposed as the *authority of the group* [*genre*] and of its *generosity* (which in less moral terms could be called, with Canguilhem, its neguentropy) as a non-inhuman group.

Hans Jonas had a significant influence on this debate in Europe by introducing the matter of responsibility for future generations at the same time that Jean-François Lyotard published *The Postmodern Condition*, which announced "the end of meta-narratives." Jonas sketched out the terms of the debate as it would be pursued throughout the 1980s, most notably with Ulrich Beck, which dominated the world political scene and went to the heart of political discourse everywhere in the world.[18]

Like Foucault, but coming to opposite conclusions, Jonas says not a word about marketing, nor about the organization of the political economy as such—any more than he focuses on the libidinal economy in general and on consumerist capitalism in specific. These are the questions that must be addressed in order to draw to a conclusion here and to lay out the problems to be addressed in the following volume of *Taking Care*, which will examine the stakes of "transformational" technologies on which Jonas frequently focuses his thought: the central question of *The Imperative of Responsibility*, for example, is the rapport between ethics and technics. But for Jonas this rapport is essentially negative: ethics is presented there as what must *contain* technics, particularly when technics becomes an industrial technology. Out of this question regarding ethics via technics as technology (i.e., as industry), Jonas engages the problematics of an essentially intergenerational responsibility, but he addresses the concept of responsibility, even while inscribing it within Heidegger's teachings on *Sorge*, without paying sufficient attention to what I believe is the prerequisite to all thinking on responsibility today, to all claims of responsibility—that is, to know

1. that what Heidegger calls *Sorge*, taking charge of one's existence as one's own, what can be called *ipseity*, is constituted as attention in that attention is always already at once psychic and collective and constructs

a *condition of individuation* that is itself always already psychic and collective;

2. that attention is thus precisely *constructed technically*, meaning that any ethics is in an essential relation to technics (but in an essentially *accidental* relation, if technics is irreducibly artifactual);

3. that attention emerges from a formational process that is a social organization, constitutive of the transindividual and transindividuation, transindividuation being transmitted as much technically as ethically from generation to generation.

The question of responsibility for future generations, as implied by technological power, can be understood only as what I have here called the *long term*. But I believe that Jonas's thesis does not take account of the literally extraordinary fact that a generation is always projected beyond itself—and the following one, and all potentially existing generations: it is inherently projected out toward potentially infinite generations. If there is, even at the furthest horizon of Jonas's reasoning, a gesture toward infinity, he leaves it in the shadows of a mystery whose mystagogy he does not point out. And at the same time, Jonas's question of responsibility is not *truthfully* asked as such: for him responsibility is in fact not a *question* but a *dogma*. If responsibility is what is imposed in advance and in some way defines itself as "the infinity of generations," the *practical* problem is a long-term one within which one must be able to *make decisions*, that is, to *make calculations*. But "infinity" is by definition incalculable.

In the second volume of *Taking Care* we will see that Jonas *cannot* address these questions because, beyond the fact that he does not identify the "dogma" he is using or whether he is trying to hide it (see CP, 168), he never confronts the *philosophical* sense of the question as it concerns Heidegger, who is Jonas's teacher on the subject. My aim in *Taking Care 2* is to confront the question of responsibility for the next generations and to take on the problem of what today we can call the long term, which will require revisiting *in depth* the connections between what Heidegger calls the ontic—the domain of *Besorgen*, which can be the object of positive and calculable determinations—and the ontological, accessible only within the sphere of *Sorge* and the *undeterminable* condition of all *determinations*, that is, of all appearance presenting itself as *what is*, which Heidegger calls *beings*.[19]

The question of what allows for and even insists on the distinction between long term and short term arises through the economy—first the political economy but also the libidinal economy (as différance). This is not a question that is asked *in abstracto*: it is reconfigured permanently as a function of the evolution of instrumentalizations and the organizations they make possible:

1. instrumentalizations such as the plow or the canal, giving the Mesopotamians and the Egyptians access to the floodwaters of the Tigris, the Euphrates, and the Nile in the same way that, today, financial instruments that have brought a good deal of world finance to its knees, along with everything—such as psychotechnology—resulting from grammatization's most recent stages;

2. organizations constituting the psychic apparatus, based on and in a vital organ, the central nervous system, itself configured by the interiorization of collective secondary (language) and tertiary (writing) retentions throughout synaptogenesis as the period of primary identification, then ceaselessly reconfigured throughout life as a succession of identifications;

3. social organizations through which these identifications produce transindividuations; these today include the World Trade Organization, Nike, Channel Y, and universities fighting the battle for intelligence (at the Sorbonne as in Saudi Arabia)—in addition to the various organizations of the European Union.

But the *economic* distinction among these determinations, and among these terms, the long and the short term, which are terms that concern the libidinal economy just as much as the political economy in that they form *investment apparatuses*, raises the question of temporality, addressed as such since Augustine, and then with Heidegger as the conjunction of being and time within which context Jonas works—but without ever interrogating it *en soi*. My thesis here is that this absence of problematization invalidates any discourse on responsibility, making an analysis of it all the more necessary, but then undermining it when it becomes clear that lurking tacitly within it, the Heideggerian conception of time has from the outset circumvented the true problem.

For Jonas, the impossibility of confronting the question of time—absent which the question of responsibility cannot even be asked—results from the fact that desire (as waiting [*l'attente*] and as time-as-attention) is not thinkable from a strictly Heideggerian perspective; it requires, like the question of the archive and its retentional technicity, the support of practices of the self through various apparatuses of care and an extension of Foucault's reflection on techniques of the self, going beyond the

Besorgen/Sorge opposition resulting from that of hypomnesis/anamnesis as inherited from Plato.

Today, the entire question of temporality must be rethought not only through the *gnôthi seauton*, the "rationality" originating in Platonic metaphysics and all that followed it as dialectics (including the Hegelian and the Marxian), finally becoming rationality as *ratio*, calculation—but equally, as Foucault shows us, as *epimēlesthai sautou*. Yet this is

1. doubtless what is inscribed in Heidegger's own initial gesture (which thus assigns understanding to being's ontic region, whereas *Sorge* is the experience of the very question of being—and the test of its ontological difference from all knowable being: the test of its mystagogy);

2. precisely what Jonas never questions (thus leaving his own mystagogy in the shadows).

The question of attention, and of its formation—and of its technicity—is at the base of all of these avoidances and diversions of attention, and it is time to initiate another direction of thought that, without forgetting the sense of privilege Heidegger accords to the future,[20] includes the issue of a technics that constitutes, as *Weltgeschichtlichkeit* (apparatuses of tertiary retention), techniques of self as well as psychotechnologies (such as radio, which Heidegger attempts to think through after 1927) and the nootechniques of *epimēleai* forming systems of care, which could be called "ages of being" and which, as (primary and secondary, psychic and collective) assemblages of retentions and protentions, *historically* construct temporality as originarily individual *and* collective.

Heidegger radically opposes *Besorgen*—preoccupation as calculation and precaution determining short- and long-term behaviors—and *Sorge*—concern and care projecting the indeterminability of all true, proper, and authentic resolution (its incalculability) out of originary temporality. But this opposition excludes the forming of *drives* (and tendencies, and principles) as a matter of desire. And Hans Jonas, like Marcuse, who interiorizes this opposition in his discourse on Freud, limits himself to the extent that he cannot even ask the question of the long term, a question that remains, for Heidegger, an *ontic* problem, or at least an ontic formulation of an entirely different question; in fact, a trivial and impertinent question relative to the thought of *Sorge*.

Jonas is thereby condemned to construct his ethics of technology and responsibility on a heuristic of fear. Because it recoils before all these questions, Jonas's thesis, tacitly grounded in Heidegger, cannot be adequate, because it rests on fear—on a drive that, when it is not linked to desire (which is thus always a form of sublimation), is similar to what makes the wild stag a victim (always lost when faced with a predator who is a desiring non-inhuman being), hence inspiring shame. This drive, fear, emerges in Jonas's work instead of and in place of anxiety. Heideggerian anxiety, so important to Lacan, is here a psychoanalytic issue of first importance: the thought of anxiety is at the bottom of Freud's "second topic."

But Jonas's regression of anxiety to fear has its origins in the most important flaw in the existential analytic: not thinking *Dasein* as desiring individuation as a *process* capable of transforming drives into objects of desire and sublimation in accord with the irreducible mystagogy that defines the desired object as structurally *incomparable* to anything else it might be.[21] The object of *Dasein*—as of the *Sorge* that constructs *Dasein* as the object of concern, solicitude, care, and as it is *not* thought as an object but as *being-to* . . . , as *being-for* . . . , as what Heidegger calls the existentials—is the non-object of attention that Heidegger calls ontological difference and that *Dasein* "encounters" in being-toward-death—itself an assemblage of protentions and retentions given, preceded, passed along, and succeeded [*cédé, précédé, accédé, et succédé*] by, through, and in the organological conditions formulating the archaeological and pharmacological reality of historiality (*Geschichtlichkeit*).

56. The pharmacology of development underlying industrial politics

After the time of irresponsible individuals must come the time of responsibility, as a political and libidinal economy working through a noo-politics concretized in *an industrial politics of technologies of the mind*. Such an economic politics, understood in the sense of a general economy such as the one Bataille suggests faced with the process of modernization, initially led by the U.S. Marshall Plan of 1948, must necessarily *make decisions distinguishing the short from the long term* and must provide (and exhaust) [*fournir et fourbir*] all the possibilities of this distinction. But such criteria can be produced only by a collective intelligence resulting in a new kind of attention and a new formation (*Bildung*) of that attention: a new organization of maturity.

Questions regarding the difference between "right" and "left" tend to push the great political questions into the background. But politics was not always structured by this difference, and it is not impossible that the right/left issue will recede to secondary status in terms of what differentiates them, and what in the future will (increasingly) differentiate "the curious," those who have the "cure," from the "incurious," the I-don't-give-a-damn-ers. But there are certainly more curious and incurious on the right than on the left, given that the denunciation of care-less-ness is clearly often part of the extreme right's fundamental(ist) position—and the triumph of care-less-ness is the historic cause of its success. The discussion of care-less-ness and care, more than any other, is pharmacological: this discourse on evils and remedies could be the worst of all poisons.

The sociotherapy now needed by contemporary society requires the theoretical and practical elaboration of a *pharmacology of development,* in the sense in which we can speak, with Piaget, of developmental psychology. From Winnicott's "space" and "transitional object," to the "heroine," moving through the hypomnesia of the machine tool, there are pharmaceutical usages and practices that contribute as much to social and psychological development as to its destruction. In this domain, in our own age we have encountered previously unknown problems, as the synaptogenetic analysis of attention deficits has shown us: if the pharmacology of psychotechniques has always been the very heart of society, more ancient than modern, the advent of psychotechnologies nonetheless introduces entirely specific (and still entirely unknown) effects onto the psychological development of the juvenile, and then the adult, psychic apparatus; that is, onto societal development, what I have called "ungrowth."

We have seen that what is good for one age can be toxic for another. And we now know that the misuse of psychotechnologies can have catastrophic effects on juvenile consciousness. Our political representatives, particularly those in power, are thus faced with exceptional responsibilities. If these synaptogenetic analyses of the effects of media on attention demonstrate that there are indeed *ages* of the *pharmakon,* of public and private powers, then psychopowers and noopowers have an enormous responsibility for public health, juvenile and adult—but also for what constitutes the most precious living noetic potential: to know the younger generation of non-inhuman beings, for the very survival of the non-inhuman that is possible only through the global elevation of intelligence.

If consciousness has neurological bases, then it is possible to *intervene* on these neurological bases, and to do so *ceaselessly* by organological means, just as since the Neolithic, planters and growers have intervened in the development of living organisms through biotechnical hybridizing techniques at the recombinant, chromosomal level; if psychopowers and noopowers do not take appropriate action in parallel circumstances, public (and private) psychopower and noopower will encounter difficulties very similar to those recently seen in those economic sectors that have long been (or seemed) quite prosperous.

Just as cigarettes have caused a number of generations to suffer many kinds of cancers and other illnesses, and as the automobile industry has been indicted by the state of California for having contributed to global warming, and having been found guilty in Japan of causing respiratory illnesses in the citizens of Tokyo, at some point in the future such a case will be brought against the programming industry if—now that we know about its effects on both children and society in general—and uniquely on programming institutions, as the sole guarantors of a system of care worthy of the name and the supporters of the battle for intelligence—these programming industries and the public powers who regulate them in the name of noopolitics and public (and mental) health are taking no action against the attentional deficits and intergenerational problems to which they are contributing.[22]

If Al Gore, former vice president of the United States, and Nicolas Sarkozy, current president of the French Republic (and president of the European Union in 2008), are in agreement regarding the necessity of protecting the environment and of making a priority of a new industrial politics, if French Prime Minister François Fillon expresses the will to engage in the battle for intelligence, this is very positive: it thus becomes possible to fight against care-less-ness; the results can be seen; no one could deny them. But it is important to understand the consequences of recent information on the state of contemporary minds, on what destroys them, and on the possibility of reconstructing them *out of* what has destroyed them—on condition of profoundly reversing the power that has become a psychopower, placing it under constraints prescribed by a psychopolitics in service to a noopolitics and through an industrial politics of the technologies of *esprit*.[23]

Notes

Chapter 1

1. [Trans.] Throughout the book, I have translated Stiegler's *majorité* (as opposed to *minorité*) variously as "majority," "the age of majority," or "adulthood," depending on the context.

2. Dolto cited by Jacques Hintzy, president of UNICEF France, in *Libération*, 18 July 2007. Henceforth Hintzy.

3. [Trans.] *Philia* is central to Stiegler's sense of both *esprit* and transindividuation. It is *philia* that distinguishes drives from desire and short-circuits from knowledge. As Stiegler says in *Réenchanter le monde*:

Capitalism is a libidinal economy that, in making dissociation a general condition, destroys desire (that is, the libidos *energy*): it destroys the social as *philia*. *Philia*, as the libido's most socially sublimated form and, as such, as organization and result of transindividuation as a communal effect, is what Aristotle calls what I am here calling the *association* from which the social milieu is produced. It could also be called *society* as such. (*Réenchanter le monde*, 60; henceforth RM)

4. [Trans.] "Les enfants mérite mieux que ça." It is vital to the following discussion of Canal J and its strategy of infantilization to understand from the outset that *ça* has a very powerful "second" meaning in French: it is not only "that" but also the French word for the Freudian "id," the home of preconscious drives. In the following, *ça* is generally translated as "id," though in the French text each iteration maintains its lamination with "that," as in the advertisement.

5. [Trans.] Stiegler's Canal J appears here as Channel Y: the point is that this is a channel specifically for the young, for minors: in French, *les jeunes*; in English, "the young" or "youth." Though this is a rather crude appropriation to another language, since Canal J is instantly evocative in French, it would make

no sense in terms of Stiegler's point about the "sublimity" of Canal J to call it "Channel J."

6. [Trans.] The distinction between "brain" and "mind" is central to the argument presented here. Stiegler will develop the case that only the mind is "conscious"—that the "available brain" is short-circuited and potentially, at the very least, incapable of thought and thus of will—chiefly the will to know and to learn. Given that the brain is itself a technical entity, its distinction from "mind" becomes even more central, particularly remembering—another vital point for Stiegler—that the French for "mind" is *esprit*, also translated as "spirit."

7. I developed this theme of the subversion of primary identification at greater length in *Mécreance et discrédit 2*, 130–35. Henceforth MD2.

8. http://blogantipub.wordpress.com/2007/06/15/eduquer-soit-meme-ses-enfants-cest-nul/. Henceforth BlogAntiPub.

[Trans.] The illustration shown at the BlogAntiPub Web site, of the father and (distressed-looking) daughter, has him assuming an apelike stance and expression—with two long stalks of asparagus dangling from his nostrils. His attempt to amuse his daughter shows him as not only unfunny but subhuman, as the daughter's facial expression clearly indicates. *He* is the child, not *she*. And these posters (ten feet by six feet) are on display for the captive audience in Paris Metro stations.

9. Preconscious: memories that can be recalled to consciousness.

10. Unconscious: repressed memories that cannot be recalled to consciousness.

11. We will return to these issues in greater detail in Chapter 3.

12. See Freud, *The Ego and the Id*. Henceforth Ego.

13. [Trans.] Stiegler is using this still much-contested term in its sense of orgiastic pleasure, orgasm.

14. In general, différance is "the spacing of time and the temporalization of space." Différance as relation governing the links between the pleasure principle and the reality principle is what Jacques Derrida has described, chiefly in *The Post Card*. Henceforth PostCard.

15. This concept of the *pharmakon*, which is at the heart of this book, is theorized by Jacques Derrida ("Plato's Pharmacy," in *Dissemination*) through commentary on Plato's *Phaedra*, in which Plato writes that writing itself is a *pharmakon*, at once what remedies the failures of memory and what weakens memory. Derrida does not emphasize the sense of "scapegoat" that the word *pharmakon* also has in ancient Greek.

16. Freud, *Moses and Monotheism*. Henceforth MM.

17. I laid out this case in "Perséphone, le chant de l'âme, 'l'autre temps,'" in *L'Inactuel*, Calmann-Lévy, 1994, and at greater length in "Perséphone, Oedipe, Épiméthée," *Tekhnema: Journal of Philosophy and Technology* 3:69–112 (1998). I

will return to the question of the transindividual and of its transmission down the generations, and on the failure of psychoanalytic theory to think it correctly (just as it fails to think technics), in *La Technique et le temps 5: La guerre des esprits*, forthcoming from Galilée.

18. Pontalis, *Après Freud*. Henceforth AF.

19. For an explanation of epiphylogenesis, see *Technics and Time 1*. Henceforth TT1.

20. See *De la misère symbolique 2*, 29, 99. Henceforth MS2.

21. See *Mécréance et discrédit 3*, 58–59. Henceforth MD3.

22. On Antigone, see MD2, chap. II, "Le complexe d'Antigone," 53.

23. [Trans.] The Revised Standard Version of Matthew cited in the translated text differs from the French version, which reads:

Voici quelles furent les origines de Jésus, le christ. Marie, sa mère, était promise à Joseph. Ils ne vivaient pas encore ensemble quand le saint souffle agit en elle et la fit mère. Joseph, son mari, était un homme droit. Pourquoi compromettre sa femme? Mieux valait la renvoyer en secret.

[These are the origins of Jesus, the Christ. Mary, his mother, was promised to Joseph. They did not yet love together when the holy breath moved in her and she conceived. Joseph, her husband, was an upright man. Why compromise his wife? Better to send her back secretly.]

24. Mann, *Tables of the Law*, 5. Henceforth Mann.

25. Symbol of the Christ, of which the Church will become the body after his Crucifixion and Resurrection, through the intermediary of a book that announces itself as the "new testament": as a new legacy. This symbol, as an institution, is thus an institution of the book. We will see near the end of this inquiry (248) how it is deployed in this hypomnesic technique, which Sylvain Auroux calls a process of grammatization.

26. "The world these advertisers presents us is totally disenchanted. She will habitually 'pig out' on fast food: we can clearly see her obesity, which has currently begun to be a preoccupation. The heap of vegetables on the table only adds to her next depression. So why shouldn't we just continue on from where we are now, conferring on the television this child's protection and education? Television, the virtual world in which parents are super-nags, merchandise is queen, desires mandatory, and the system unique and liberal" (BlogAntiPub).

27. Knowledges of which the ego is the contact point with the exterior world as the system of perception/consciousness whose *living knowledge*, as the introductory lens for primary retentions, integrating them into secondary retentions, and thus transforming and enriching this heritage, occurs through the subject's new experiences. See *De la misère symbolique 2*, 232ff.

28. For a full discussion of transindividuation, see my preface in Simondon,

Individuation psychique et collective (henceforth IPC), xiii, and RM, 122; *La Té-lécratie contre le démocratie* (henceforth TCD), 33ff., 107ff., 157ff.; *De la démocratie participative* (henceforth DDP), 102. And as a reminder, for Jean-Bernard Pontalis the unconscious, as defined by Freud, is transindividual.

29. See Deleuze, *Negotiations*, 242. Henceforth Neg.

30. I explore this viewpoint in developing the concept of the adoption process in *La Technique et le temps 3*, 138ff.

31. Winnicott, *Playing and Reality*, 19. Henceforth PR.

32. For more on this idea, see note 39; and *Philosopher par accident*, 81. Henceforth PPA.

33. [Trans.] Télévision Française 1, or TF1, was the first nationwide television channel in France. Established as a public service in 1935, it was the sole national channel for twenty-eight years, going through a number of name changes, initially Radio-PTT Vision prior to World War II, Paris-Télévision during the German occupation, Télévision française in 1944. It was the first RTF (Radiodiffusion-télévision française) when a second channel emerged in 1963, and finally TF1 with the opening of the national bureau in 1975. TF1 was privatized in 1987.

34. [Trans.] In 2004, TF1 CEO Patrick Le Lay clarified the channel's aims, announcing that

there are many ways to speak about TV, but in a business perspective, let's be realistic: in the end, TF1's job is helping Coca-Cola, for example, sell its product. What *we* sell to Coca-Cola is *available human brain time*. This is where permanent change is located. Nothing is more difficult than getting access to it: we must always be on the lookout for popular programs, follow trends, surf on tendencies, all in a context in which information is speeding up, getting diversified and trivialized. [emphasis added]

35. [Trans.] The phrase "by the book" indicates, for Stiegler, that the proper understanding of x is invested in the *social narrative*, i.e., in the stories culture tells about itself, in various forms.

36. *Le Figaro*, 2 June 2007.

Chapter 2

1. Mendelssohn and Kant, *Qu'est-ce que les Lumières?* Henceforth QL. [Trans.] For citation specifics in "An Answer to the Question: What Is Enlightenment?" (henceforth WEK), see Kant.

2. For further discussion of this point, see *Mécréance et discrédit 1*, §31. For more on culture as the transmission of collective secondary retentions, see 152ff. Henceforth MD1.

3. See TT1, 185; and PPA, 49ff.

4. Freud, *On Metapsychology*, 38, 94. Henceforth OM.

5. *Scilicet* 1/1, 35. Henceforth Scil.

6. See Section 22.

7. Ibid.

8. [Trans.] "*Pouvoir, devoir, vouloir*, et surtout *savoir* le *croire* et l'*esperer* sont les infinitifs de la majorité."

9. [Trans.] It is important to note that for Kant "the Symbol" has numerous symbolic meanings and connections, in this case linking *Aufklärung* to the Catholic Church. One must ask whether this makes the notion of the Symbol more or less helpful.

10. [Trans.] Stiegler's case regarding the *pharmakon* is clearly made here; unclear in the transition from French to English is the transition, alluded to in Chapter 1, from *esprit* to its senses in English. This slippery word is vital to Stiegler's presentation; three short passages from *Réenchanter le monde* may help clarify things:

> 1. The *re-enchantment of the world* . . . is manifestly a reference to Max Weber, and to his analysis of disenchantment as an operation through which capitalism imposes itself on the world.
>
> But it is precisely also a reference to what Weber called the *spirit* [*esprit*] of capitalism: capitalism, according to Weber, initiates the process of disenchantment through an *enchantment*, through a new religious spirit [*esprit*] at capitalism's very origin under the names of *Protestantism, Reformation,* and *Lutheranism*—themselves preceded in large part by the appearance of a "techno-logy" of the spirit: the printing shop, which provided access to books *for all* (particularly the "faithful"), which also led to the origin of the "republic of letters," and finally to modern industrial democracy. (RM, 18)
>
> 2. We, the members of *Ars Industrialis*, think that a politics must be capable of espousing an industrial economy of the spirit [*de l'esprit*], without substituting it for an economic initiative but rather furnishing the framework for social regulations and public investments crystallizing a political *and spiritual* will—that is, elevating the level of individual and collective intelligence through the agency of a new form of public power that itself moves toward a new form of public will. (RM, 23)
>
> 3. Our age is menaced, throughout the world, by the fact that "*la vie de l'esprit*," "the life of the mind/spirit" [Trans.: now it becomes impossible to distinguish them], to use Hannah Arendt's words [Trans.: from *The Life of the Mind* (*La vie de l'esprit* in French), 1978], has completely succumbed to the imperatives of the market economy and of the return of investments of business concerns based on technology. . . . We will call them the "sector of technologies of the *esprit*" [*le secteur des technologies de l'esprit*] (despite the

metaphysical and theological overload weighing on this word, "*esprit,*" which we must also understand in its English sense, as "mind"). (RM, 27)

In other words, *both* "mind" and "spirit" are not only proper but vital translations of *esprit*, and simultaneously, since for Stiegler (and not just in the French) they are identical.

It is vital to remember that in translating *esprit* as "spirit," one is attempting to be (nearly) free of that "metaphysical and theological" loading Stiegler mentions, but that one must still attempt to maintain the sense of *esprit* in the sense in which Derrida uses it in *Specters of Marx* and which echoes Stiegler's, as a haunting (and brittle) energy all too easily lost, as either "mind" or "spirit."

11. For a further discussion of this connection, see TCD, 259ff. See also Anthony Giddens, who defines modernity differently, as a mode of expertise. I am in fundamental disagreement with him on this point, since expertise is what accomplishes what I call the *dissociation* of associated milieux. I develop this theme further later on (see p. 240) and in volume 2 of *Taking Care*, forthcoming [in French].

12. This idea forms the very core of *Ars Industrialis*; see http://www.arsindustrialis.org.

13. See *Le Figaro*, 2 June 2007; and Section 10.

14. The course was published by the *Magazine littéraire* two hundred years after the appearance of Kant's response to the investigation of the *Berlinische Monatsschrift*. It was then republished in *Dits et écrits 2*, 415ff. Henceforth DE2.

15. On the concept of an associated milieu, see RM, 52ff; TCD, 29ff; DDP, 74ff.

16. See references to A. Leroi-Gourhan in *Technics and Time 2*. Henceforth TT2. As we will see, Leroi-Gourhan is translating, as anthropology, what Aristotle had already said as philosophy.

17. To speak in Bachelardian terms. On this point, see also Lecourt, *Pour une critique de l'épistémologie*, 30. Henceforth CEL.

18. Foucault, *The Order of Things*, 87. Henceforth OT.

19. In the introduction to his edition of "What Is Enlightenment?" translated by Jocelyn Benoist, Dominique Lecourt emphasizes that "at the beginning of the 1730s, . . . a sense of the 'public' was created within an active bourgeoisie that wanted to be enlightened; this public began to extend into other levels of society that had recently become literate. Thus the wave of didactic books and dictionaries that were published, along with the publication of small literary works that fit into one's pocket."

20. See Kintzler, *Condorcet*. Henceforth Con.

21. "These are the forces of the intelligence that will bring about and augment . . . stronger, more durable, more ethical economic and social growth,"

François Fillon declared during a visit to the Orsay astrophysics laboratory (*Figaro*, 2 June 2007). See also my comments on E.-A. Seillière in MD2, 104–6.

22. Fillon, policy statement, 3 July 2007. The statement's concluding sections would have benefited from inclusion of more precise details. Henceforth FF.

23. [Trans.] In English in the original.

24. On the toxicity of human media, see my comments on Freud in MD3, §19, 89ff.

25. One of the premier conceptions of stupidity as a historical form was developed by Gustave Flaubert, first laid out in *Madame Bovary*, in which the figure of historical stupidity is the pharmacist, M. Homais. It is duplicated in *Bouvard et Pécuchet*, where the two central characters with these names finish by writing a *Dictionary of Received Ideas* in which historical stupidity is itself the focus of thought. It is for this reason that Raymond Queneau, in *Bâtons, chiffres et lettres* (henceforth RQ), can write: "If Madame Bovary is Flaubert . . . it is less evident that he is also Bouvard and Pécuchet. The requirements for taking this encyclopedic expedition with them—he tells us that he read more than *fifteen hundred volumes* in pursuit of this goal—could but confirm this connection." Flaubert writes in one of his letters: "Bouvard and Pécuchet invaded me to such a point that I became them. Their stupidity is mine and I am bursting with it" (RQ, 110). Bouvard and Pécuchet are copyists like him; like him they practice the *pharmakon* that is writing and that engenders that *always-minor* form of thought, literature (such as the *Dictionary of Received Ideas*), always minor in the eyes of philosophers—who nonetheless are writers (though such copyists hardly exist today). Who are the "pharmacists of the soul" if not doctors (if it is true that, as Kant tells us, one can be another's doctor only by teaching that soul to care for itself; this is precisely what Kant calls adulthood. Being able to take care of oneself presumes the capability of taking care of others—of being *responsible*).

26. Here I must specify that all technical media, insofar as they are epiphylogenetic, are also psychotechnical media insofar as they are mnemotechnical. This is how a world is constituted through its technicity: it configures forms of thought and psychic equipment according to psychomnesic characteristics that it misreads as a medium. Even so, all technics is not, properly speaking, psychotechnics: all technics is not aimed at capturing or forming attention, even if all technics contributes to this capture and this formation (or deformation).

27. Saudi Arabia this summer (2008) announced its intention to create a great university of international studies.

28. And this stupidity, like the Hydra, is always proteiform: it takes multiple forms, and these forms are those of heads, faces, mouths. Along these historic forms, and for our own times, and here in France, there is what Braudel calls French capitalism.

29. Fillon, *Déclaration de politique générale*.

30. This is the subject of *Réenchanter le monde* and the reason for the existence of *Ars Industrialis*.

31. I will return to this point, which is at the heart of the politics of the Institute for Research and Innovation at the Pompidou Centre, in *Le Temps des amateurs*, forthcoming.

32. See *De la misère symbolique 1*, 111–14ff.; and Section 15.

33. See TCD; RM, 41, 133 ; and Sections 17 and 18.

34. The problem is less one of *ontological* difference, which cannot think despite Heidegger's efforts, these *pharmaka* forming what he calls *Weltgeschichtlichkeit*, than of *pharmacological* difference. But this is not simply a matter of an impotence of aporia and undecidability that pervades Derrida's *infra*minor epigonality: it is, rather, as impotence's différance, a retreat of this impotence, a conquest of majority that is not, here, autonomy opposed to heteronomy but an individuation within an associated symbolic milieu that is also and always already a technical milieu.

35. [Trans.] SMS is the acronym for Short Message Service, by which short text messages are sent on cell phones and other devices, including pocket PCs. It was first developed in the early 1990s to connect a cell phone to a PC, then evolved into its current form.

In certain parts of the world SMS can be utilized to send voice messages as well. It is specifically designed for very short messages. Originally developed for telephone operators' service messages, it is now in universal use, with everexpanding applications (such as making submissions to television programs' polls). Many businesses have also adopted SMS for both internal and external communication.

Chapter 3

1. [Trans.] Stiegler's word here, and throughout this section, is *âme*, but the English "soul" does not resonate with his sense of mind control, in Kant, Plato, etc.; I have thus in the following translated it variously as "soul," "spirit," or "mind" (*esprit*) as sense and context dictate.

2. It would be important here to pay particular attention to the psychosomatotechniques found in Asian systems of self-care in which mind and body are not separated, giving rise to therapeutic systems completely different from the symptomatic one developed in the West since Hippocrates.

3. [Trans.] Constantin Guys, born in the Netherlands in 1802, was a cartoonist-illustrator with a long career in nineteenth-century France. He was famous for his illustrations of the "fashionable" world of the French Second Empire (1852–70). He had been part of the famous fight for Greek independence in his youth and had reported (in illustrations) on the Crimean War (1853–56) for *The*

Illustrated London News. Finally settling in Paris in the 1860s, Guys continued to work for the *News* as an illustrator, though at the same time achieving renown for his drawings of the artificial elegance of Parisian life under Napoleon III. Guys died in Paris in 1892. Baudelaire's "The Painter of Modern Life," his elegy to Guys published in 1863, was the first work of "art criticism" in the modern sense, placing Guys' work in its historical and aesthetic context and defining "modernity" as such.

4. [Trans.] The French text of Kant's short essay is radically divergent from the standard English translation used here: Kant's original and Stiegler's French are much more derisory and ironic. Stiegler:

Guardians who very amiably (through kindness) have taken it upon themselves to apply a high direction to humanity . . . after having made their cattle quite stupid, have then carefully ensured that these peaceful creatures are not permitted to dare to take the least step outside of the baby carriage in which they have been put, showing them the dangers threatening them should they try to venture out alone.

Note the echo of Plato's "guardians" in the *Republic,* enjoined to train the "heroes" who will govern the carefully censored *polis;* Kant exposes their *other side,* just as Stiegler does in the immediately following paragraphs.

5. Heidegger returns to this program in his account, citing Plato (*Sophist,* 242c), at the beginning of *Being and Time* (henceforth BT): "The being of beings 'is' itself not a being. The first philosophical step in understanding the problem of being consists in avoiding the *mython tina diēgeisthai,* in not 'telling a story,' that is, not determining being as beings by tracing them back in their origins to another being—as if being had the character of a possible being" (BT, 5). But this is in order to open the question of a *new mystagogy:* that of the *difference,* called "ontological," of a [sense of] being that is not *a* being—that is, according to my analysis, of a being not yet finished, whom I understand to be infinite in constituting *the object of desire.* On this point, see chapters 5 and 6 for my inquiry into the object of attention as the object of all desires; see also *Mystagogie—De l'art contemporain,* forthcoming.

6. *Règles pour le parc humain,* 44. Henceforth PS.

7. Fragment CXXIII, in *The Presocratics,* Gallimard, 173. Henceforth Pre.

8. *Meno,* 80a. Henceforth PM. "Since to research and to learn is nothing other than to remember oneself . . . there is no such thing as teaching, but only reminiscing."

9. On the question of identity, see Section 19.

10. On this subject, see in particular *Constituer l'Europe 1* (henceforth CE1), 63, 96; *Constituer l'Europe 2* (henceforth CE2), 11, 48, 90, 122; RM, 180, 240.

11. This is why, contrary to François Fillon, who imagines that "the education system no longer needs legislative reform; it needs to complete the structural

reform begun in 2005," I believe that France's project must be to redefine itself through an entirely different educational project, which does not simply require structural reform but a veritable revolution.

12. With the exception of the totalitarian structures of the social apparatus, contemporary with the birth of the cultural industries, whose goal is also the elimination of the psychic apparatus through psychotechnologies.

13. See MD1, 82–87.

14. On this subject, François Fillon says: "Faced with a culture of violence, I have only one order: yield to nothing! I use the word 'culture' intentionally, since our entire culture is implicated in its values and morals. We would have promised to act against the multi-recidivists: the legal project we will present respects our engagement. The delinquent instigators of serious acts, as recidivists, will be the object of painful reactions. We have also promised you to consider the delinquency of minors. Henceforth, minority will no longer be an official alibi for juvenile delinquents. By dint of having been released unpunished, certain young delinquents have concluded that society has neither the courage to re-try them nor the generosity to put them back on the right road. This is what must stop!"

15. If the question is one of cultural violence, i.e., the violation of culture, of which the "culture of violence," as François Fillon calls it, is but a part, and if "it is actually our entire society that is challenged in terms of values and morality, precisely to the extent that this "culture of violence" is produced through the psychopower of capture of brain time only "available" because it is *violence stripped of consciousness*: properly seen, it is not simply a question of asking that "audiovisual public service . . . clearly assumes its proper role," which would moreover necessitate from the outset that the prime minister specify how he conceives of this vocation. Whatever it is, such a vocation could be assumed only through, on the one hand, defining one part of a new legislative framework for audiovisual media in general, private as well as public, and, on the other, through implementation of an industrial politics of new media, whose elements were outlined in *Réenchanter le monde: La valeur esprit contre le populisme industriel.*

16. [Trans.] Stiegler's reference here is to organ-ology rather than to the standard sense of "organization"; hence the intrusive hyphen.

17. "Creation of a Ministry of Ecology, Development, and Long-Term Planning is part of the structuring of global policy we are going to implement. The 'point-man of the environment' to be named in the autumn will announce it." F. Fillon.

18. Sarkozy famously declared, on the evening of 6 May 2007, that "friendship means to accept that friends can think differently, and that . . . a great nation like the United States needs not to be an obstacle to the struggle against

global warming, but on the contrary to take the lead against it, since what is at stake is the end of humanity."

19. [Trans.] Throughout this section, Stiegler uses *liquidation* both as an echo of the liquidation of a business enterprise, the final dispersal of assets, and the Derridean "dissemination" of power, the spreading out of intensity toward not only entropy, in the sense of the Second Law of Thermodynamics, but also in Deleuze's sense, a "liquidation" on the plan of immanence that, inhabiting the phenomenological arena, has to do with the relationship between consciousness and the unconscious, between the sociocultural and the individual.

20. This generational confusion leads irresistibly to the discourse of "growth" and to the *global* malaise of which it is a symptom. François Fillon is entirely correct to emphasize the dynamism of the new industrial nations, and in particular that of their youth. But it would be wrong to underestimate their various problems, which are being revealed at such a vertiginous pace (e.g., the results of China's growth rate). These problems are storm clouds gathering on the world's horizon, in a sky full of future storms that will soon be weighed down with hundreds of millions of tons of carbon dioxide that contemporary culture is jettisoning there, and that the dark and inevitably destructive industrial methods are filling with toxic molecules. The destruction of intergenerational structures is now taking place in Asia and the rest of the world as well as in the older industrial countries, with the same effects: incivility and negative sublimation (cf. MD2, 74, 88–89; and MD3, 95).

21. François Fillon, who generally appeals to reason, addresses himself particularly to his more erudite representatives (to those who make public use of their rationality, in addressing a public that reads: "The national energy would produce only very imperfect accomplishments if it were deprived of its principal resource: I mean French intelligence. . . . The immense group of our academics, biologists, mathematicians, philosophers, jurists, and historians who have made us shine must not be halted at the threshold of a new century where, precisely, the power of grey matter will determine our future"). Furthermore, Fillon asserts, with regard to necessary reforms in the universities: "I will not be one of those who will sacrifice fundamental research on the pretext that it would be unproductive *in the short term.*"

22. On the vast question of fear and its current exploitation, see Lecourt, *Contre la peur* (henceforth CP); and Crepon, *La Culture de la peur.*

23. See Sections 32 and 50.

24. See Heidegger, *Poetry, Language, Thought.* Henceforth PLT.

25. On this point in particular, see MD2, 20; and on the difference between consistence, existence, and subsistence, see MD1, 69–70, 125–27.

26. As Cyril Morana notes in *Eclairer les Lumières* (henceforth CM): "For Mendelssohn, there indeed exists simply 'a danger of catastrophic diversions

from the effort of understanding, from the acquisition of knowledge,' an abuse of reason whose disastrous consequences would consist of the development of egoism and immoralism. Do Enlightenment thinkers think themselves to be the definitive progress of reason, or of decadence, systematically consecutive in the development of human knowledge?" (CM, 47).

27. On these questions, see MD1, 123.

[Trans.] The French *motif* translates as "reason," in the sense of "the reason for doing x." Stiegler's, and Weber's, indication here is that "reason" has become detached from causality, let alone social or cultural causality, and is thus in aid of destructive psychotechnologies.

28. See Section 39.

29. Grammatization as becoming discrete, which characterizes the development of hypomnesic systems as techniques of attention capture, as psychotechnics and then as psychotechnologies. On this process of grammatization, see TCD, 157.

30. The second volume of *Prendre soin*, and *Le Temps des amateurs*, both forthcoming.

31. Neg, 245.

32. Weber, *The Protestant Ethic*. Henceforth PE.

33. I have analyzed a number of aspects of this in CE1, 12, 20.

34. See MD1, 92–94, 143–47.

35. On the question of design, see CE1, 59; Flamaux, *Le Design, Essais sur les théories et les pratiques;* and *Les Entretiens du nouveau monde industriel,* a conference co-organized at the Pompidou Centre (27 and 28 November 2007) by the *l'Institut de recherche et d'innovation* (IRI), *l'École Nationale Supérieure de Création Industrielle* (ENSCI), and Cap Digital. Proceedings forthcoming.

36. See Section 2.

37. On the superego and a critique of the law in general, see MD2, 53.

38. Technologies of a collective intelligence are in the process of development in a number of ways. Sadly, their conception and creation are not being accompanied by a scientific and industrial politics worthy of the name. As a result, given that such technologies are also *pharmaka*, they are often used to weaken individual as well as collective intelligence. Barbara Cassin has explored this problem in *Google-moi* (henceforth Cassin). I will return to it in *Le Temps des amateurs*, forthcoming.

39. This issue is what *Ars Industrialis* calls "technologies of the spirit" in both the technical and the symbolic context that has appeared along with numeric networks.

40. Regarding economic warfare it will be necessary to address internationally, as is the case with all wars, the question of this war's rules and those of any possible peace treaty.

41. [Trans.] "Suffrage," in the sense in which Condorcet uses it, was one of the central ideas of the Enlightenment. The "Condorcet method," though specifically aimed at producing fair elections, extended to many other ideas as well, such as the adoption of a liberal economy; free and equal public education for all, regardless of race, gender, or class; constitutionalism in the form of equal legal rights for women and people of all races. Condorcet was particularly interested (within the Enlightenment context of an informed citizenry, "the literate world") in the defense of human rights in general, and of the rights of women and blacks in particular: as an abolitionist, he became an active participant in the Society of the Friends of the Blacks in the 1780s. Somewhat ironically, given his use by Stiegler, Condorcet was very much in favor of the (Enlightenment) ideals espoused by the newly formed United States (Benjamin Franklin was a close friend) and throughout his adult life proposed numerous economic, administrative, educational, legal, and political strategies aimed at transforming France. Because of his long-term association with the monarchy, during the Revolution Condorcet first went into hiding, then, when he felt increasingly unsafe, attempted to escape. He was caught, captured, and imprisoned at Bourg-la-Reine, where he died under ambiguous circumstances in 1792 (quite possibly murdered to prevent his being brought back to Paris for execution, which, given his general popularity, might have been felt to be dangerous). He was buried in a common grave in Bourg-la-Reine. He was reinterred in the Pantheon in 1989, but since all record of his body's location had been lost in the nineteenth century, his coffin there is empty.

42. I will explore further into this issue in *La Technique et le temps 5, La guerre des esprits*, forthcoming.

Chapter 4

1. "*Consciousness*," whose initial meaning is "with knowledge" (*con-scientia*), within the community of a shared knowledge, also has the sense of "moral consciousness" or "conscience," a usage that spread rapidly throughout the seventeenth century, along with the philosophy of the subject.

   [Trans.] The French *conscience* means both "consciousness" and "conscience," as Stiegler indirectly indicates here. Both meanings have central importance in the battle for intelligence and the formation of long circuits of psychosocial knowledge, attention, and the formation of maturity.

2. To read more on the logic of the worst, see MD2, 41, 74, 94.

3. See RM, 20ff., 112ff.; and TCD, 145ff., 151ff.

4. Livingstone and Bovill, *Children and Their Changing Media Environment*, cited by Dufour in *On achève bien les hommes*.

5. See *Archive of Pediatrics and Adolescent Medicine*, vol. 161, May 2007.

6. See *Pediatrics*, vol. 113, 708.

7. [Trans.] Inserm, Institut nationale de la santé et de la recherche médicale (National Institute of Health and Medical Research), is the sole French organization dedicated entirely to biological and medical research and to general health. It specializes in the study of human maladies, from the most common to the rarest.

8. I have commented extensively on this subject in MD2, 130.

9. And through the systems of care that are also mechanisms of social assistance. In this regard, the current political system in Great Britain for single mothers is entirely scandalous and indicates what kinds of social and moral regressions can result from a dominant populist discourse. Under the pretext that delinquency is more frequent in these families, the mothers are now obliged to subject themselves to a system of oversight that involves putting them and their children on an "index" [of likely delinquency].

10. [Trans.] Jules Ferry (1832–93), lawyer, statesman, and politician, as an ardent republican, participated in the first republican ministry of the Third Republic, serving from 1879 to 1885 first as minister of education and then of foreign affairs. Ferry remains well known today for his work in both of the following positions: (1) his energetic support of French imperialism and (2) his reform of the French education system. In the present context these seem strange bedfellows:

1. In 1870, after France's military defeat by Germany (and at least in part as compensation for it, given France's economic conditions at the time) Ferry first articulated the idea of France's building a global colonial empire. He declared that "the superior races have a right because they have a duty: it is their duty to civilize the inferior races." He then led the negotiations that established the French "protectorate" in Tunis, the occupation of Madagascar, the exploration of the Congo and Niger, and the conquest of what was to become known as Indochina.

2. Vehemently opposed to the clerical/religious education then offered in France, Ferry was responsible for reorganizing the entire French system of public education. The "Ferry Laws" of 1881 and 1882 made primary education in France free, nonclerical (laic), and mandatory; as a republican, Ferry (somewhat schizophrenically) championed universal education as a way of uniting the French "nation" as a concept (what Stiegler might call an "ideal object"). These laws established both universal access to education and French as the Republic's sole language; though these laws were certainly important in unifying the French nation-state under the Third Republic, they also brought about the virtual extinction of a number of regional languages that have only recently begun to be studied again.

11. See Section 19.

12. [Trans.] *La Troisième République*, an ostensibly republican parliamentary democracy that governed France for seventy years, from May 1870, during the Franco-Prussian War, to July 1940, with the Nazi invasion and the country's subsequent fall, lurching from crisis to crisis, between the Second Empire and the Vichy regime. Adolphe Thiers, *le Libérateur du Territoire* and the first leader of the Third Republic, called 1870s republicanism "the form of government that divides France least," not a ringing endorsement. In general, France seemed to agree to being a republic again, though the Third Republic was never terribly popular. Nonetheless, it was the first genuinely stable republican government the French had ever seen, and the first to win the support of the majority of the population. Ironically, it was initially intended to be a temporary government, "filling in" until a new king could be crowned; therefore, most monarchists played a part in the republican institutions of government, thereby giving those institutions significant (though not universal) elite support (the "Legitimists" were virulently antirepublican, and *Action française*, a monarchist movement founded in 1898, was influential through the 1930s). No king was ever crowned.

The failure of the Third Republic came about not as a result of its "liberal democratic" institutions, modeled on Enlightenment ideas with which we are concerned here, but because it did not successfully resist the Nazi invasion.

13. I develop this point in TT3, 142.

14. [Trans.] Leroi-Gourhan's 1943 work, remarkably, has not been translated from the French.

15. [Trans.] The veins of cross references here, from Rimbaud back to Pindar then forward to Nietzsche, each of which has its own set of valences, are forbiddingly dense. Briefly:

In his letter of May 1871 to Paul Demeny, following his famous declaration, Rimbaud says that "j'assiste à l'éclosion de ma pensée: je la regarde, je l'écoute" [I witness the blossoming of my thought: I look at it, I listen to it]; this is a new sense of the "making" (*poeisis*) of art-as-thought. As Stiegler suggests, this is indeed "the very poetry of human being," in a number of senses ancient and modern.

The Pindaric odes form the basis of much of Rimbaud's poetry, i.e., his thought, and of the "Sophoclean" aspect of Nietzsche's.

Nietzsche's "comment deviens ce que tu es" [How to Become What You Are] is the subtitle of *Ecce Homo*, which Nietzsche wrote in October/November 1888 (one year before his "break" in Turin). The book title's reference (John 19:5) to Pilate's words regarding the Messiah brought low ("Behold *the man*") resonates through Nietzsche's entire sense of the subject ("a fiction") and of the "soul" (a bundle of chaotic *treiben*) "redeemed" by art.

Ecce Homo is an "autobiography," but unlike any other ever written: it is a work of (nonnaturalistic, Dionysian) art that should be compared to Van Gogh rather than to any other *writer* of Nietzsche's day (or ours). On the one hand, it is all about style; on the other hand, *that is the portrait.*

For Rimbaud as for Nietzsche (and Stiegler), the chimera of identity resides both in and outside language.

16. See Section 15.

17. Marcuse, *Eros and Civilization.* Henceforth EC.

18. All symbolic activity is idiomatic in this sense, and all human activity is symbolic.

19. On this issue, it is possible to download the conference containing the seminar "Finding New Weapons" at www.arsindustrialis.org, in particular the session of 18 October 2006 entitled "Idiomatic Amnesia."

20. I return to this point in *Mystagogies. De l'art contemporain.* Henceforth Myst.

21. See my preface to IPC, xi.

22. Husserl, *Crisis of European Sciences,* 196. Henceforth Huss.

23. For more on this formation, see particularly Foucault, *Discipline and Punish.* Henceforth DP. I will spend a good deal of time on this question in volume 4 of *Technics and Time* in order to show that the founders of cities, "nomothetes," are at once legislators and geometricians, and that it is impossible to think of political individuation, which begins with the pre-Socratics, independently of the scientific thought that also emerged from them and their movement precisely because writing constitutes the very organology that is common to both the law and all rational forms of knowledge. This is why Kant could write (wrongly, but not without reason) that "one could truly call the advent of writing the advent of the world" (*Réflexions sur l'éducation,* 106; henceforth RE).

24. See TCD, 158ff.

25. Already, as I have pointed out a number of times, the organological stage of literary grammatization appearing first in the seventh century BCE was transformed so as to produce either an intensification of symbolic life and the associated milieux of which it consists or the decomposition of that life through the hypomnesic and logographic dissociation of those same milieux. And it is essential to note here that the "Sophist" was originally *grammatistēs,* the one who taught hypomnesic logographia. Equally, it should be noted that in the Gospels, the scribes are regularly contradicted by the Messiah (see, e.g., Mark 12:38). I will not comment further here on this last point; on the other hand, I have often analyzed the conflict between philosophy and sophistics, laying out the consequences for the current problems in the educational system.

26. "Dissociation" is the analytic moment of knowledge that is, however, only an effective knowledge if it is capable of engendering a moment of *synthesis.*

27. [Trans.] Though it is true that *otium* is generally translated as "leisure," it is useful to remember that it can also be translated as "literary study," since the

latter was (and significantly may still be) thought to be a function of the former: no reflective literary study without the leisure time in which to do it.

28. That do not exist in the sense that they are mental constructions not to be found in what they allow to be thought, and that is a dimension of or in the world, such as "space." The objects of reason, like the geometric point that cannot exist since it is not spatial, are thus both absolutely necessary artifacts and the infinite objects of desire, in the double sense that not being in the world, they are in a different domain from that of finite, calculable objects, and in the sense in which these objects are "unfinished" in that knowledge is only rational as comprehension of the individuation transformed by this comprehension— and thus again always already unknown.

29. See Kintzler, *Condorcet.* [Trans.] *Refonder,* "to reconstruct on new bases with new objectives."

30. Kant, *Critique of Pure Reason.* Henceforth CPR.

31. See *le Bailly: methodeuô* means "to follow closely, in a race," derived from *odos,* "road." [Trans.] *Le Bailly* is the great Greek/French dictionary.

32. This is the law of the process of adoption, producing unity within the nonidentical. I have developed this point further in *Technics and Time 3,* chapter 3, "*I* and *We,* the American Politics of Adoption."

33. On the question of the *one,* see *Aimer, s'aimer, nous aimer,* 17, 42, 51, 53, 69. Henceforth ASN.

34. The domain of the *one* is the desymbolization inherent in dissociated milieux.

35. See TCD, 221.

36. See RM, 124ff.

37. I mean three things here:

1. that the transformation of an instrumental medium that consists of hypomnesic knowledge in general could be accomplished only through a sharing of the research and construction of its objects as well as their discourse (their critique), and of the diffusion of all methods and results (theorems, new discoveries, etc.) by which they claim to be objects of knowledge. This diffusion could not be limited to teaching;

2. that these objects are no longer merely those of regional or fundamental ontologies nor even ontogeneses, but of genealogies in which *gignesthai* and the fictionalizing of *what is,* in light of the *artifactual transformation* of *what is,* is the reality of technoscientific knowledge *as* knowledge itself in hyperindustrial democracies;

3. that this hypomnesic fact, which Bachelard called "phenomenotechnics," obfuscated at the very origin of these democracies through the education system in the wake of metaphysics in general, can now no longer remain concealed and is not thinkable within the framework of an ontology: it requires

thought as a process. Simondon's system of individuation (which is nonetheless not a dogma, which must be critiqued, which remains *onto*genetic) is the departure point for any such theory.

38. See DE4, 892, and my commentary in Section 37.

Chapter 5

1. On disaffection as disaffectation, see MD2, 124ff.

2. Hayles, "Hyper and Deep Attention." Henceforth GD.

3. [Trans.] *Flux* is both "flux" and "flow"; in some cases (e.g., Husserl), translations maintain "flux"; in others, Stiegler's clear sense calls for "flow." And because of the psychotechnologies under consideration here, "flux" can also be "stream."

4. This is an issue that Jean-Pierre Changeux, in a paragraph entitled "To Learn Is to Eliminate," addresses in *Neuronal Man: The Biology of Mind* (henceforth NM) in these terms: "Epigenesis has the power of selection over preformed synaptic manifestations. To learn is to stabilize preformed synaptic combinations. It is also to eliminate all others" (304).

5. *Deep attention*, of which there are numerous types and give rise to both critical and rational attention, is less an attitude of conservation than of observation.

6. A domestic animal is in this sense doubtless somewhat less "vigilant," less savage, and less sensitive to any dangers threatening it: less in a "multitasking mode," in part because it is misled by its principal predators: humans, who have domesticated it, cared for it (i.e., taken charge of certain of its "tasks," chiefly that of avoiding other predators—but only after having hunted the animal down and, in the end, domesticated it; we will see, in *Taking Care 2*, that hunting is itself, in certain conditions, a system of care), after having been a predator very close to the animal, and without doubt quite savage.

7. [Trans.] To "bootstrap" is "to pull oneself up by one's own bootstraps," i.e., to advance or rise with little or no assistance from others.

8. In the final analysis, hyperattention shares many traits with the solicitations of audiovisual objects, including monochannel, whose effect is the loss of a certain kind of attention, leading to surfing; on this matter, Jacques Brodeur explains that contemporary Hollywood cinema employs very tightly structured sequences, ceaselessly soliciting and stimulating attention.

9. This process gives access to the transindividual that attentive consciousness can achieve only by returning it (i.e., individuating it) according to the rules governing the simultaneous construction of anamnesis and dialectic, and thus a *dianoia*: an individuation of the subject *and* of its object (the object of observation, not simply of self-preservation). See the beginning of this section.

10. [Trans.] Stiegler's use of *littéralement*, literally "literally," which in *Technics and Time* distinguishes the written/literary from the oral, here has a slightly different meaning. Linked to Kant's sense of "a public that reads," it should catch the sense in which Kant/Stiegler means it: available to those who can read and write, who are literate. I have therefore translated *littéralement* as "literately"; thus, further on, *littéralisé* becomes "literatized." Kant despised neologisms and felt we should all be speaking Greek, Latin, and of course German, but in a hypertechnological age, "ized" nicely depicts the transformative process of grammatization.

11. Gould, *Écrits 1*, 52 (henceforth Gould); and During, "Logics of Performance" (henceforth LP).

Gould's "accident" is in certain respects comparable to what happens when one goes to the library or a bookstore to search for a book, and what one finds is a different book and is thus thrust into a dilemma that also produces a sort of accidental attention, which is often a source of invention. This also often happens on the Internet as the site of constant surfing. Quite interesting possibilities for surfing exist there, a virtue of accidental exploration and exploitation within numeric organology just as there is virtue in video games Katherine Hayles tries to learn.

12. Barbara Cassin's book on Google's grammatization of the world—which she does not analyze as grammatization—opens up a useful critique of Google's entrepreneurial ideology but neglects these aspects, which greatly limits the force of a critique that is, moreover, very Platonic, which is surprising coming from a philosopher who has contributed a great deal to the reevaluation of sophistics. Aristotle recommends taking the Sophists literally at their word when they pose their problems, then turning them into questions of logic: to reverse them as psychotechnical, noetic questions. We must do the same thing today with psychotechnologies—and remember that in the Academy, Aristotle is reputed to have taught rhetoric (cf. Robin, *Platon*, 9; henceforth Robin).

13. An international program of research into these questions should be initiated, for example, in partnership with the University of Southern California and involving, in France, the Instituts Universitaires de Formation des Maîtres (IUMF) as well as the École Normale Supérieure (ENS) and the Centre national de documentation pédagogique (CNDP).

14. Contrary to what Wolfgang Iser claims in *The Act of Reading*.

15. This is a matter of what, when I was at INA, I called "multisupport editions"; it was in that framework that Jacques Derrida and I published *Ecographies of Television*, which was first a video recording for which I had envisaged a numeric edition in which the book would have been a mode of access to the recording, which in turn would give access to other Derridean resources through an index created in hypertext. I had launched such a program at the Institute

for Research and Innovation at the Pompidou Centre, where I developed the software *Timelines* designed for recording what are called *lectures signées, regards signés, écoutes signées*, objects of deep attention that are not books. See www.iri. centrepompidou.fr.

16. See Section 36.

17. See TCD, 129ff.

18. [Trans.] Both words Stiegler uses here, *élément politique*, obviously have multiple senses; as for the second, though, "policy" resonates with the re-creation of the central education system. Since Stiegler bases so much of his program on a Greek root, I have chosen to emphasize a resonance with *polis* and the political instead.

19. MD2, 74, 89.

20. Aristotle, *Metaphysics A*, 980b30. See my commentary on this text in the concluding section of *Mécreance et Discrédit 1*.

21. See RM, 117.

22. Brodeur, http://data.edupax.org/precede/public/Assets/divers/documentation/1_articles/1_067_Autre_Avenue_fin_novembre06.pdf. Henceforth Brodeur.

23. *Métro*, 5 June 2007.

24. Ibid.

25. Cited by Al Gore in *Time*, 16 May 2007.

26. *Métro*, 6 June 2007.

27. *Télévision et fonction parentale*, http://www.unaf.fr/IMG/pdf/Television_et_fonction_Parentale.pdf.

28. babyfirsttv.com/fr/parents.

Chapter 6

1. I addressed this subject in MD2, 124, as a particular case of what is called a process of disaffection and disaffectation through cognitive as well as affective saturation.

2. [Trans.] "Agribusiness" generally refers to the combined elements of the "food industry," from farming (seeds, equipment, chemicals, fertilizers) to distribution (trucking, processing) to consumption (marketing, wholesale and retail sales, regulation). It has two connotative senses: (1) descriptive: the group of activities and industries involved in food production, and (2) pejorative: the industrialized mass production of food, ranging from corporate farms to huge chains of supermarkets.

3. Gasmi and Grolleau, *Économie de l'information*.

4. The Gasmi and Grolleau article shows precisely this: "This paper is also an

argument in favor of a reconciliation of the cognitive sciences, economics, and marketing, allowing for a pluri-disciplinary approach to things in real time."

5. [Trans.] The vital connection here, apart from the *attention/attendre* connection, is that "waiting" is the negative theology of action: as the act of inaction *and* as anticipation *attente* is itself infinite, in that as a condition it is not reliant on any *end to waiting*: waiting *is*. That waiting, anticipation, is endless means that when one is "in" it, one should be patient: waiting means patience. But to be patient requires reflection (overcoming immediate gratification); reflection requires an object, i.e., focus. Thus, "attention" connotes "patient, focused waiting." Each of these elements contributes to Stiegler's sense of attention and attention formation: immaturity must overcome impatience and lack of focus to become mature, patient, and focused. To learn this means learning *critical attention*, which must be learned (is not "natural," in Babyfirst terms).

To see the other (parodic) side of this phenomenon, see *En attendant Godot*, in which the waiting (*attendant*) is endless/patient: the play's two acts could easily become two million, and Didi and Gogo are "resigned" to (patient about) their "assignment" (this might require another volume on both "attention" and the "sign")—not focused, however, but dispersed across all of world thought and literature (from the Bible to Baudelaire), or else focused only on Godot and his "arrival," though "he" (?) never arrives and may not exist—*qui sait?*

6. The expression "structural coupling" comes from Humberto Maturama and Francisco Varela.

7. We might recall that a former minister of education, François Bayrou, opposed the "regression" to mental calculation in primary education.

8. In terms of agribusiness, it is as though these economic "normatives" are like a herd of cattle, consisting of specific, calculable, definite amounts of attention no longer a function of the indeterminate, open nature of the human brain's plasticity—as if it were possible to reduce this indeterminability in order to control it more closely. The basis of this reasoning is the exclusion, a priori, of the possibility of any choice of foodstuffs outside of the intelligence associated with agriculture and of food itself.

9. [Trans.] "Proletarian" for Stiegler does not mean "worker" nor "exploited worker" in the traditional Marxian sense, but rather the cog in the social wheel that has been deprived of all skills, let alone expertise, thus of knowledge, and *thus* of any participation in the critical process of collective intelligence (and thus of identity). The Stieglerian prole has no *savoir-faire* and thus no *savoir-vivre*.

10. See MD1, 116, 187ff.

11. On this point, see ASN, 64ff.; PPA, 48ff.; *De la misère symbolique 1*, 134 (henceforth MS1).

12. Neotenics is a central focus of Dany-Robert Dufour's *On achève bien les*

hommes. [Trans.] Neotenics, in biology and zoology, is the retention of immature traits into adulthood or the reaching of sexual maturity prematurely, e.g., during the larval stage.

In Stiegler's sense, the neotenic extension of immaturity would *prevent* the reaching of any maturity other than the chronological: mental children in adult bodies, precisely the central goal of the psychotechnologies of control employed by programming industries and combated by programming institutions.

13. Structural couplage is a particular case of transductional relations. [Trans.] Transduction, as employed by Gilbert Simondon and Stiegler, is, as Simondon says, "an operation, physical, biological, mental, social, by which an activity is gradually disseminated within a particular domain, this dissemination being based on local structuring of the domain: each region of this structuration is then used as a structuring principle in the following region" (*L'individu et sa genèse psycho-biologique*, 30; henceforth IG). Simondon also calls transduction a "method for mental discovery. The method consists of following a being's emergence in order to engender thought simultaneously with the object's development" (IG, 32). Transduction is thus an unending process (operation) of the development of knowledge and intelligence through the combined forces of technics and the mind.

14. [Trans.] Stiegler's double-play with *majority* should not be lost here: "democracy" is inherently governance by those who are capable of taking responsibility—who are mature in the Kantian sense. Stiegler's ubiquitous distinction between *minorité* ("minority status," or "immaturity") and *majority* ("adult status," or "maturity") means that democracy is *règne de la majorité*, both "rule by the majority" and "rule by those who are mature."

15. Gilles Deleuze's sense of marketing as "the science of societies of control" is clearly evident here. Heidegger says the science he calls the *Ereignis* of the *Gestell* is cybernetics.

16. Cited by Guiland in *S'intéresser à l'attention*. Henceforth HG.

17. The "economy of attention" is a new field of cognitive science as applied to management and marketing, following technologies of motivation that I have shown (CE1, 100) have led to general demotivation.

18. I am employing this word in the sense in which it is used in connectionist cognitive theories.

19. Programs in which the cognitive sciences and artificial life also model attention through robots that can understand only what is already preloaded into their nervous systems and who do not model early, then adult synaptogenesis, nor processes of identification, the robot's attentional behavior appearing to be far less attentive than that of a stag taking care of its herd: "the mechanisms involved in managing the robot's attention are absolutely clear. For example, it is easy to teach a robot the names of certain red objects so long as the robot

is 'innately' attracted to the color. If such an inclination is absent from the robot's attention mechanisms, interacting with it becomes much more complex" (see Kaplan, *Automates intelligents*). What is missing here is the question of an individuation that requires the preindividual and transindividuation. However, it is very interesting to see how Frédéric Kaplan describes the research done on robots as possible modalities of what I call *general experimental organology*—and then to inquire into the genetic modeling of anamnesis through the hypomnesic processes of a new genre, the robotic. I mean *general experimental organology* in the prehistoric sense in which it was an experimental technology practiced as a method for remaking paleohuman behavior (on this theme, see Eric Boëda's work), and in the sense in which the COStech laboratory (UTC) laid out the procedures of experimental phenomenology (see the work of Charles Lenay). As in all models of behavior, robotics is here a specific stage of the grammatization process. Grammatization is before all else a formal modality of reproducibility; and the robotic, especially as Frédéric Kaplan implements it, is a form of the mechanical reproducibility of human psychomotor phenomena to some extent constructing an experimental heuristic of the models of human existence through their reproduction—that is, through their modeling. The problem here, as in cognitive science in general (with the exception of spatial cognition; see TT2), is that the robotic paradigm neglects to think the status of the robotic *for the robot reproducing what amounts to psychomotor human behavior* as it develops, reproducing the human, from the essential human *and thus robotic* capacity, itself to produce artifacts before anything else, first of all tools (of which robots are the automatized hypomnesic extensions), but also language as the artifactual fruits of transindividuation. In other words, what establishes a model are not functions themselves but the capacity to reproduce functions and while doing so to transform them; this means reproducing their evolutionary dynamics (what I have described elsewhere as a process of defunctionalization and refunctionalization) as psychomotor correlates of technical evolution. This approach would require thinking in terms of a libidinal economy and an organization of desire, neither of which seems to be envisaged by the experimental organology previously described, and this is particularly striking when Frédéric Kaplan evokes the mother/nourisher relationship while making no reference to Winnicott's work.

20. See CE2, 100.

21. *Prise de forme*: taking form in the sense Simondon gives it. See IG, 42ff. [Trans.] Simondon's idea here is that the *relation* between attention as the flow of consciousness and the *object* of attention as that which captures this flow is transductive, that the latter does not proceed from the former; rather, the latter is constituted *in* the former. This is what distinguishes *object* from *thing*: the thing is outside of attention, but not the object, which is only an object for a subject. The relation between the two is a world that transcends

this relation (and in which there are things), but this world is itself fabricated organologically, in part as a symbolic retentional deposit (i.e., as tertiary retentions), and as such constitutes the medium or element of this relation as well as its preindividual ground. In other words, I am not here suggesting a return to a metaphysics of the subject but a rethinking of the subject in terms of individuation; the relation of attention and its object is the very course of individuation in its narrowest sense, but also where it is fabricated, properly speaking, as the formation of circuits of transindividuation, since this "psychic" attention can truly be produced only insofar as it becomes collective and as such literally takes part in transindividuation.

22. Analyses such as Jeremy Rifkin's in the *Age of Access*, 126. Henceforth Rifkin.

23. These circuits are traced in the discursive practices Foucault describes in *The Archaeology of Knowledge*, 260. Henceforth AK.

24. Husserl, *Origin of Geometry*. Henceforth OG.

25. On collective secondary retentions, see MD2, 35n1.

26. [Trans.] In the following, Stiegler is ranging across the various senses of *lettre*, from "the letter itself" (as prior to meaning) to the specifics of any disciplinary knowledge (which must be learned *à la lettre*, i.e., exactly, but also through letters as both written and spoken language and "letters" in the sense of "arts and letters," as a disciplinary body of literate knowledge). In order to pursue maturity, one must be *lettré*, well read—which also means capable of critical thought as part of the process of becoming literate.

Chapter 7

1. Plato, *Lesser Hippias*, 363a. Henceforth LH.

2. A *dogmatic* rational attention becomes, by that very fact, irrational: reason is what remains open to its unfinished nature. But this very unfinishedness opens out the permanent possibility of a mystagogic reversion since it is itself not explicable or understandable: it can only be experienced and individuated. It is not possible to understand individuation, says Simondon, other than by in-dividuat*ing* it, making it escape from itself through its very understanding itself, which means that an unknown that remains in principle unknowable is the very principle of its knowability.

3. [Trans.] Stiegler's phrase here is "son sommet comme *embarras*, ce que le Grec nomme l'aporia"; *embarras* can of course be translated as "embarrassment," but also as "difficulty" or "perplexity"; since *aporia* has come to be so closely associated with its Derridean usage, as *impasse* (which is also derived from the Greek notion of *aporia* as "impassability"), I have simply left it to do its own work, with the occasional reference to barriers or limits.

4. PM, 81a.

5. But this *défaut*, this impasse, is not a lack [*faire défaut* is commonly translated as "lack"]. I am closer here to Deleuze than to Lacan.

[Trans.] Stiegler's phrase is *où elle lui fait défaut*; *défaut* is such a key word for Stiegler that one can never limit it to a single meaning, particularly since he immediately points out that *défaut* should not be seen as "lack"; his point is that the philosopher never sees wisdom whole or clearly but always partially, faultily, in default. But even though wisdom can never be totalized, it can be *theorized*; "it" is a chimera; thus my translation of *elle lui fait défaut* as "chimerical."

6. "The object of desire" as Plato and Aristotle present it, Plato defining philosophy as love (*The Symposium*), Aristotle making of *theos* the object of *all* desires (*On the Soul*), where philosophy is an ontotheology as the discourse on what is desirable—on what can only give itself through a *process* leading from *dunamis* (power) to *energeia* (action). And the route to action [*passage à l'acte*] is clearly the route to desire. Hegel, and Spinoza before him, understood that Aristotle's idea of desire is linked to that of processuality in which being can only be thought as the movement to action of a power Simondon analyzes as the preindividual. For more on this issue, see Simondon's "L'inquiétante étrangeté de la pensée et la pétaphysique de Pénélope," the preface of *L'Individuation psychique et collective*.

[Trans.] Stiegler's own route to action occurs in a double sense in his *Passage à l'acte* (*Acting Out*): first as the "acting out" of criminal behavior in the context of which Stiegler's life was altered to what might be called a *passage au-delà de l'acte*—the life of the philosopher. The Aristotelian *energeia* Stiegler devotes to the aporia of philosophy, the teaching of philosophy, indeed to education in general, is a living manifestation of the process he describes here.

7. It might be objected here that what distinguishes knowledge from technics, for Greek philosophy, is that it is apodictic, while technics is precisely *not* demonstrable and remains the fruit of inductive, and therefore empirical, knowledge. Consequently, one might say that technics is what remains mysterious, like magic, whereas knowledge is by nature clear, distinct, etc. But one would be mistaken: if the understanding could become an automatizable technique (like technology), exactly reproducible through an algorithm and thus calculable, it would be because, as Husserl shows (in *The Crisis of European Sciences*), it has lost its intuitive dimension, and because this is irreducibly affective: reason is a motif that is initially *an emotion*.

8. These are the transformations reproduced in the pedagogic process in the course of a collective individuation within a regulated, and ideally associated, milieu: the construction of the object in a class, whether in an individual tutorial or a collective classroom, is a co-individuation (1) of the object, (2) of the subject studying the object, (3) of the educator accompanying the subject and

providing access to the object—always according to the disciplinary rules covering many differing forms but that are always subjected to the constraints of explication and argumentation. The attention constructing this object works through a process not only of co-individuation but of *trans*individuation as the sharing of significations and, in fact, of significations that can be made explicit and can be argued, which is why the process must properly be called *critical transindividuation*.

9. All kinds of new physical and psychic maladies proliferate here.

10. Plato, *Alcibiades*, 127c–127d. Henceforth Al.

11. Foucault, *Birth of the Clinic*. Henceforth BC.

12. Foucault, "The Meshes of Power." Henceforth Meshes.

13. Biopower had been a Foucauldian commitment from his first texts, on medicalization in Georges Canguilhem's work, and from the first questions regarding the "norm" in *Discipline and Punish*.

14. See DP, 190.

15. See Section 20.

16. Foucault himself emphasizes that this is a radical sense of *epimētheia*, meaning both self-care, as we have already seen, and administration.

17. See Section 20.

18. This was the case when one day I disagreed with one of my professors in the midst of an oral exam, which is usually and appropriately called an "interrogation." I am thinking here of Mme Risbec, my fourth-form mathematics teacher, who was also my main teacher. I particularly remember one day when she had me demonstrate a theorem on the basis of a lesson in a geometry text by MM. Lebossé and Hemery. At the end of my demonstration, it turned out that she and I disagreed on the answer to the problem from the book. At the end of the school year, Mme Risbec made me repeat the class on the pretext that I was too much younger than my friends in the class. From that day on I was disgusted with school; I quit junior high school three years later, in 1968, after having spent a short time on the barricades in the rue Guy-Lussac, without ever having believed in it. Having become a father, I started working early, and became militant both about cultivating myself without the public schools but in the school of life and about fighting against what appeared to me to be a menacing stupidity. It was only when my stupidity landed me in prison that I could finally go back to geometry, to the spirit of contradiction, and to the logic of demonstration of what we philosophers call apodictic judgment. I have often thought of Mme Risbec and several other teachers and professors from my younger years; to certain of them, like M. Passage, a beautifully and properly named French teacher, I owe a great deal.

19. [Trans.] Nietzsche's conception of *ressentiment* is ideal here: more than "resentment," *ressentiment* has a burning, active core that not only "explains"

Zarathustra but Nietzsche's more straightforwardly autobiographical works as well, beyond *Ecce Homo*, but relying on their extraordinary insights, as an active resentment that leads both to action and forgetting. Since Nietzsche was reading Dostoevsky in his last period, it is not pure speculation to imagine that *ressentiment* includes the sense in *Notes from Underground*, where it indicates action without thought and, thus, the forgetting of any (Aristotelian) sense of individuality. Thus *ressentiment*, as laid out in *Zarathustra* and elsewhere, is *active resentment* leaping out whenever the "individual" is brought into conflict with self, other, or the collective; it is the *action* that counts, and that makes the figure of *ressentiment* into one through which the active sense of *competition* turns into one of *self-dissatisfaction*.

20. [Trans.] The ENS (École Normale Supérieure) was created during the French Revolution. Its original mandate was to serve the new Republic by providing it with teachers educated and trained in the Enlightenment's secular, critical value system. As a *grande école* it functions outside France's university structure; it does not give degrees in the ordinary manner but prepares a very select group of students (approximately one hundred enter per year) for careers of public service as philosophers, writers, scientists, diplomats, politicians, etc. Students are paid a stipend to attend the school.

The first and still the main ENS, in the rue d'Ulm in Paris's fifth arrondissement, now has several other campuses as well. Three other *écoles normales supérieures* were established in the nineteenth century: ENS de Lyon, specializing in the sciences; ENS Lettres et Sciences Humaines (also in Lyon), in the humanities; and ENS de Cachan, in pure and applied sciences, sociology, economics and management, and English language.

The ENS has the reputation of being among the finest educational establishments in Europe, though its ranking has slipped in recent years (it is currently ranked third in France).

21. The criminal underworld's term for this is *affranchissement*: an *affranchi* is someone who "knows the score," knows that this is really *only* or *rather* that; for example, this bar is a front for other activities, so-and-so is a police spy, or some influential figure is corruptible, etc. This is an image of a world essentially constructed on the basis of lies and tricks; those not "wised up" are called *caves*, outsiders and/or dupes. For more on this vocabulary, see for example *Touchez pas au grisbi*, one of Simonin's crime novels, or *Le Petit Simonin*, the best-known dictionary of French slang.

[Trans.] *Affranchir*'s two meanings, "to free" (as a slave) and "to stamp or frank" (as a letter) both contain elements of the sense in which the word is used in criminal slang. The *affranchi* is both free of the normal constraints of language and appearance *and* "stamped" or "validated" as an insider, a "wiseguy," and not a *cave*.

Déniaiser, literally, "to make less naïve, through instruction or training," i.e., to reduce or eradicate one's innocence, on a darker level also means to deflower, to take someone's virginity. Loss of innocence can mean increased knowledge and thus extended consciousness, but through the *destruction* of a state of innocence. The latter sense contributes significantly to the *déception* that education through industries of control produces.

22. "Then appears, across disciplines, the power of the Norm. New law of modern society? Rather say that since the 18th century, it has been added to other powers, giving them new limitations. . . . The Normal has been established as the principle of coercion through teaching, with the initiation of standardized education and the establishment of public schools" (DP, 187).

23. *L'Oeil du pouvoir,* interview with Michelle Perrot. In *Dits et écrits 3,* 196. Henceforth DE3.

24. I have explained this more fully in "Les prothèses de la foi," 237; and in "La peau de chagrin," 103.

25. In *Discipline and Punish,* as in *The Order of Things,* the blackboard plays a major role in the archaeology of surveillance: "[It is of] decisive importance because of its techniques of notation, recording, file-construction, ordering into columns and then on blackboards, with which we are familiar but which have allowed for the epistemological blockage of the sciences of the individual" (DP, 190). Writing on the blackboard results in the pagination of printed books and creates a *space* of objectivation that supports a *time* of subjectivation (what I prefer to call psychic and collective individuation); this is a product of what Auroux designated as "grammatization's second technological revolution."

Chapter 8

1. See *The History of Sexuality 1.* Henceforth HS1.

2. "The Discursive Regularities" is the title of the second part of *The Archaeology of Knowledge.*

3. Especially in epistolary form; cf. DE4 and Section 45.

4. How would it be possible to think modern medicine without thinking the role of medication, and how could we *not* think medical biopower as the birth of the pharmaceutical industry? Yet Foucault gives no place to these questions in *The Birth of the Clinic.*

5. I have explored this theory of schematism more thoroughly in *Technics and Time 3.*

6. The similarity of Foucault's analyses in *Discipline and Punish* and Weber's is quite striking.

7. DE4, 987. When Foucault writes that it is necessary "not only to do the history of industrial techniques but that of political techniques as well," he refers

just as much to an organology of social organizations as to material artifacts that are called techniques; this is what Deleuze misunderstands (cf. MS1, 24). The rifle, as a technical organ, requires a social organization both compatible with its usage and capable of ensuring proper training in its use, as well as the rational management of such competent individuals (their competence *is* their individualization).

8. Simondon, *Du mode d'existence des objets techniques*, 115–19. Henceforth MEOT.

9. On this issue, see RM, 41.

10. See Heidegger, *Questions 1/2*, 116 (henceforth Q1/2); and *Langue de tradition, langue technique* (Paris: Closterman, 1990).

11. Nicolas Sarkozy: "Our job is not to help our children remain children or even big children, to help them become adults, to become citizens. We are all educators" ("Lettre aux éducateurs," 4 September 2007, http://www.jeunesse-sports.gouv.fr/IMG/pdf/lettre-educateurs.pdf).

12. Cf. Michael Aglietta, "Le capitalisme de bulle en bulle," an interview in *Le Monde*, 2 September 2007.

13. Published in 1988 as *La Technologie politique*.

14. [Trans.] Johann Heinrich Gottlob von Justi (1717–71) published over fifty books on a wide variety of areas, including geology, chemistry, physics, philosophy, literature, technology, politics, and economics. Though he has been influential in a number of these areas, Foucault's interest in him has to do with von Justi's effort to theorize the creation of "modern commercial monarchies" within the Holy Roman Empire, states that could compete militarily (he wrote during the Seven Years' War), politically, and economically with France and England. Von Justi stressed that only a "moderate monarchic government" dedicated to the right to private property and open trade could succeed, while autocratic or oligarchic governmental forms inevitably lead to poverty, corruption, and military defeat.

Von Justi's economic theory fell within this political framework: he argued in favor of a growing population and private consumption as economic generators, and open competition and trade, even that sponsored by government, as essential to financial growth and economic robustness.

Policing and the relationship between police and citizen were of central importance to von Justi.

15. Cf. "'Omnes et singulatim': vers une critique de la raison politique," in DE4, 143ff.

16. And since then a significant body of mathematical thought whose rigor Catherine Kintzler recalls in full Foucauldian years. Cf. Con.

17. [Trans.] "Management" in this work should be seen in the current (2009) context: as business management, the management class, administration (as in

schools and universities), and governance (as in government as such and the governing of markets, as, for example, the Federal Reserve).

18. Cf. Bernays, *Propaganda*. Henceforth Prop.

19. Cited by Packard in *The Hidden Persuaders*, F63. Henceforth HP.

[Trans.] At the end of the first decade of the twenty-first century, as "we" (now not just the industrialized world, but *the world*) go through the current iteration of this cycle, we are confronted not only by an overabundance of *things* not being bought but by an overabundance of *debt*, since the most recent phase of market capitalism has involved "financial instruments," such as mortgage-backed derivatives, whose "value" is literally undeterminable (though certainly less than zero).

20. See Section 18.

21. Cf. EC, 89, and my commentary on it in MD3.

22. Giddens, *Consequences of Modernity*, 21ff. Henceforth AG.

23. Foucault, "Tehran: Faith Against the Shah." Henceforth Tehran.

24. To say nothing of the pathological effects on bodies themselves of this biopolitics that has become evident in States, let alone environmental questions in general, as consequences of care-less-ness.

25. As will be the case with Manicheanism; cf. DE4, 789. In the life of the monk, "contemplation is the supreme good" (790). Everything is about concentration and attention, "for Cassien, the perpetual mobility of the spirit ["esprit"] is a sign of its weakness. It is what distracts the individual from contemplation of God." The remedy: "to immobilize consciousness; . . . to eliminate the spirit's movements, which turn away from God."

26. [Trans.] Cassien—Saint John Cassien (Joannes Cassianus [360–433 CE])—was a monk about whom little is known, wrote an important doctrinal treatise in the Pelagian mode, and founded the Abbey Saint-Victor in Marseille. Originally known as Cassien, "Jean," "John," was later added in homage to Saint John Chrysostom. According to legend, Cassien was born in Scythia, between Romania and Bulgaria, *or* in the Nile delta, confusion between the two being the result of confusion between Scythia and the Scete desert in Egypt, which he visited later.

In 403 CE, in Constantinople, he received the teachings of Saint John Chrysostom, making him deacon (and giving him control) of the cathedral.

His preaching was contrary to Augustine's: Cassien believed in the "four senses of the Writings," based on the ideas of Origen. He was an adherent of Cenobitism, a *communal* monastic form opposing itself to the hermitic Anchorites who lived alone and consecrated their lives to solitary contemplation. Cenobitists traced their worldview to two Greek words, *koinos* (in common) and *bios* (life). Cassien brought this sense of communal life to the West ca. 400 CE.

27. Dobbs, *Greeks and the Irrational*. Henceforth GI.

28. [Trans.] In 1660, the grammarians of Port-Royal, an influential monastery near Paris, published a grammar book based not on usage judged then to be "the best," but on "reason." This work was entitled *General and Reasoned Grammar*, "general" because it embraced all languages, "reasoned" because it explained reason's function relative to language itself. It was the opposite of what was considered "good usage" in its day.

Stating that universal mechanisms of logic pervade every language, the *Grammar* marked the birth of what would become modern linguistics. *The Logic of Port-Royal* was published in 1662, anonymously in Paris (it was written by Antoine Arnauld and Pierre Nicole). The book was at once a success, as an intellectual grammar book and a compendium of philosophical epistemology from Descartes and Pascal. It was divided into four sections, corresponding to the four aspects of rational thought: understanding, judgment, decision, and order.

Its claim is that all of our knowledge occurs through ideas reflecting things, and judgment of things expressed in proportions invented by a subject and a predicate. It examines the "justness" of various propositions and of syllogistic deduction itself. The determination of various judgments and conclusions leads to the modern notion of science itself, the scientific method (analysis and synthesis).

Port-Royal logic has had a significant influence on contemporary mathematics, which considered itself able to inform all other domains of knowledge through language, thus proposing an ideal of *rational* language harmonizing the "spirit of *finesse*" and of geometry: classic discourse par excellence.

29. Auroux, *La Révolution technologique de la grammatisation*, 71. Henceforth RTG.

30. Cf. particularly Auroux's commentary on the Castilian politics of language in 1492, 93.

31. Cf. RTG, 74–75, the table showing the grammatization of European vernaculars.

32. Loyola, *The Spiritual Exercises*. Henceforth SE.

33. Cf. Derrida, "Faith and Knowledge," 1–78, 29. Henceforth FK.

34. All diachronization of language constituted in a discourse that tends to transindividuate that language, eventually as a specialty language and discipline, is idiomatic. Idiom is not necessarily a dialect; in Spanish, it gives its name to the language itself.

35. I will return to this theme in *Technics and Time 5: The War of the Spirits*.

36. See *Des Alexandries*, Christian Jacob (Paris: Bibliotèque nationale française, 2002 and 2003).

37. Cf. Gille, *Histoire des techniques*, 70. Henceforth HT.

[Trans.] Boulton (1728–1809) owned a sheet-metal-rolling plant in Birmingham, England. Through a series of purely financial events, Boulton the factory owner became Watt the inventor's partner in producing the steam engine for which Watt is famous. Their relationship was strictly business: contracts, partnerships, various business ventures. As it happens, Boulton was a very "enlightened" factory owner, providing a clean, well-lit working environment and refusing to hire children. He worked in partnership with Watt until both of them retired in 1800.

Chapter 9

1. The diachronicity of knowledge is what is at stake in this work, as opposed to Bachelardian, Structuralist, and Althusserian positions on the rupture, as Dominique Lecourt has shown in his excellent *Pour une critique de l'épistémologie*, 98–133, a significant part of this chapter's inspiration. Lecourt writes about "the notion of *epistēmē* which lays out 'configurations of knowledge' as the large regions obeying specific structural laws against thinking the *history* of ideological formations other than as abrupt 'mutations,' enigmatic 'ruptures,' sudden 'tearings.' This is the kind of history . . . from which Foucault now wants to break."

2. In *Archaeology*, the *domains* of interest to Foucault are not *disciplines* in the sense in which the word means "the group of statements taking their organization from scientific models that aim at coherence and demonstrability, and that are received, institutionalized, transmitted, and sometimes taught as sciences" (AK, 206). The object of archaeology is to make these disciplines (e.g., psychiatry) *possible*, "at a time when . . . a whole set of connections appeared between hospitalization, internment, the conditions and procedures of social exclusion, the rules of jurisprudence, work-place standards, and bourgeois morale; in short, the entirety of what characterizes the formation of these statements for this discursive practice" (206). This "set of connections" is what Foucault calls knowledge. Much more than a discipline or a group of disciplines, it is "the field of coordination and subordination of statements in which concepts appear and are defined, applied, and transformed" (208).

3. This concept was investigated by Jacques Virbel.

4. On this matter, see B. Stiegler, "L'inquiétante étrangeté de la pensée et la métaphysique de Pénélope," the preface to Simondon's IPC, ix.

5. "Today it is history that transforms documents into monuments. . . . It might be said, were one to play with words a bit, that history, today, leans toward archaeology—toward the intrinsic description of the monument" (AK, 7). Notice here how the educational institution is a *documentary monument*.

6. "History is a particular manner for a society to give status and elaboration to a documentary mass from which it cannot separate itself" (AK, 138).

7. Cf. MS1; MD1; and RM.

8. Simondon indicates that this field is like the electromagnetic field *transductively* constituted by a bipolar tension that structures *all* processes of individuation. Cf. IPC, 44–47, 76; and my comments on it in the preface to this work, ii.

9. Cf. MS1, 141–42.

10. A science is itself an individuation process as a collection of documents in just the sense in which Foucault understands it in *Archaeology*.

11. In this printed materiality, the book is a "node in a network" (AK, 34) forming a "system of references." But it is also the concretization of a transindividuation process performed by retentional devices, a process that itself requires tertiary retentions forming a hypomnesic structure; Foucault discusses these *hypomnēmata* extensively in *L'Écriture de soi*.

12. Cf. Derrida, *The Problem of Genesis*; and my commentary in TT2.

13. Cf. Deleuze, *Anti-Oedipus*, 169. Henceforth DAO.

14. It would be necessary here to demonstrate how the law itself is a fruit of grammatization, and how contemporary rights are upset by new forms of grammatization and *hypomnēmata*.

15. [Trans.] IPv6, "Internet Protocol version 6," is the Internet "layer protocol" for "packet-switched internetworks." Ipv4, still the network standard, has far less "address space" than version 6, as a result of using a 32-bit rather than a 128-bit address. The greatly expanded band width of version 6 would mean much greater flexibility in many applications, from assigning addresses to routing Internet traffic, in addition to doing away with network address translation. Version 6 has many other advantages, though at present it is still more hypothetical than real, in that it is in very limited use.

IPv6 was anointed in 1998 by the Internet Engineering Task Force as the successor to version 4. By late 2008, however, after ten years of development, IPv6 had just begun to be recognized globally. In 2009 it is still in its "infancy," still virtually invisible worldwide.

16. On this subject, see *L'Économie de l'hypermatière*. Henceforth EH.

17. See HE.

18. See Section 25.

19. See Section 36.

20. "By 'ideological practices' I mean the complex formations of montages of notions-representations-images, on one hand, and montages of behaviors-conduct-attitudes-gestures, on the other. The totality functions as the practical normatives governing attitude, and the concrete human standpoint regarding real objects and the real problems of their social and individual existence, and of their history" (cited in CEL, F120).

21. See MD1, F88.

22. Cf. in the same vein regarding multipolarity Simondon's IPC, 159–63, 240; and my commentary in its introduction, xiii.

23. [Trans.] *Comput*, deriving from the Latin *computus*, "to reckon or cal-culate" (i.e., to compute in its original sense), is in the sense in which Stiegler uses it a term from Christianity meaning "the calculation of the dates of non-fixed holidays or feast days." It is therefore used also to designate the (fictional) moon, the *comput* or "paschal" full moon used in such calculations. The "paschal moon," for instance, is the fourteenth day of a lunar month occurring on or af-ter March 21; it is unrelated to actual lunar cycles. *Comput*, then, is a reckoning/calculating (technical) apparatus.

24. [Trans.] *L'individuation à la lettre, à la lettre* means "literally" in the sense of "actually" or "really," and also "of or to the letter" in the sense of "precisely," "exactly." *L'individuation à la lettre* can have the sense of "individuation, liter-ally" or "precise individuation"; my translation of it as "literal individuation" derives from Stiegler's sense of the *littérale* and its connection to literacy, through Kant's Enlightenment sense that maturity rests solidly on literacy, *alphabétisa-tion*.

25. See Section 40.

26. Here it is useful to invoke Winnicott: interiorization is a matter of a tran-sitionality that is to some extent regressive.

27. This is precisely how Simondon defines the "spiritual."

28. Derrida, *Edmund Husserl's "Origin of Geometry,"* 84. Henceforth HOG.

29. As Derrida himself says regarding the relation of desire to its object; cf. PostCard.

Chapter 10

1. On these topics, see DM2, 79ff.

2. See RM, 74, 88, 99ff.

3. [Trans.] In its plural form this is a very awkward word; though *dispositif* can be translated in a number of ways, Foucault chose to make it very clear that "apparatus" was his choice. Since Agamben takes Foucault up on his use and definition of the word, I have chosen to stay with it in both singular and plural form when Stiegler cites either Foucault's or Agamben's texts. Elsewhere, when *dispositif* appears in other contexts, it may be translated as "device" or "opera-tion."

4. Agamben, *What Is an Apparatus?* Henceforth WA.

5. Foucault, "The Confession of the Flesh," 195–96. Henceforth CF. The in-terview is also cited in Agamben.

6. I made the same connective translation in TT1.

7. [Trans.] Stiegler's *la navigation*, from Agamben's *navigazione*, becomes "Web browsing" in the English translation. This is perfectly correct; however, because Stiegler makes so much of the maritime reference here and in TC2, I have left "navigation," of which "Web navigation" or "browsing" is one kind.

It is also worth pointing out that "browsing" is "navigating" only in the loosest sense: very few marine "navigators" are "browsing"—or wouldn't be for long. In the maritime context, "navigation" means the opposite of "browsing." Further, Stiegler goes on to equate navigation with "transport," thus connecting it to agribusiness.

Not incidentally, Heidegger's use of the "marine" in *Antigone*, to which Stiegler refers here, a twenty-page interpretation of one of the play's choruses, deals with humans "navigating" life despite being "the uncanniest of the uncanny." The choral passage on which Heidegger focuses begins

> Manifold is the uncanny, yet nothing
> Uncannier than man bestirs itself, rising up beyond him.
> He fares forth upon the foaming tide
> Amid winter's southerly tempest
> And cruises through the summits
> Of the raging, clefted swells.

8. Heidegger, *Introduction to Metaphysics*. Henceforth IM.

9. "Binary streams" are the flux of zeros and ones circulating through numeric networks.

10. Objects on which Agamben comments regarding their arrival in Italy: "For example, I live in Italy, a country where the gestures and behaviors of individuals have been reshaped from top to toe by the cellular telephone (which the Italians dub the *telephonino*). I have developed an implacable hatred for this apparatus, which has made the relationship between people all the more abstract. Though I have surprised myself by thinking on more than one occasion about ways to destroy or deactivate those *telephonini*, as well as ways to eliminate or at least to punish or imprison those who do not stop using them, I do not believe that this is the right solution to the problem" (WA, 16).

11. [Trans.] Stiegler's equating here of *disposition* and *kosmos* begs a word or two. Κοσμος invokes "universe" or "world" in its usual sense, but also "order" (as in *logos*), "arrangement." Thus, *kosmos* (*à la* Plato's *idein*) is an idea, a concept, ineluctably abstract and thus universal. As such, it is not a function of space and time, *dispositioned*, *dispossessed* of any material facticity and corporeality (though it remains an *object* in Heidegger's and Stiegler's sense). One might even think here of the nature of *position* (and thus disposition) as Derrida employs it in *Positions*.

12. Canguilhem, *The Normal and the Pathological*, 178. Henceforth NP.

13. [Trans.] "Soigneux et je-m'en-foutistes devant 'l'Ingouvernable.'" Stiegler's *soigneux* here has to do with *concerned*, caring, *care-ful* citizens—those who take an active (literate) role in a healthy society's long-term circuitry and the building of maturity through intergenerational understanding and differentiation. *Je-m'en-foutisme* is literally an I-don't-give-a-damn attitude, though *foutre* has many uses in French: certainly implicit in Stiegler's seemingly standard use of

je-m'en-foutiste includes the profanity that all high school French students learn, which would result in the *profane* translation of "I don't give a fuck," using language in its roughest and most profane sense to indicate the speaker's (and it would be a *speaker*, not a *writer*, in the Kantian sense) *level* of indifference to "societal values."

14. [Trans.] Read Derrida, Heidegger, Marx, and Shakespeare, in that order.

15. Melancholy is the pathology that cannot transform this polarity into a dynamic, and it is doubtless initially this pathology that must be treated in many ways.

16. On this theme, see RM, 117.

17. Refusal to work against the inclination to abandon responsibility, and against the concessions made to a very subtle inclination to remain immature that lives within every mature adult until death, is an extraordinarily serious and common temptation. Could we imagine that twentieth-century men and women, confronted by an implacable process of Nazification, resolved to abandon all "resolution" (*Entschlossenheit*) and to claim that there was *nothing to be done*, that this process was—one might say after the fact—the concretization of *Gestell*, the gas chambers having been somehow produced by the "apparatuses" of the Industrial Age? This position was taken, and still is, but now in a new context. I must admit that it happens more often to me that it appears to make me reason thus myself. I even say to myself that I must be able to think that way in order to be able to *fight against what is true* in this reasoning. But the danger is thus to *stop* at this "truth" and to find it sufficient justification for inaction and the renouncing of all struggle. The danger is making *the argument justifying one's own care-less-ness*.

18. I will return to these questions, and to the concepts of profanation and sacrifice in Agamben, in the second volume of *Taking Care*. For the moment, I would specify that for me one of the difficulties his thought poses is his use of the concept of usage in *Profanations*, especially F107–8.

19. And which was part of a public debate with Derrida in Rio de Janeiro. See MD1, chapter 1 ("Vouloir croire"), 173ff.

20. [Trans.] *Passer à l'acte*, as is evidenced by Stiegler's own life (and his *Passer à l'acte*, from Stanford), is not just to *act* but to *act out*: to manifest through action an "interior" that, as Judith Butler reminded us, is "nothing" without its expression, its acting out. In the current context, *passer à l'acte* relates to the action needed to transfer knowledge from one generation to another, which can only be accomplished *actively*, in a living discourse between/among the generations; without this interaction, no *passage à l'acte* is possible, and thus no maturity.

21. I have amplified this idea in a variety of circumstances, first of all in *Acting Out* (henceforth AO), but I must add here that profanation is also the "becoming-profane" that Jean-Pierre Vernant describes in analyzing the consequences of the historic expansion of writing in ancient Greece and, through it, what is

always concretized in the process of grammatization: *becoming profane* is a public becoming, not at all mysterious, which most notably opens the possibility of a *public that reads.*

22. In the next chapter, and above all in volume 2 of *Taking Care.*

23. I am not sure that something can legitimately be said of desire separate from pornography, as Agamben does (e.g., in *Profanations*). The risk is, on the contrary, to have always and in advance lost sight of the question.

Chapter 11

1. On *soft power*, see Noyer, proceedings of a conference at the Théâtre de la Colline.

2. This is also the grammatization in play for Weber with regard to the *hypomnēmata* of the techniques of compatibility without the rationalization of which disenchantment consists would never have been possible.

3. This question, the focus of the three volumes of *Mécréance et discrédit*, is introduced in volume 1, 95, 157.

4. This problematics provides the context for Agamben's reflections in *What Is an Apparatus?* but that he does not thematize.

5. This is the age of what Valéry describes as a political economy of the mind, even while observing that its value is being reduced.

6. [Trans.] The "Popular Front," a common term in the history of many countries worldwide, has a specific history in France. An uneasy alliance of left-leaning and left-wing groups, including the French Communist Party (PCF), the Socialist SFIO, and several others, formed in France between the two World Wars, during a time in which various versions of "socialism" were being tested worldwide. Somewhat surprisingly, the Front populaire (FP) won the May 1936 elections for the Assemblée Nationale (three months after the victory of the Frente Popular in Spain) and constructed a French government led by the Socialist/SFIO leader Léon Blum. A number of important outcomes ensued, including a general strike and the Matignon Agreements, central to the evolution of French social rights. One of their rallying cries was "Tout est possible!" (Everything is possible).

But internal struggles (related to the Spanish Civil War, opposition from the right, and the pervasive effects of the Great Depression) brought an end to the FP as a political power by mid-1937 and to the movement as a whole by autumn 1938.

Memorably, the short ascendancy of the FN (for the first time in France) included women ministers (French women did not have voting rights until 1944).

7. Cf., for example, Fleury, *Le TNP et le Centre Pompidou.*

8. In 1939, 45% of the French owned a radio, on which the first public station appeared in 1923.

9. This produces more and more frequent short-circuits. And it is more than ever the case, in France with SkyRock radio (the principal advertiser of blogs, talk radio, the Internet, and cell phones—that is, for creating the hyperattentional apparatuses Katherine Hayles and Giorgio Agamben analyze). On this subject, see "Révolutions industrielles de la musique."

10. This is the context for Isidore Isou's *Le Soulèvement de la jeunesse* [*Youth Uprising*], which develops Situationist thought.

[Trans.] Isidore Isou, born Ioan-Isidor Goldstein (1925–2007), the founder of Lettrism, was a Romanian-born poet, visual artist, filmmaker, and film critic. He lived and worked in Romania as an art journalist and cofounder (with social psychologist Serge Moscovici) of the art journal *Da*, which was quickly banned and closed down by the authorities. After World War II, Isou moved to Paris to further his work on concepts involving the complete transformation of art from the ground up. He created the movement he called "Lettrism" (he was the movement's only member), having written the *Lettriste* manifesto at age sixteen; he then developed a systematic Lettrist "hypergraphics." The movement attracted others and currently continues to grow (under a variety of names). Throughout the 1960s, Isou and the Lettrists became very influential in France; Guy Debord and Gil Wolman were members before Wolman broke away to form the Lettrist International, which over time developed into the dissident Situationist International, whose influence on the visual aspects (e.g., posters, film, clothing, etc.) of the 1968 uprising was central, eclipsing such movements as existentialism and surrealism in its involvement with social change. Since Isou's death in 2007, many of his print and film works have been reissued (along with a great deal of previously unpublished material), including the fourteen hundred–page *La Créatique ou la Novatique*. Kino International has now released a DVD collection of Isou's films: *Avant-Garde 2: Experimental Films 1928–1954*.

11. Cf. Ross, *May '68 and Its Afterlives*. Henceforth Ross.

12. This is created through public health organizations, hospitals, the politics of hygiene, health insurance, and the pharmaceutical industry, the "normatization" of modern life, the food-service industries, public security, insurance and anticipation of various risks, and more generally modern, democratic creature comforts by which the "petite-bourgeoisie" can be identified.

13. [Trans.] Europe 1 (formerly Europe No.1) is a private radio channel founded in 1945. During the May 1968 uprising it became known as "Radio Barricades" as a result of its largely favorable live coverage of the strikes and other events. French authorities accused it of broadcasting slanted coverage that created a "threat to public order" and banned its being played on car radios for a period of time. A further result was that the French minister of the interior cut the number of frequencies available to suburban and other radio stations in order to counteract live broadcasts of the disturbances. As the uprisings subsided, the ban eased.

Somatization is a concept in clinical psychology in which a psychic conflict is translated into bodily (re)action.

14. [Trans.] Stiegler's use of "profane" here has many facets, starting with its derivation from Latin (*pro*, "before"; *fanum*, "temple"): i.e., relative to but outside the sacred, holy, religious. The fact that *laic*, secular Enlightenment and then bourgeois culture (including education) is therefore inherently profane relates to the shame Stiegler associates with pharmacological being.

15. In order to think the possibility of non-inhuman beings requires the thinking of the possibility of the inhuman in the human well before thinking of the human in human beings, in the sense in which this issue is raised by cognitivism. This means to be given the possibility of thinking the human outside a humanism that cannot see its being pharmacological, and thus organologically subjected to the process of autoindividuation. But this is what produces a process of metastable evolution between two tendencies without which no freedom can exist: good and bad. On this point, I return to my introduction of Simondon's *L'Individuation psychique*. The non-inhuman being is dynamically sensitive to this duplicity, which is endemic to human pharmacology—that is, through the originary relation to apparatuses.

16. It has often been said in the press that no one saw the current crisis coming; this claim is absolutely astonishing. The reader who would like to verify that it is false could, for example, glance at the *Ars Industrialis* of 16 December 2006, "L'investissement durable," with Jean-Luc Gréau. One might also read Michael Aglietta and Laurent Berrebi's *Désordres dans le capitalisme mondiale* (Paris: Odile Jacob, 2007).

[Trans.] *Prendre Soin 1*, published in fall 2009, has anticipated the Great Downturn of 2009 and has presented the results and outcomes of Stiegler's (and many others') comments on both the shallower and deeper implications of unregulated "global market economics," which have been (at least since the Reagan years in the United States) in the hands not of the non-inhuman but of the inhuman. The deregulation that began in the United States in the late 1960s and culminated with the removal of the last banking regulations in 1998 and 1999 (under Democrat Bill Clinton) led during the George W. Bush years to excesses of *financial* inhumanity (pace Bernard Madoff) unimaginable only ten years earlier—but whose substructure had been building for forty years.

17. I have explored this theme at greater length and more positively in *Réenchanter le monde*, particularly in the final chapter.

18. Just as I completed the manuscript for this book, the Nobel Prize for Peace was awarded equally to the IPCC (Intergovernmental Panel on Climate Change), a group of experts working on planetary environmental questions, and Al Gore, about whose recent positions I have written elsewhere here. The award confirms this final chapter's findings. At the same time, unhappily, in France DNA testing used in opposing immigrant candidates for adoption has finally

been voted in by the Assembly: this is an extremely serious symbolic action, particularly when added to the denial of the difference between minor and major status in determining the sanctions against juvenile delinquency passed by the Assembly in June 2007. Immigration is a *fact* (rarely wished for: one leaves one's country because of something one is undergoing there), whereas adoption is a *voluntary act* (by those who adopt just as much as for the adoptee). Moreover, speaking of adoption, it is how analysis of what I have called a *process of adoption*, which is always a process of collective as well as psychic individuation (cf. *Technics and Time 3: The Time of Cinema*), starts out by challenging genetic filiation: the criterion for filiation is never genetic, always symbolic. This is perhaps the most profound basis for the symbolic formation of a social group, which can never be founded on an implied "ethnic purity," truly a profane transgression of all that (for example, in monotheism asserted as a founding origin of "national spirit) affirms the adoptive dimension of "children of God" (Moses adopted by Amran and Yokebed, Jesus adopted by Joseph, the Koran's insistence on the law of milk and not of blood as the principle of fraternity in the family).

The American channel Babyfirst, aimed at babies of six months to three years, started broadcasting in France in October 2007; on its Web site, in the section aimed at parents cited earlier here, one can find a very representative illustration of what needs to be analyzed as psychopower.

The 2007 Nobel Peace Prize, the juridical evolutions and psychopower discourses put out by Babyfirst, are all signs of a simultaneous convergence and contradiction—and it is these contradictions that must be thought through, in terms of what converges and what diverges, what actions are necessary, what struggles: struggle against care-less-ness, stupidity, and the *being-in-human* toward which we are heading, ceaselessly and ubiquitously.

19. Beings, for which the word *object* will no longer work—ontological difference requiring the transcendence of the subject, created in a metaphysics that must, through existential analysis, be transcended through situating it as a privileged being, which constitutes its *ethos* as well as Jonas's ethics.

20. This privilege is what makes Heidegger's philosophy of time the obligatory point of departure for all philosophic thought regarding desire, waiting attentively [*atente attentionnée*], that Heidegger himself does not authorize. On the privileging of the future, see BT, §6, §41.

21. On this issue, see my contribution, "Le théâtre de l'individuation."

22. And what is true of the programming industry and the national public powers is also true across Europe and internationally.

23. The elements of such a politics are laid out in *Réenchanter le monde*. More generally, these elements of debate on questions related to an industrial politics of technology of the spirit in Europe can be found on the *Ars Industrialis* Web site, www.arsindustrialis.org.

Bibliography

[Trans.: Bibliographical entries in French here remain untranslated; all translations from these works are mine unless otherwise indicated.]

Agamben, Giorgio. 2007. *Profanations*. Trans. Jeff Fort. New York: Zone Books.
———. 2009. *What Is an Apparatus? and Other Essays*. Trans. David Kishik and Stefan Pedatella. Stanford, Calif.: Stanford University Press.
Aristotle. 1979. *Metaphysics*. Trans. Hugh Tredennick. Boston: Loeb Classic Library.
Auroux, Sylvain. 1993. *La Révolution technologique de la grammatisation*. Liège: Mardaga.
Baton-Hervé, Élizabeth. 2004. *Télévision et fonction parentale*. http://www.unaf.fr/IMG/pdf/Television_et_fonction_Parentale.pdf.
Bernays, Edward. 2004. *Propaganda*. New York: Ig Publishing.
Brodeur, Jacques. N.d. http://data.edupax.org/precede/public/Assets/divers/documentation/1_articles/1_067_Autre_Avenue_fin_novembre06.pdf.
Canguilhem, Georges. 1991. *The Normal and the Pathological*. Trans. Carolyn R. Fawcett. New York: Zone Books.
Cassin, Barbara. 2007. *Google-moi, la deuxième mission de l'Amérique*. Paris: Albin Michel.
Changeux, Jean-Pierre. 1985. *Neuronal Man: The Biology of Mind*. Trans. Laurence Garey. New York: Pantheon Books.
Crepon, Marc. Forthcoming. *La Culture de la peur*. Paris: Galilée.
———. 2006–7. *Trouver des armes contre la peur.* "*Pour une polémologie de l'esprit.*" Conference, Amphithéâtre 43, Université Paris 7, 2 place Jussieu, Paris 5, 20 December 2006, and 17 January 2007.
Deleuze, Gilles. 1983. *Anti-Oedipus*. Trans. Robert Hurley, Mark Seem, and Helen R. Lane. Minneapolis: University of Minnesota Press.

———. 1997. *Negotiations 1972–1990.* Trans. Martin Joquin. New York: Columbia University Press.

Derrida, Jacques. 1981. *Dissemination.* Trans. Barbara Johnson. Chicago: University of Chicago Press.

———. 1987. *The Post Card: From Socrates to Freud and Beyond.* Trans. Alan Bass. Chicago: University of Chicago Press.

———. 1989. *Edmund Husserl's "Origin of Geometry": An Introduction.* Trans. John P. Leavey Jr. Lincoln: University of Nebraska Press.

———. 1996. "Faith and Knowledge: The Two Sources of 'Religion' at the Limits of Reason Alone." In *Religion,* ed. Jacques Derrida and Gianni Vattimo, 1–78. Stanford, Calif.: Stanford University Press.

———. 2003. *The Problem of Genesis in Husserl's Philosophy.* Trans. Marian Hobson. Chicago: University of Chicago Press.

Dobbs, E. 2004. *The Greeks and the Irrational.* Sacramento: University of California Press.

Dolto, Françoise. 2007. In Hintzy, Interview.

Dufour, Dany-Robert. 2005. *On achève bien les hommes.* Paris: Denoël.

During, Élie. 2000. "Logics of Performance: Cage/Gould." *Critique,* no. 639–40 (August–September).

Fillon, François. 2007. Interview. *Le Figaro.* 2 June.

———. 2007. Policy Statement, 3 July 2007. http://www.premier-ministre. gouv.fr/acteurs/ interventions_premier_ministre_9/discours_498/declaration_politique_générale_56763.html.

Flamaux, Bridgette. 2006. *Le Design, Essais sur les théories et les pratiques.* Paris: Institut français de la mode.

Fleury, Laurent. 1999. *Le TNP et le Centre Pompidou: deux institutions culturelles entre l'État et le public.* Dissertation. Paris IX Dauphine.

Foucault, Michel. 1972. *The Archaeology of Knowledge.* New York: Harper Torchbooks.

———. 1973. *The Order of Things: An Archaeology of the Human Sciences.* New York: Vintage Books.

———. 1978. *The History of Sexuality 1. An Introduction.* New York: Pantheon.

———. 1980. "The Confession of the Flesh." In *Power/Knowledge: Selected Interviews and Other Writings 1972–1977,* trans. Alain Grosrichard, ed. Colin Gordon. New York: Pantheon.

———. 1984. "What Is Enlightenment?" In *The Foucault Reader,* ed. Paul Rabinow. New York: Pantheon.

———. 1994. *The Birth of the Clinic: An Archaeology of Medical Perception.* New York: Vintage Books.

———. 1994. *Dits et écrits 1.* Paris: Gallimard.

———. 1994. *Dits et écrits 2.* Paris: Gallimard.

———. 1994. *Dits et écrits 3*. Paris: Gallimard.

———. 1994. *Dits et écrits 4*. Paris: Gallimard.

———. 1994. "Les mailles du pouvoir." In *Dits et écrits 4*.

———. 1995. *Discipline and Punish*. New York: Vintage Books.

———. 2001. "L'Écriture de soi." In *Dits et écrits 4*.

———. 2001. "Qu'est-ce que les Lumières?" In *Dits et écrits 4*.

———. 2005. "Tehran: Faith Against the Shah." In *Foucault and the Iranian Revolution: Gender and the Seductions of Islamism*, ed. Janet Afary and Kevin Anderson. Chicago: University of Chicago Press.

———. 2007. "The Meshes of Power." In *Space, Knowledge, and Power: Foucault and Geography*, trans. and ed. Jeremy Crampton and Stuart Eldon. London: Ashgate.

Freud, Sigmund. 1943. *A General Introduction to Psychoanalysis*. Trans. Joan Rivière. Garden City, N.J.: Garden City Publishing.

———. 1962. *The Ego and the Id*. Trans. James Strachey. New York: W. W. Norton.

———. 1967. *Moses and Monotheism*. Trans. Katherine Jones. New York: Vintage Books.

———. 1984. *On Metapsychology*. Penguin Freud Library, vol. 11. London: Harmondsworth.

———. 1984. "What Is Enlightenment?" In *The Foucault Reader*, ed. Paul Rabinow. New York: Pantheon.

Gasmi, Naser, and Gilles Grolleau. 2002. *Économie de l'information versus l'Économie de l'attention? Une application aux labels agro-alimentaires*. http://gis-syal.agropolis.fr/Syal2002/FR/Atelier%202/Gasmi%20%20Grolleau.pdf.

Giddens, Anthony. 1991. *The Consequences of Modernity*. Stanford, Calif.: Stanford University Press.

Gille, Bertrand. 1978. *Histoire des techniques*. Paris: Gallimard (La Pléiade).

Gould, Glenn. 1983. *Écrits 1*. Paris: Fayard.

Guiland, Hubert. N.d. "S'intéresser à l'attention." http://www.internetactu.net/.

Hayles, Katherine. 2007. "Hyper and Deep Attention: The Generational Divide in Cognitive Modes." www. nlajournab.org.

Heidegger, Martin. 1976. *Poetry, Language, Thought*. New York: Harper Publishing.

———. 1990. *Questions I et II*. Paris: Gallimard.

———. 1990. *Questions III et IV*. Paris: Gallimard.

———. 1996. *Being and Time*. Trans. Joan Stambaugh. Albany, N.Y.: SUNY Press.

———. 2000. *Introduction to Metaphysics*. Trans. Gregory Fried and Richard Polt. New Haven, Conn.: Yale University Press.

Heraclitus. *Les Présocratiques*. Paris: Gallimard (La Pléiade).

Hintzy, Jacques. 2007. Interview. *Liberation*, Paris, 18 July.

Husserl, Edmund. 1970. *The Crisis of European Sciences and Transcendental Phenomenology: In Introduction to Phenomenological Philosophy*. Trans. David Carr. Evanston, Ill.: Northwestern University Press.

———. 1978. "The Origin of Geometry." Trans. John P. Leavey. In *Edmund Husserl's "Origin of Geometry": An Introduction*. Stony Brook, N.Y.: N. Hays.

Iser, Wolfgang. 1980. *The Act of Reading: A Theory of Aesthetic Response*. Baltimore: Johns Hopkins University Press.

Jonas, Hans. 1985. *The Imperative of Responsibility: In Search of an Ethics for the Technological Age*. Chicago: University of Chicago Press.

Kaiser Family Foundation. 2005. *Generation M: Media in the Lives of 8–18 Year-olds*. http://www.kff.org/entmedia/7251.cfm.

Kant, Immanuel. [1784]. "An Answer to the Question: What Is Enlightenment?" http://www.english.upenn.edu/~mgamer/Etexts/kant.html.

———. 1993. *Réflexions sur l'éducation*. Paris: Vrin.

———. 2003. *The Critique of Pure Reason*. Trans. J. M. D. Mieklejohn. Mineola, N.Y.: Dover Publications.

Kaplan, Frédéric. 2004. *Automates intelligents*. http://www.automatesintelligents.com/interviews/2004/juil/kaplan.html.

Kintzler, Catherine. 1984. *Condorcet*. Paris: Minerve.

Lacan, Jacques, ed. 1968. *Scilicet* 1/1. Paris: Seuil.

Lecourt, Dominique. 1972. *Pour une critique de l'épistémologie, Bachelard, Canguilhem, Foucault*. Paris: Maspero.

———. 1999. *Contre la peur*. Paris: PUF.

Leroi-Gourhan, André. 1943. *L'Homme et la matière*. Paris: Albin Michel.

———. 1975 [1964–65]. *Le geste et la parole*. Vol. 1, *Technique et langage*; vol. 2, *Le mémoire et les rythmes*. Paris: Broché.

Levi, Primo. 2000. *If This Is a Man*. Trans. S. J. Woolf. New York: Everyman's Library.

Livingstone, Sonia, and Moira Bovill, eds. 2001. *Children and Their Changing Media Environment*. Mahwah, N.J.: Laurence Erlbaum.

Loyola, Ignatius. 2007. *The Spiritual Exercises*. New York: Cosimo Classics.

Mann, Thomas. 1945. *The Tables of the Law*. New York: Alfred A. Knopf.

Marcuse, Herbert. 1974. *Eros and Civilization: A Philosophical Inquiry into Freud*. Boston: Beacon Press.

Mendelssohn, Moses, and Immanuel Kant. 2007. *Qu'est-ce que les Lumières?* Postface by Cyril Morana. Paris: Mille et une nuits.

Morana, Cyril. 2007. "Eclairer les Lumières." In Mendelssohn and Kant, *Qu'est-ce que les Lumières?*

Noyer, Jean-Max. 2005. Proceedings of a conference at the Théâtre de la Colline, 5 November. http://www.arsindustrialis.org/node/1460.

―――. 2005. CRICS Activités. http://www.uf-cci.univ-paris7.fr/crics/activites. html.

Packard, Vance. 1963. *The Hidden Persuaders*. New York: Cardinal Press.

Perrot, Michelle. *L'Oeil du pouvoir*. In Foucault, *Dits et écrits 2*, 204.

Petit, Philippe, and Vincent Bontemps. 2008. *L'Économie de l'hypermatière. L'être non inhumain peut-il demeurer humain?* Interviews. Paris: Fayard.

Plato. 2001. *Alcibiades*. Cambridge: Cambridge University Press.

―――. 2004. *Charmides*. New York: Quiet Vision.

―――. N.d. *Lesser Hippias*. http://www.ac-nice.fr/philo/textes/Plato-Works/01-LesserHippias.html.

―――. N.d. *Meno*. http://classics.mit.edu/Plato/meno.html.

Pontalis, Jean-Bernard. 1971. *Après Freud*. Paris: Idées-Gallimard.

Queneau, Robert. 1965. *Bâtons, chiffres et lettres*. Paris: Gallimard.

Rifkin, Jeremy. 2001. *The Age of Access: The New Culture of Hypercapitalism, Where All of Life Is a Paid-For Experience*. London: Tarcher.

Robin, Léon. 1968. *Platon*. Paris: PUF.

Ross, Kristin. 2004. *May '68 and Its Afterlives*. Chicago: University of Chicago Press.

Simondon, Gilbert. 1964. *L'individu et sa genèse psycho-biologique*. Paris: PUF.

―――. 1999. *Du mode d'existence des objets techniques*. Paris: Aubier.

―――. 2007. *Individuation psychique et collective*. Paris: Aubier.

Sloterdijk, Peter. 2000. *Règles pour le parc humain*. Paris: Mille et une nuits.

Stiegler, Bernard. 1996. *Technics and Time I: The Fault of Epimetheus*. Trans. Richard Beardsworth and Georges Collins. Stanford, Calif.: Stanford University Press.

―――. 2000. "Les prothèses de la foi et le fidélité aux limits de la déconstruction." *Alter*, no. 8.

―――. 2003. *Aimer, s'aimer, nous aimer*. Paris: Galilée.

―――. 2004. *De la misère symbolique 2. La catastrophe du sensible*. Paris: Galilée.

―――. 2004. *Mécreance et discrédit 1: La décadence des démocraties industrielles*. Paris: Galilée.

―――. 2004. *Philosopher par accident*. Paris: Galilée.

―――. 2004. "Révolutions industrielles de la musique." *Cahiers de médiologie*, no. 18. Paris: Fayard.

―――. 2005. *Constituer l'Europe 1*. Paris: Broché.

―――. 2005. *Constituer l'Europe 2*. Paris: Broché.

―――. 2006. *De la misère symbolique 1. L'epoque hyperindustrielle*. Paris: Galilée.

―――. 2006. *Mécreance et discrédit 2. Les sociétés incontrôlables d'individus désaffectés*. Paris: Galilée.

————. 2006. *Mécreance et discrédit 3. L'esprit perdu du capitalisme.* Paris: Galilée.

————. 2006. "La peau de chagrin." *Rue Descartes,* no. 52. Paris: PUF.

————. 2006. *Réenchanter le monde: la valeur esprit contre le populisme industriel.* Paris: Flammarion.

————. 2006. *La Télécratie contre la démocratie.* Paris: Flammarion.

————. 2006. "Le théâtre de l'individuation—Déphasage et résolution chez Simondon et Heidegger." In *Technics, World, Individuation: Heidegger, Simondon, Deleuze.* Olms: Jean-Marie Vaysse.

————. 2007. *De la démocratie participative.* Paris: Mille et une nuits.

————. 2007. Preface. In *Individuation psychique et collective,* by Gilbert Simondon. Paris: Aubier.

————. 2008. *Acting Out.* Trans. David Barison. Stanford, Calif.: Stanford University Press.

————. 2008. *Technics and Time 2: Disorientation.* Trans. Stephen Barker. Stanford, Calif.: Stanford University Press.

————. Forthcoming. *Mystagogies. De l'art contemporain.* Paris: Galilée.

————. Forthcoming. *Technics and Time 3: The Time of Cinema.*

Stiegler, Bernard, and Jacques Derrida. 2002. *Ecographies of Television.* Trans. Jennifer Bajorek. London: Polity.

Weber, Max. 2002. *The Protestant Ethic and the Spirit of Capitalism.* Trans. Peter Baehr and Gordon C. Wells. New York: Penguin Classics.

Winnicott, D. W. 1982. *Playing and Reality.* New York: Methuen.

Zimmerman, Frederic, and Dimitri Christakis. 2004. "Early Television Exposure and Subsequent Attentional Problems in Children." *Pediatrics* 113 (4 April): 708–13.

————. 2007. "Television and DVD/Video Viewing in Children Younger Than 2 Years." *Archives of Pediatrics and Adolescent Medicine* 161 (May): 473–79.

MERIDIAN

Crossing Aesthetics